Dr. Harrison was one of the ten chosen.

In 1949, after more than forty years of service in Arabia, he became college physician at Berea College, Kentucky. At present he resides at the Memorial Home Community, Penney Farms, Florida.

The Light that Lighteth Every Man

The Light That Lighteth Every Man

by

PAUL W. HARRISON, M.D.

Wm. B. Eerdmans Publishing Company
Grand Rapids, Michigan

PRINTED IN THE UNITED STATES OF AMERICA

TO MY FATHER

who served God
not after the law of carnal commandment
but after the power of an indissoluble life.

PREFACE

Around the year 95 A. D. there appeared a new account of the life and teachings of Jesus. The Church added this to the three accounts already in hand. The author was the Apostle John, writing for the early Christians of his day.

We know why John wrote this book, for he tells us, "These are written that ye may believe that Jesus is the Christ, the Son of God, and that believing ye may have life in his name." This double conception, "the Christ, the Son of God," seems out of place in a book written for a Greek church. That church would not understand the Jewish hope for a Messiah. Those hopes as Jesus found them were wholly mistaken, being pointed toward a military leader who would set up an earthly kingdom. More important still, the destruction of Jerusalem was twenty-five years in the past when this Gospel appeared, and the Jewish nation with its dreams was a faded memory.

"Son of God" was a term better suited to John's Greek audience. It is better suited to us. But the division of thought which we read into the passage may not have been present in John's mind. The term "the Christ" means simply "the anointed," that is, anointed by God. It comes from the Old Testament, and was applied to priests and prophets as well as to kings. No doubt in Jesus' own time it had come to be used as the title of their expected deliverer, but when John sent this Gospel to the Greek church all that was forgotten.

John faced a difficult task. For decades he had lived immersed in Greek thought. He spoke of "the Jews" as a foreign race. But inside John was very much a Jew. It was the task of this Jew to show to the Greek world that the carpenter of Nazareth was the Son of God, not the son of Zeus. Jesus must be seen as the Son of the Old Testament Jehovah. The words "the anointed" give a Jewish slant to the story. They point to the past, to a Jewish past.

7

Jesus was Jehovah's anointed. That much comprehension must be included in the most elementary faith.

Here we see John, a Jew, faced with the necessity of seeing a duality in the unity of God. John was really arguing with himself. His Greek audience would have accepted without protest a half-dozen incarnations if they were needed. But the incarnation of a semi-human Greek god was not at all what John was announcing. The Old Testament Jehovah, power, holiness, complete otherness and all, must be brought down from heaven to earth, and recognized in the unimpressive figure of this common human carpenter. "These are written," says John, to make that recognition possible.

CONTENTS

The Light that Lighteth Every Man

JOHN 1:1-18

In the beginning was the Word, and the Word was with God, and the Word was God. The same was in the beginning with God. All things were made by him; and without him was not any thing made that was made. In him was life; and the life was the light of men. And the light shineth in darkness; and the darkness comprehended it not.

THE OLD ORDER of relationship between God and Man.
The Divine Nature of the Word.
The Eternity of the Word.
His Association with God.
His Identity with God.
His Power Creating the Material Universe.
His Life the Source of the Moral Order.
The Failure of the Old Order.

There was a man sent from God, whose name was John. The same came for a witness, to bear witness of the Light, that all men through him might believe. He was not that Light, but was sent to bear witness of that Light. That was the true Light, which lighteth every man that cometh into the world. He was in the world, and the world was made by him, and the world knew him not. He came unto his own, and his own received him not. But as many as received him, to them gave he power to become the sons of God, even to them that believe on his name: which were born, not of blood, nor of the will of the flesh, nor of the will of man, but of God.

THE INCEPTION OF A NEW ORDER.
The Forerunner.
His Source.
His Name.
His Function.
His Purpose.
The Forerunner's Message.
The Earthly Visit of the Light.
His Arrival.
His Hostile Reception.
His Purpose. To make men children of God, that is, to introduce a NEW ORDER.

And the Word was made flesh, and dwelt among us, (and we beheld his glory, the glory as of the only begotten of the Father,) full of grace and truth. John bare witness of him, and cried, saying, This was he of whom I spake, He that cometh after me is preferred before me: for he was before me. And of his fulness have all we received, and grace for grace. For the law was given by Moses, but grace and truth came by Jesus Christ. No man hath seen God at any time; the only begotten Son, which is in the bosom of the Father, he hath declared him.

METHOD OF INTRODUCING THE NEW ORDER.
The Incarnation of the Word.
Deity Himself Involved.
Normal Humanity Assumed.
Ordinary Human Association and Life Practiced.
Means for His Identification.
We Beheld His Glory.
We Received His Grace.
We Received His Truth.
The Witness of John.

COMPLETENESS AND FINALITY OF THE NEW ORDER.
A Perfect Revelation of God.

THE INTRODUCTION

JOHN 1:1-18

In studying the Gospel of John, our first need is an analysis of its introduction. In the outline on the opposite page we can see the general lines of John's argument. We must grasp these if we desire to understand the Gospel itself.

THE OLD ORDER

In the beginning was the Word, and the Word was with God, and the Word was God. The same was in the beginning with God. All things were made by Him; and without him was not any thing made that was made. In him was life; and the life was the light of men. And the light shineth in darkness; and the darkness comprehended it not.

THE OLD ORDER OF RELATIONSHIP BETWEEN GOD AND MEN

The Nature of the Word.
> (1) His eternity.
> (2) His association with God.
> (3) His identity with God.

The Work of the Word.
> (1) Creator of the material universe.
> (2) Source of the moral and spiritual order.

The Old Order's Failure.

"The Word" — what is meant by this term? The curiosity of the philosopher is not satisfied. We are told simply that through the Word relationships between God and men are mediated. In the old order and in the new as well, through Him and not otherwise, men come into contact with the Divine.

We begin with a bird's-eye view of the previous order. The material universe, the world in which man lives, is the creation of the Word. Man's moral nature, that is, his conscience, is nothing less than the presence of the divine Word in his heart. Sometimes it is a faint spark, but we are assured that this spark is present in every man.

The old order did not succeed. The light did not triumph. "The darkness apprehended it not"; or "overcame it not" — a still more complete admission of failure. The best which could be said was that the light itself was not extinguished.

Why is man's heart "dark"? And whence came this darkness, so dense that the indwelling light of the divine Word, the Creator of the universe, did not illumine it? The question comes from the philosopher and the theologian. It is left unanswered. Followers of the Old Testament and students of comparative religion alike are left dissatisfied.

A new order was needed, that is, a new relationship between God and man. The remaining sections of the introduction give us short outlines, first of the inception of the new order, and second of the method of its introduction.

There was a man sent from God, whose name was John. The same came for a witness, to bear witness of the Light, that all men through him might believe. He was not that Light, but was sent to bear witness of that Light. That was the true Light, which lighteth every man that cometh into the world. He was in the world, and the world was made by him, and the world knew him not. He came unto his own, and his own received him not. But as many as received him, to them gave he power to become the sons of God, even to them that believe on his name: Which were born, not of blood, nor of the will of the flesh, nor of the will of man, but of God.

THE INCEPTION OF THE NEW ORDER.

The Forerunner.

      (1) His source.
      (2) His name.
      (3) His function.
      (4) His purpose.

The Forerunner's Message: The Light is coming.

The Light's Earthly Visit.

      (1) His arrival.
      (2) His hostile reception.
      (3) His purpose: to introduce a new order.

The Nature of the New Order.

      (1) Entrance: a free gift.
      (2) Entrance requirement: reception of the light.

(3) Essence of the new order: men becoming God's children.
(4) Method of the new order: a divine new birth.

The second paragraph of Chapter I tells of the new order's inception. God sent a forerunner. He announced a visit of the "light which lighteth every man," so that when this Light appeared men might believe.

Such provision seems absurd. The Creator of the universe hardly needs argument or evidence to identify him. Nevertheless, God sent the forerunner. And shortly after this forerunner delivered his message, the Light came for an earthly visit. And He required identification, for He came to the people accompanied by no divine manifestations. Nothing indicated from whence He came.

The need for the forerunner was the greater because the purpose of the divine visit was no impersonal execution of a distant divine program. God's will was accomplished only as men recognized and received the Light. Then they became children of God.

We catch a glimpse of God's great eternal plan. He was introducing a new order of relationship between Himself and men. The old order had failed. In the new order, on the one condition of recognizing and receiving the Light, men were to be born into the family of God.

This is the most important paragraph. This is the theme of John's Gospel. The life of God is entering the life of men. In contrast, the old order had been a reign of law. "The law was given by Moses." And outside the Jewish circle were laws still more rigid and forbidding. "The soul that sinneth, it shall die." "Every transgression and disobedience received a just recompense of reward." Wherever men looked, there was nothing but law.

In the new order we feel the thrill of a different atmosphere. We have climbed a mountain and come up above the fogs and miasma of the valleys into freshness and beauty and fragrance. We are dealing with life. Men are to be born. They will be children of God.

The boldness of this conception dazes us, and at first our minds refuse to take it in. Yet we see its illustration every day as the thrill and joy of human life find their supreme expression in a beautiful wedding. Every loveliness that we know is mustered for the occasion — beautiful clothes, lovely flowers, music, fragrance, and joy. The bloom and exquisite happiness of life are there. The pure joy of the occasion brings tears to our eyes. And why? Because two life streams are to join, and a new life will be the result.

It is a beautiful picture, a symbol of something still more beautiful and miraculous. "I bow my knees," says Paul, "unto the Father . . . of whom the whole family [fatherhood] in heaven and earth is named." The new birth with its beauty is important because it is the beginning of our eternal life, "an endless [indissoluble] life" Paul calls it.

A new birth comes only from the union of two streams of life. In Jesus God brings His stream of divine life to join ours. From that union new men are born, "not of blood, nor of the will of the flesh, nor of the will of man, but of God." New life has appeared. Such men and women are God's children.

Jesus came to His own. Some of them received Him. From that union of God's life with theirs new life resulted. But what about us? Jesus is not here now, and to us now, as to the people then, Jesus must come so that we can receive Him. But Jesus *does* come to us. One of God's miracles is the vivd impression Jesus makes through the Gospel account.

Jesus does not make the same impression on all men alike. But He comes to each one, and that vivid figure which we see is the real Jesus. All the mistaken efforts of friends and all the hostility of enemies have failed to distort the divine figure which has walked down through the centuries — a figure, simple and perfect and divine.

We must spend a moment on this matter of "receiving" the light. It is the human Jesus whom we receive, the Jesus whom we can see, and to whom we listen. "Eating His flesh" is the way He once put it. Our view of Jesus is always incomplete; that cannot be otherwise, of course. But our acceptance of Him must be absolute. Everything contrary to Him is cast out.

This seems simple enough. One point must be further considered. An American citizen in the depths of Arabia does not receive a visiting American consul just by giving him dinner. Passports and birth certificates are brought out to be signed and registered. The consul is not "received" except as his connection with Washington is recognized. The point is important. As we shall see, John's Gospel was written for the purpose of making this complete reception of Jesus possible.

And the Word was made flesh, and dwelt among us, (and we beheld his glory, the glory as of the only begotten of the Father,) full of grace and truth. John bare witness of him, and cried, saying, This was he of whom I spake, He that cometh after me is preferred before me; for he was before me. And of his fulness have all we received, and grace by grace. For the law was given by Moses, but grace and truth came by Jesus Christ. No man hath seen God at any time; the only begotten Son, which is in the bosom of the Father, he hath declared him.

METHOD OF INTRODUCING THE NEW ORDER.

The Incarnation of the Word.
    (1) Deity involved.
    (2) Normal humanity assumed.
    (3) Ordinary human association practiced.

Means for His Identification.
    (1) We beheld His glory.
    (2) Of His fulness (grace and truth) we all received.

The Epoch-Making Nature of the New Order.
    (1) Introducing a new dispensation as Moses did.
    (2) Bringing a complete and final revelation of God.

We have seen the introduction of the new order. The Light made an earthly visit. He purposed bringing men into the family of God. That could only be accomplished if the Light were recognized and received.

But how are men to recognize the divine Light so they can receive Him? This section answers that question. "The Word became flesh" — not animal flesh, and not "spiritual" flesh, if there

is such a thing, but human flesh. What does that mean? The
Word, God Himself, became a human being, and lived in the
normal way with other men so that they could know and understand Him. "And tented among us" says the author, emphasizing.
in this way the intimacy of the association. Certainly this is the
ideal way, perhaps indeed the only way to bring divine truth
within human reach. But the question remains, If God incarnates
Himself as a normal human being, how is He to be recognized?

The more this problem is considered, the more serious it appears. Christ is an everyday man, associating easily with other
men. What conceivable words or acts could lead to the conclusion that He is God incarnate? But it is here that the necessary
evidence must be found! Philosophy and metaphysics cannot
furnish it.

This is how it became manifest: Jesus' companions, men like
ourselves, have left reports of his words and deeds which first
convinced them. The remaining fraction of the introduction tells
us what convinced John. First, "We beheld his glory, glory as
of the only begotten of the Father." God's glory consists not
principally in His power. Even Moses was shown that. It is
in His inner nature, His moral character. Jesus' glory, too, was
seen in His character. The writer of this Gospel had seen and
meditated on it for months and years. He puts this evidence first.
Probably every disciple who lived with Jesus put it first. The
beauty of a sunset we see by looking at it. The glory of Jesus
was like that.

Separated by nineteen hundred years from Jesus' human pilgrimage, we find the supreme evidence for His divinity in His
grace and truth. We think of Jesus' teaching. His grace and truth
both come to us through His teaching, as John divides Jesus'
teaching into these two fractions.

When we study this Gospel we feel some of the thrill the early
disciples felt and our hearts melt in the sunshine of the grace
Jesus revealed. God's grace has to do with men's salvation. Jesus
had no time for any smaller subject. Jesus brings life, eternal
life, God's own life indeed. Men have no other need. We will

marvel many times at the beautiful contributions from our Heavenly Father which this supreme gift involves.

"And truth." That was the second gift that Jesus gave to men. There is no other truth. That is because there is no reality except God our Creator, our Sustainer, and most of all, our Heavenly Father. Words will fail us as we gaze on these majestic peaks.

Jesus' principal activity was teaching, patiently conveying these truths to men. His glory they could see, but His grace and truth they received. They were transformed by them.

Finally there was the witness of the forerunner. This evidence was available to all. Any man who wished to follow Jesus was welcome. But God's plan was not fulfilled by bringing a few of Jesus' contemporaries into God's family. The new order is for all men, and for all time. At that time only a few could come into close contact with Jesus and know Him, and enter God's family. He remained only a few years, and visited only a few places.

For the myriads who could not come into contact with Jesus it is necessary to preserve the picture which God presented in Christ's life, so that later generations can see His glory. Jesus' message has been recorded, too, in order that we can receive His grace and truth.

We now see the purpose of the Gospel of John. Those who knew Jesus were able to recognize Him for what He was and understand Him and receive Him. By means of this Gospel we can do the same. If this analysis is correct, we may expect to find the following in John's Gospel:

(1) An adequate picture of Jesus' glory, that is, His divine character.

(2) An adequate record of His teaching, that is, His grace and truth.

(3) An adequate reproduction of the testimony of John the Baptist.

For the law was given by Moses, but grace and truth came by Jesus Christ. No man hath seen God at any time; the only begotten Son, which is in the bosom of the Father, he hath declared him.

The philosopher and the theologian are disappointed again, and this time the historian with them. What would we not give for an analysis of the difference between the old reign of law

and the present rule of grace. Evidently God could not be fully
revealed till grace came. The law did not fully reveal Him.

Many questions emerge here. What was the purpose of the
law? It was a temporary thing, useful for its time but completely
unsuited to men as a permanent way of life.

Jesus brought grace and truth. Neither Moses nor the prophets
could bring these in their fulness. And the most unbelievable
statement of all is John's simple word that Jesus succeeded in
declaring God to limited men.

A word may be said here about the composition of John's
Gospel. We have been looking at the introduction. Splendid
ideas are mentioned and then dropped, with no discussion at all.
We would like to know more about "the Word" and God, and
about the law and grace.

But the writer has a definite purpose in mind. Like Paul, he
does "this one thing." He wants to demonstrate that Jesus is the
Christ, the Son of God. Not a paragraph or a word is put in
except as it ministers to that end. A discussion of law and grace
would afford us no help and therefore there is no such discussion.
We will see many such omissions as we study John.

One omission we must note. To Paul the resurrection was the
one and sufficient proof of Jesus' divinity. John sees it differ-
ently. He records the resurrection casually. It was simply one of
the things that witnessed to Jesus' divinity.

This Gospel is put together with the smallest amount of what
we might call literary connective tissue. "After these things,"
"again therefore Jesus passed by," or indeed the simple connective
"and" is all that joins different episodes together. When we find
something that looks like padding, or a mere recitation of an
interesting story, we can be sure that we have missed the writer's
mind.

So, having told us what lines of proof are to be brought forward, the writer brings up Number 1 without wasting a word,
"And this is the witness of John."

JOHN 1:19-51

And this is the record of John, when the Jews sent priests and Levites from Jerusalem to ask him, Who art thou? And he confessed, and denied not; but confessed, I am not the Christ. And they asked him, What then? Art thou Elias? And he saith, I am not. Art thou that Prophet? And he answered, No. Then said they unto him, Who art thou? that we may give an answer to them that sent us. What sayest thou of thyself? He said, I am the voice of one crying in the wilderness. Make straight the way of the Lord, as said the prophet Esaias. And they which were sent were of the Pharisees. And they asked him, and said unto him, Why baptizest thou then, if thou be not that Christ, nor Elias, neither that Prophet? John answered them, saying, I baptize with water: but there standeth one among you, whom ye know not; He it is, who coming after me is preferred before me, whose shoe's latchet I am not worthy to unloose. These things were done in Bethabara beyond Jordan, where John was baptizing.

The next day John seeth Jesus coming unto him and saith, Behold the Lamb of God, which taketh away the sin of the world! This is he of whom I said, After me cometh a man which is preferred before me; for he was before me. And I knew him not: but that he should be made manifest to Israel, therefore am I come baptizing with water. And John bare record, saying, I saw the Spirit descending from heaven like a dove, and it abode upon him. And I knew him not: but he that sent me to baptize with water, the same said unto me, Upon whom thou shalt see the Spirit descending, and remaining on him, the same is he which baptizeth with the Holy Ghost. And I saw, and bare record that this is the Son of God.

Again the next day after, John stood, and two of his disciples; and looking upon Jesus as he walked, he saith, Behold the Lamb of God! And the two disciples heard him speak, and they followed Jesus. Then Jesus turned, and saw them following, and saith unto them, What seek ye? They said unto him, Rabbi, (which is to say, being interpreted, Master,) where dwellest thou? He saith unto them, Come and see. They came and saw where he dwelt, and abode with him that day: for it was about the tenth hour. One of the two which heard John speak, and followed him, was Andrew, Simon Peter's brother. He first findeth his own brother Simon, and saith unto him, We have found the Messias, which is, being interpreted, the Christ. And he brought him to Jesus. And when Jesus beheld him, he said, Thou art Simon the son of Jona: thou shalt be called Cephas, which is by interpretation, A stone.

The day following Jesus would go forth into Galilee, and findeth Philip, and saith unto him, Follow me. Now Philip was of Bethsaida, the city of Andrew and Peter. Philip findeth Nathanael, and saith unto him, We have found him, of whom Moses in the law, and the prophets, did write, Jesus of Nazareth, the son of Joseph. And Nathanael said unto him, Can there any good thing come out of Nazareth? Philip saith unto him, Come and see. Jesus saw Nathanael coming to him, and saith of him, Behold an Israelite indeed, in whom is no guile! Nathanael saith unto him, Whence knowest thou me? Jesus answered and said unto him, Before that Philip called thee, when thou wast under the fig tree, I saw thee. Nathanael answered and saith unto him, Rabbi, thou art the Son of God; thou art the King of Israel. Jesus answered and said unto him, Because I said unto thee, I saw thee under the fig tree, believest thou? Thou shalt see greater things than these. And he saith unto him, Verily, verily, I say unto you, Hereafter ye shall see heaven open, and the angels of God ascending and descending upon the Son of man.

Chapter I

THE WITNESS OF JOHN

And this is the record of John, when the Jews sent priests and Levites from Jerusalem to ask him, Who art thou? And he confessed, and denied not; but confessed, I am not the Christ. And they asked him, What then? Art thou Elias? And he saith, I am not. Art thou that prophet? And he answered, No. Then said they unto him, Who art thou? that we may give an answer to them that sent us. What savest thou of thyself? He said, I am the voice of one crying in the wilderness, Make straight the way of the Lord, as said the prophet Esaias. And they which were sent were of the Pharisees. And they asked him, and said unto him, Why baptizest thou then, if thou be not that Christ, nor Elias, neither that Prophet? John answered them, saying, I baptize with water: but there standeth one among you, whom ye know not; He it is, who coming after me is preferred before me, whose shoe's latchet I am not worthy to unloose. These things were done in Bethabara beyond Jordan, where John was baptizing.

The introduction finished, the author begins at once, "And this is the witness of John." In the introduction this witness seemed important. Here it is much less so. This Gospel appeared among the Greek churches, and in a way it is a surprise to find a Jewish fragment like this in it at all. For the Greeks of the writer's time, and for the generations to come, the testimony of John the Baptist would not be of outstanding value.

John's testimony was a simple thing. He predicted the coming of an unbelievably great Visitor. He identified Him on arrival.

We will understand the Baptist better if we remember the series of inspired prophets who God sent to the Jewish nation at different times. They were of many types, but they were alike in this respect that they carried a message from God. Each had a tremendous influence in lifting the nation. There was always backsliding afterwards. The prospect seemed discouraging at times, but in the light of history we can see that the nation's understanding of God gradually increased. Toward the end of the prophetic succession, probably indeed from the very beginning, there was a feeling that a Messiah would come. He would lead the nation back to God. He would be the nation's ruler.

The next day John seeth Jesus coming unto him, and saith, Behold the Lamb of God, which taketh away the sin of the world! This is he of whom I said, After me cometh a man which is preferred before me; for he was before me. And I knew him not: but that he should be made manifest to Israel, therefore am I baptizing with water. And John bare record, saying, I saw the Spirit descending from heaven like a dove, and it abode upon him. And I knew him not: but he that sent me to baptize with water, the same said unto me, Upon whom thou shalt see the Spirit descending, and remaining on him, the same is he which baptizeth with the Holy Ghost. And I saw, and bare record that this is the Son of God.

What were the Jewish people expecting at this time, and what was John expecting? The Messiah was to be a great and magnificent king, a victorious military leader. The disciples clung to this dream up to the shadow of the cross, and, indeed, beyond it. But how much of God did they expect to see incarnated in the Messiah? David was Israel's hero. He was a very wonderful king, but no one thought of him as an incarnation of God. Some minds, that of India for instance, turn easily to the idea of God incarnating Himself as a man. The Hebrew mind is poles apart from that. It is blasphemy to suppose that God and man can be united in one person.

John was the last and greatest of the prophets, according to Jesus' own statement. He brought the last and the greatest of the prophetic messages. The others had said that in the future the leader would come. John said, "He is here." John may well have been the greatest, too, in this impact on the nation. He was born into a cultured priestly circle, but after his years in the desert, he burst on the nation as a shaggy Beduin preacher of repentance and remission of sins. The country was full of natural amphitheaters where thousands could hear his powerful voice. He "shook them over hell" as did Johnathan Edwards centuries later. The religious leaders and the contemptuous agnostics came in hundreds to hear themselves called, "Ye offspring of vipers, who warned you to flee from the wrath to come?" Edwards at his best scarcely surpassed that. The tax collectors and the soldiers with them bowed in repentance. The king himself trembled before this terrible preacher, and the whole community was shaken.

Again the next day after, John stood, and two of his disciples; And looking upon Jesus as he walked, he saith, Behold the Lamb of God! And the two disciples heard him speak, and they followed Jesus. Then Jesus turned, and saw them following, and saith unto them, What seek ye? They said unto him, Rabbi, (which is to say, being interpreted, Master,) where dwellest thou? He saith unto them, Come and see. They came and saw where he dwelt, and abode with him that day: for it was about the tenth hour. One of the two which heard John speak, and followed him, was Andrew, Simon Peter's brother. He first findeth his own brother Simon, and saith unto him, We have found the Messias, which is, being interpreted, the Christ. And he brought him to Jesus. And when Jesus beheld him, he said, Thou art Simon the son of Jona: thou shalt be called Cephas, which is by interpretation, A stone.

We must remember the prophetic stature of John the Baptist, for otherwise his testimony is not impressive. He repudiated any idea that he himslf might be the Messiah. He was only a forerunner. The one to come was indescribably greater. John was not worthy to loose his sandal straps.

We wish that the Baptist had told us something about his own position in Old Testament prophecy. The writer of this Gospel was surely familiar with Jesus' statement that John the Baptist was the Old Testament Elijah. But this Gospel is not writing about John the Baptist. It is writing about Jesus, and the only interest it has in the Baptist is the testimony he brought to Jesus.

This is the second part of John's testimony. He had predicted the coming of an indescribably great leader. Here he identifies Him on arrival. The basis for this identification is disappointing. It seems a trivial incident. From the other accounts we learn more. The heavens were opened, a portent of great impressiveness. Every one of the other gospel writers mentioned it, and also Peter in his epistle. Peter evidently was an eye witness too.

John's conception of Jesus surprises us: "The Lamb of God that taketh away the sin of the world." What connection did this have with the expected Messiah? Probably none. In any case, when this Gospel appeared it was a mere memory. But where did this conception come from? It was doubtless an inspiration directly from God. This was John's message.

The day following Jesus would go forth into Galilee, and findeth Philip, and saith unto him, Follow me. Now Philip was of Bethsaida, the city of Andrew and Peter. Philip findeth Nathanael, and saith unto him, We have found him, of whom Moses in the law, and the prophets, did write, Jesus of Nazareth, the son of Joseph. And Nathanael said unto him, Can there any good thing come out of Nazareth? Philip saith unto him, Come and see. Jesus saw Nathanael coming to him, and saith of him, Behold an Israelite indeed, in whom is no guile! Nathanael saith unto him, Whence knowest thou me? Jesus answered and said unto him, Before that Philip called thee, when thou wast under the fig tree, I saw thee. Nathanael answered and saith unto him, Rabbi, thou art the Son of God; thou art the King of Israel. Jesus answered and said unto him, Because I said unto thee, I saw thee under the fig tree, believest thou? thou shalt see greater things than these. And he saith unto him, Verily, verily, I say unto you, Hereafter ye shall see heaven open, and the angels of God ascending and descending upon the Son of man.

The people as a whole took no interest in this. So far as we can see they remained quite ignorant of the greatness of Jesus. None stepped through John's baptism into a fellowship with Jesus. However, a half-dozen of John's intimate followers did. They were probably John's leading disciples.

Much space is given to the circle around the Baptist, and their response to Jesus. Some of the surprising missions in John's testimony receive an explanation here. John refuses to say anything about the Messiah. We can see why he would make his replies to the Pharisees intentionally obscure but we would have expected greater clarity in his explanations to his disciples. But John himself was probably puzzled. There simply was no resemblance between the Messiah he had been expecting, and the Jesus who now stood before him.

We get some idea of John's expectation from the different things that his disciples said. They found what they were waiting for, and they were waiting for what their master had taught them to wait for. "We have found him of whom Moses in the law and the prophets wrote." "Rabbi," said Nathanael, "thou art the Son of God, thou art the King of Israel." John may not have been quite sure that this was the coming Messiah, but at least here that specific hope emerges. It was Andrew who said,

"We have found the Messiah." Probably John was very much puzzled then already for we know that he became so later. He probably was sometimes up and sometimes down, as mercurial souls frequently are.

John guided some of his disciples into a contact with Jesus. They were receptive men and followed practically at first sight. Their faith was deep and their loyalty unswerving. They were the nucleus of the group which followed Jesus during His earthly life, and it was to them that the leadership of the Church was eventually given.

Jesus understood the universal nature of His mission from the start. John the Baptist never attained to that, and the men whom he had trained scarcely did. As the event showed, this was their greatest defect. Eventually God had to bring Paul in from the outside to universalize Jesus' message and carry it to the world.

With the Baptist's testimony finished, the writer turns to other lines of evidence. First, he paints a picture to show Jesus' glory, that is, His likeness to God. This is something that men can see, and in Jesus' day everyone could see it for He lived in full view of the people. The disciples saw it best and concluded that Jesus was the Christ, the Son of God. The writer must paint a picture so vivid that we, nineteen hundred years later, can see His glory too.

Second, the author reports Jesus' teachings. Men can receive these, and some who listened, did. We might suppose that men trained in religion would make better reporters. But the wisdom of the world is foolishness with God and Jesus' teachings have been written down for us by men who had nothing to recommend themselves except a most transparent intention to tell the truth. They were utterly unable to insert deep meanings of their own into the words they were recording.

We are surprised by the brevity of these accounts of how Jesus taught and walked up and down the roads and paths of Palestine. However, we marvel at their vividness and beauty even today. Nothing extraneous is put in. The author of this Gospel is never a mere hero worshipper, and never the pure historian. He is an evangelistic debater, trying to give men eternal life by proving certain points to them.

Throughout the Gospel, painting the picture of Jesus, and recording His teaching proceed side by side. In each chapter, then, our effort will be to look carefully at the portrait given there, and to study the teaching which the chapter records.

In most of the chapters we find both Jesus' picture and His teaching. Chapter 2 is an exception. There is no mention of what Jesus taught. We are given, as it were, three candid camera snapshots, vivid and beautiful, and shockingly contrasting. We move from the peace of a marriage feast, to the violent cleansing of the temple.

The Gospel of John is almost as significant in what it omits as in what it includes. Organized government, organized religion, organized industry never seem to catch Jesus' attention, nor John's. The picture is made up of Jesus' personal relationships to different men and women, and to God. He moved in a complicated society, but Jesus' life was as free from the pressure of institutions as that of a roving Bedouin in the deserts of Arabia. In Jesus' mind, as in the Bedouin's, institutions are semi-mythical illusions, lacking all real significance. The world's only reality is men and women. Christ's relationships to them and to the Heavenly Father do not simply reveal Jesus' character, they constitute His divine character.

This chapter is an outline. In it are the elements which make up the complete picture. Jesus associated with the common people, with the disciples, with the Pharisees, and with His Heavenly Father. These elements are all introduced here, and can be traced through the entire book.

And the third day there was a marriage in Cana of Galilee; and the mother of Jesus was there: And both Jesus was called, and his disciples, to the marriage. And when they wanted wine, the mother of Jesus saith unto him, They have no wine. Jesus saith unto her, Woman, what have I to do with thee? mine hour is not yet come. His mother saith unto the servants, Whatsoever he saith unto you, do it. And there were set there six waterpots of stone, after the manner of the purifying of the Jews, containing two or three firkins apiece. Jesus saith unto them, Fill the waterpots with water. And they filled them up to the brim. And he saith unto them, Draw out now, and bear unto the governor of the feast. And they bare it. When the ruler of the feast had tested the water that was made wine, and knew not whence it was, (but the servants which drew the water knew,) the governor of the feast called the bridegroom, And saith unto him, Every man at the beginning doth set forth good wine; and when men have well drunk, then that which is worse: but thou hast kept the good wine until now. This beginning of miracles did Jesus in Cana of Galilee, and manifested forth his glory; and his disciples believed on him.

After this he went down to Capernaum, he, and his mother, and his brethren, and his disciples; and they continued there not many days.

And the Jews' passover was at hand, and Jesus went up to Jerusalem, And found in the temple those that sold oxen and sheep and doves, and the changers of money sitting: And when he had made a scourge of small cords, he drove them all out of the temple, and the sheep and the oxen; and poured out the changers' money, and overthrew the tables; And said unto them that sold doves, Take these things hence; make not my Father's house a house of merchandise. And his disciples remembered that it was written, The zeal of thine house hath eaten me up.

Then answered the Jews and said unto him, What sign shewest thou unto us, seeing that thou doest these things? Jesus answered and said unto them, Destroy this temple, and in three days I will raise it up. Then said the Jews, Forty and six years was this temple in building, and wilt thou rear it up in three days? But he spake of the temple of his body. When therefore he was risen from the dead, his disciples remembered that he had said this unto them; and they believed the Scripture, and the word which Jesus had said.

Now when he was in Jerusalem at the passover, in the feast day, many believed in his name, when they saw the miracles which he did. But Jesus did not commit himself unto them, because he knew all men, And needed not that any should testify of man; for he knew what was in man.

Chapter II

JESUS WITH INDIVIDUALS AND GROUPS

And the third day there was a marriage in Cana of Galilee; and the mother of Jesus was there: And both Jesus was called, and his disciples, to the marriage.

John pictures Jesus in His contacts with individuals and with groups. The incidents are selected well, and the portraits are vivid and complete. John writes as a child writes: this happened,

and this, and this. First in the series is a marriage feast in Cana.
In it Jesus' mother carried some responsibility. Perhaps it was
given by a relative. Jesus was invited. He was not a hermit or
a fanatic. He was one of many acceptable guests. He mingled
with the others on the basis of simple equality.

We realize with a start that here we have a view of the silent
thirty years. Jesus spent those years as a carpenter. His public
ministry extended over only three years. Christ left us an example
that "we should follow in His steps." Not many of us are to
follow Him in His public ministry. We all try to follow Him
as He lived during those thirty years. The two little pictures
which John gives us here are almost our only material to go by.

Jesus did not preach to the people at the feast. Through the
silent years, He never had done so. We might suppose that a
wedding feast would afford a good opportunity. Why had He
come?

The question is very important. He came because He loved
men and enjoyed being with them. His life's purpose, to be sure,
was giving men eternal life. Here as a guest, we see His sense
of comradeship with them. The desire to give men eternal life
can be a treacherous thing. Every Pharisee was anxious to give
men eternal life. Zeal for men's souls while we detest their
company and try to keep them as far away as possible is simple
hypocrisy. Jesus loathed such an attitude.

Jesus loved men, loved to be with them, loved them for their
own sakes, and found pure joy in associating with them. He was
like the Arab pearl dealers who love to see and handle and admire pearls entirely apart from sales and profits.

The central lesson here is hospitality. We of the West do not
know much about that. Yet it is one of our major obligations, if
we are to live as God wants us to live. Jesus accepted with
pleasure the invitation to this feast, and accepted the obligations
of a guest. Those are just as binding, though not so obvious, as
the obligations of a host.

Jesus was often seen at feasts. He enjoyed them. Love and
joy and brotherhood are there, and the essence of hospitality.

And when they wanted wine, the mother of Jesus saith unto him, They have no wine. Jesus saith unto her, Woman, what have I to do with thee? mine hour is not yet come. His mother saith unto the servants, Whatsoever he saith unto you, do it. And there were set there six waterpots of stone, after the manner of the purifying of the Jews, containing two or three firkins apiece. Jesus saith unto them, Fill the waterpots with water. And they filled them up to the brim. And he saith unto them, Draw out now, and bear unto the governor of the feast. And they bare it. When the ruler of the feast tasted the water that was made wine, and knew not whence it was, (but the servants which drew the water knew,) the governor of the feast called the bridegroom, And saith unto him, Every man at the beginning doth set forth good wine; and when men have well drunk, then that which is worse: but thou hast kept the good wine until now. This beginning of miracles did Jesus in Cana of Galilee, and manifested forth his glory; and his disciples believed on him.

After this he went down to Capernaum, he, and his mother, and his disciples; and they continued there not many days.

It is a time of harmony and peace and the relief of hunger, a time of good fellowship and pure democracy. He approved of it all, even the conviviality, for He contributed to that very element.

If they had asked for it, Jesus could have made a further contribution to these friends of His, who were finding joy and brotherhood in neighborly hospitality. He could have given them an effective contact with God, which would have made the emotions and attitudes at this feast permanent and growing things.

John begins his portrayal of Jesus with this simple story. Nothing of importance is seen. It is a beautiful example of common, everyday life. Jesus spent many years living as an ordinary citizen. The family was not one of wealth, but it was not one of bitter poverty either. He was a self-respecting, hard working, conscientious artizan who supported, in a frugal way, a considerable family.

In this little story John gives us a remarkably vivid view of that long silent period. There is one thing that we wish he had put in. Jesus was a good carpenter, one of the best. Why did not John put into the story one of His honestly and beautifully made benches? It would have meant a great deal to us.

It was a frugal feast. Artizan's incomes are meager. Perhaps more guests came than were expected. Such things often happen in that part of the world. So the wine ran out, and Jesus suddenly found Himself asked to carry the responsibility of a guest. A guest must come to his host's assistance in any way the situation requires.

The bridegroom would be put to very great shame by this failure in the entertainment. To be sure, no one's life was in danger. Nobody was even ill. But there was one young man who faced disgrace before all his fellows, and there was one little bride who would certainly cry all night. Hospitality is the supreme obligation in that part of the world, and the situation was serious.

Jesus' mother looked Him up. She was the bridegroom's agent. Now we are to see the obligations of a guest. We would like to ask a question. Was no one available to run and get some more wine? One of the disciples would do. On some account such a simple solution was not possible. Perhaps it was night by this time, or the shops were far away.

Jesus' mother brought the matter to Him, because He was the only one who could take care of it. Their host was in trouble. His mother's word was brief: "They have no wine." She added no comment, for none was needed. Some obligations are very plain.

Jesus' reply is puzzling, perhaps on account of an idiom brought to us from the Aramaic and distorted by its translation into Greek. It came from the intimacy of a home. "As between you and me, taking care of this will amount to nothing at all." His mother was satisfied with the reply. The situation would be taken care of, immediately. Mary was a woman of few words. To the servants — not slaves this time, but retainers of some sort — she simply said, "Do what He tells you."

Jesus realized as He stood there that His mother was right. He turned to the servants: "Fill them up, all of them." Yes, all of them, and right to the brim, too, for the servants caught some of Mary's confidence. Then they took that water to the ruler of the feast. That was all there was to it. It was the best wine they ever tasted.

Mary was accustomed to giving the disciples orders. Their faith was notably reinforced. Fifty years later when John wrote this Gospel, he remembered it as one of the half-dozen episodes to which he owed his unshakable faith in Jesus. He helped to carry the water to those jars, and he helped to take it to the governor of the feast.

There is something tremendously adequate about Jesus' miracles. He fed the five thousand all they could hold. Here he gives his host a hundred and fifty gallons of wine. That was surely enough to make them convivial. But a feast is supposed to show abundant hospitality. Much was left over — a nice wedding present for the newlyweds.

After this he went down to Capernaum, he, and his mother, and his disciples; and they continued there not many days.

Here is another picture of Jesus before His ministry began. It shows His family life. We know very little about this. The meagerness of the material makes what we have the more valuable. One verse. It is a charming little picture. Jesus is the head of a family. His mother and His brethren are there. From a later mention we know that sisters were in the group. Joseph is not seen. Probably he had died.

Jesus' mother was a woman of great force of character. She led a mixed group with both brothers and disciples in it. The brothers were not much younger than Jesus, and no doubt a good part of the family support came from them.

The scene is significant also in that it is our first view of Jesus, leading His disciples. He had been the support of the family for years, but lately, probably for a few months, disciples had begun to follow Him. We estimate their number as, most likely, six, coming from the group around John the Baptist. They lived together and they travelled together.

So far as we know, none of the disciples was a carpenter, so their help toward the family support would be small. Perhaps they caught fish and brought them. Arrangements of this sort seem to make less trouble in the East than they do with us, but even so, it is most unlikely that the disciples' continued presence was appreciated. Jesus' brethren did not accept His "pretensions," as they would have termed them. The attitude of devoted adoration on the part of the disciples would be very irritating, and feeding them a most unwelcome burden.

Jesus' departure seems abrupt, but probably it caused no distress to His brethren, even if His mother did weep secretly. They were able to assume the support of the family, and probably welcomed the separation. Jesus had to leave the family behind. The old relationship was never resumed. But from this little interlude of a few months we gain one insight of importance. To become a disciple was to become a member of Jesus' family. He did not rule over a group of sons, and still less a group of employees or slaves. Jesus led the group as an elder brother. It is well to remember this as we observe Jesus, living and working with His disciples through the years of His ministry. That is the essence of our discipleship too. Jesus is our elder brother.

Jesus never had a harbor of return where His wounded and torn soul could come for comfort. His brethren, of course, would have been of no help, but it is easy to imagine His mother stroking the wrinkles out of His troubled forehead, and out of his hard-pressed soul at the same time. We see as a dreadful reverse image the loneliness He never escaped when He occasionally rested back onto the confidence and faith of the Bethany home where the sisters Mary and Martha understood Him better by far than the disciples did.

"And the Jews' passover was at hand, and Jesus went up to Jerusalem."

Here we meet a surprise. Jesus went up to Jerusalem. The Passover was coming in a few days and the city was crowded. In those days the dispersed Jewish community had money enough to travel. Josephus tells us that sometimes the pilgrims numbered two to three million. The temple records do not quite bear him out, but from them we learn that the pilgrims paying the required shekel were between half a million and a million. They

And the Jews' passover was at hand, and Jesus went up to Jerusalem,
And found in the temple those that sold oxen and sheep and doves,
and the changers of money sitting: And when he had made a scourge of
small cords, he drove them all out of the temple, and the sheep, and
the oxen; and poured out the changers' money, and overthrew the
tables; And said unto them that sold doves; make not my Father's house
a house of merchandise. And his disciples remembered that it was written, The zeal of thine house hath eaten me up.

---

gained a tremendous financial reinforcement from this annual
gathering.

Jesus knew of this before He went. The crowds were no surprise. But perhaps He had never been there at a time when He
could see with His own eyes the selling of the animals in the
outer temple court. This preceded the actual feast. The animals
must be brought and the temple shekels secured before the feast.
The preceding few days were very busy with ths merchandising.

Indeed, we feel here an unmistakable element of surprise.
Jesus most likely had never realized the extent of the traffic.
Sacrificial animals were brought in and sold literally in thousands. They had to be officially passed as perfect, and no one
could do this but the temple officials. The monopoly created in
this way was extreme. A dove, worth five cents in the open market,
sold for five dollars.

Mixed with those who sold the animals were dozens and scores
of money changers. Their tables were piled high. Every sort of
foreign money had to be changed into temple currency. It was a
place of dust and noise and confusion.

The profits of this merchandising went to the priests. They were
enormously wealthy. Abuses of this sort often develop in connection with religious pilgrimages. Mecca has been a sink of
wickedness for centuries. However, the account does not indicate
that the Jerusalem of Jesus time was on a level with modern
Mecca. Immorality and drunkenness were not there. Extortion
there surely was, but this does not seem to be uppermost in Jesus'
mind. He did not find any searing infidelity. The Roman eagles
had been kept out.

Moreover, Jesus lived in a very wicked world. Alien oppressors ruled the country with a harsh and autocratic hand. Slavery was universal, and even more dreadful then than now. Jesus looked on these things in silence. No doubt He disapproved but He uttered no word against this situation.

But for some reason the temple scene stirred up a tremendous reaction. In fierce indignation He made a small whip out of little cords, and drove away the whole unsavory company. He overturned the tables of the money changers, spilling on the floor quarts, indeed pecks of copper and silver and gold coins. Hundreds of animals bolted, trod under foot numbers of fleeing men. There was a mad scramble for the scattered money, and finally a reverent silence, after the loudly protesting tradesmen had gone.

To many of us this is the most astonishing event in Jesus' life. His emotions were strong, but always under control. Here He embodies the very fury of God. There was no violence. The avaricious crowd fled simply from the frown on His face.

What did Jesus see here that stirred Him so terribly? He saw the laws which regulate temple worship being violated, and He saw the priests getting rich, but His reaction cannot be explained by that. Most sins roused in Jesus nothing but pity.

The longer we study the account, the more puzzling it seems. Jesus standing there, the embodiment of the wrath of God, must have seen before Him nothing less than the world's supreme means to wreck men. Our puzzled surprise will recur many times as we see Him dealing with these religious leaders.

Careful meditation shows us something of what was in Jesus' mind. "You must not make my Father's house a house of merchandise" was the indictment. The temple was His Father's house. Its services and sacrifices were for the purpose of giving the people a picture of God. Our worst, most deadly sin is entertaining within ourselves, and passing on to others, a degraded and evil picture of God.

The Old Testament and its services were intended to show that God is infinite, eternal and holy, reasonable and ethical in His demands, and loving in His attitude toward men. Repentant ahd

Then answered the Jews and said unto him, What sign shewest thou unto us, seeing that thou doest these things?   Jesus answered and said unto them, Destroy this temple, and in three days I will raise it up. Then said the Jews, Forty and six years was this temple in building, and wilt thou rear it up in three days?   But he spake of the temple of his body. When therefore he was risen from the dead, his disciples remembered that he had said this unto them; and they believed the Scripture, and the word which Jesus had said.

---

sincere worshippers were given a real path to reconciliation with God, and the forgiveness of their sins.

But the scene that Jesus surveyed gave the impression that the essential part of religion was buying an animal, and by its sacrifice placating a selfish, stupid, and childish God. Even with the element of extortion being absent, making God's house a market place must have this effect, for the worshipper is purchasing God's favor with a few pieces of money. The Pharisees believed just this, and they labored night and day to teach it to the worshippers. Every missionary to the Mohammedans understands at least part of the reason why Jesus reacted thus against this caricature. Repentance is made almost impossible. Men are shut away from God almost completely. The degraded conception of God presented by the temple service which Jesus saw, was no whit better than that found in any heathen temple of the Romans.

The Jews were furious. John remembers it vividly after fifty years. They demanded some evidence from Jesus to show that He had authority to cleanse the temple. Jesus discussed such things with no one. So He made a reply which was unintelligible to them, as He intended it should be. The disciples understood it eventually, and it reinforced their faith.

"Make not *my Father's house* a house of merchandise." One important element in John's picture is Jesus' love and devotion to His Heavenly Father. Jesus spoke of "my Father," "your Father," "the Father." This beautiful word was on His lips continually. It embodied the conception of the Creator. Jesus used this term three times as often as the more impersonal word "God" in John's Gospel.

"God" comes from the old order, when the law was given through Moses. Omnipotence is in it, and justice, with just a trace of love. We still find this picture of God today among the Jews and Mohammedans.

We must not miss the significance of the new picture of God. It is one of Jesus' most important contributions. Even the word "Father" is a poor symbol. Earthly fathers are never perfect. But it was the best figure that Jesus' earthly experience had given Him. Joseph no doubt was a good father. We love to think of God as a King and as a Judge. David even pictured Him as a Shepherd. Jesus passed all of these by. His prayers and thoughts and love were directed toward His Heavenly Father.

What light does this give us? What does a father do? He takes care of his children, is devoted to them, and loves them. Children show love to their fathers in return. God's devotion to us is more than ours to Him can ever be. He lives for His children.

Nothing is farther from the mind of a father than to desire arbitrary, unthinking obedience from his children. He wants them to develop their every possibility. Therein he finds his greatest joy. He hopes for full and free comradeship with them eventually. Light shines on many theological puzzles if we worship, not in the first place a Creator and not a distant divine Judge, but our Heavenly Father.

There was a man of the Pharisees, named Nicodemus, a ruler of the Jews: The same came to Jesus by night, and said unto him, Rabbi, we know that thou art a teacher come from God: for no man can do these miracles that thou doest, except God be with him. Jesus answered and said unto him, Verily, verily, I say unto thee, Except a man be born again, he cannot see the kingdom of God. Nicodemus saith unto him, How can a man be born when he is old? can he enter the second time into his mother's womb, and be born? Jesus answered, Verily, verily, I say unto thee, Except a man be born of water and of the Spirit, he cannot enter into the kingdom of God. That which is born of the flesh is flesh; and that which is born of the Spirit is spirit. Marvel not that I said unto thee, Ye must be born again. The wind bloweth where it listeth, and thou hearest the sound thereof, but canst not tell whence it cometh, and whither it goeth: so is every one that is born of the Spirit. Nicodemus answered and said unto him, How can these things be? Jesus answered and said unto him, Art thou a master of Israel, and knowest not these things? Verily verily, we speak that we do know, and testify that we have seen; and ye receive not our witness. If I have told you earthly things, and ye believe not, how shall ye believe, if I tell you of heavenly things? And no man hath ascended up to heaven, but he that came down from heaven, even the Son of man which is in heaven.

And as Moses lifted up the serpent in the wilderness, even so must the Son of man be lifted up: That whosoever believeth in him should not perish, but have eternal life.

For God so loved the world, that he gave his only begotten Son, that whosoever believeth in him should not perish, but have everlasting life. For God sent not his Son to condemn the world; but that the world through him might be saved.

He that believeth on him is not condemned: but he that believeth not is condemned already, because he hath not believed in the name of the only begotten Son of God. And this is the condemnation, that light is come into the world, and men loved darkness rather than light, because their deeds were evil. For every one that doeth evil hateth the light, neither cometh to the light, lest his deeds should be reproved. But he that doeth truth cometh to the light, that his deeds may be made manifest, that they are wrought in God.

After these things came Jesus and his disciples into the land of Judea; and there he tarried with them and baptized.

And John also was baptizing in Enon near to Salim, because there was much water there: and they came, and were baptized. For John was not yet cast into prison.

Then there arose a question between some of John's disciples and the Jews about purifying. And they came unto John, and said unto him, Rabbi, he that was with thee beyond Jordan, to whom thou bearest witness, behold, the same baptizeth, and all men come to him. John answered and said. A man can receive nothing, except it be given him from heaven. Ye yourselves bear me witness, that I said, I am not the Christ, but that I am sent before him. He that hath the bride is the bridegroom; but the friend of the bridegroom, which standeth and heareth him, rejoiceth greatly because of the bridegroom's voice: this my joy therefore is fulfilled. He must increase, but I must decrease. He that cometh from above is above all: he that is of the earth is earthly, and speaketh of the earth: he that cometh from heaven is above all. And what he hath seen and heard, that he testifieth; and no man receiveth his testimony. He that hath received his testimony hath set to his seal that God is true. For he whom God hath sent speaketh the words of

God: for God giveth not the Spirit by measure unto him. The Father loveth the Son, and hath given all things into his hand. He that believeth on the Son hath everlasting life: and he that believeth not the Son shall not see life; but the wrath of God abideth on him.

Chapter III

NICODEMUS

The Picture

There was a man of the Pharisees, named Nicodemus, a ruler of the Jews: The same came to Jesus by night, and said unto him, Rabbi, we know that thou art a teacher come from God: for no man can do these miracles that thou doest, except God be with him. Jesus answered and said unto him, Verily, verily, I say unto thee, Except a man be born again, he cannot see the kingdom of God.

This picture is simpler than many, for Jesus is dealing with an individual. We are surprised by some of the things which He says, and more by what He leaves unsaid. In our effort to understand Jesus, this is a portrait of great importance.

Nicodemus is a striking figure. He was a great man. Middle-aged to elderly, he had devoted his whole life to the study of the Scriptures. He was a Pharisee, and conspicuous among them for learning and ability. He was a member of the Sanhedrin, that council of seventy members which ruled the political as well as the religious life of the nation.

Nicodemus was courteous and humble. He greeted Jesus cordially as a fellow Rabbi, and showed great respect for His achievements, new upstart as He may have seemed to some. He did not ask Jesus to come to him, but took the initiative and came himself, by night, doubtless with a retinue of his disciples, as religious teachers in that part of the world do to this day. Jesus, too, was surrounded by an informal *mejlis* as the Arabs term their evening receptions. Friendly visitors, a dozen or two of them, listened.

Thus the conversation had a considerable audience, men of religious convictions and training. They could compare notes afterward and reproduce the scene and dialogue very accurately. Nicodemus came by night, because there was leisure then. He assumed correctly enough that the same was true of Jesus. The discussion lasted through an entire evening.

Nicodemus' opening remark is courtesy at its best. A great figure in the scholarly and religious world was recognizing with all cordiality a new arrival. And this opening remark had in it elements deeper than simple courtesy. Nicodemus had heard of Jesus and His work, doubtless knew it very well. He would not have thought of claiming for himself that which he recognized in Jesus. "We know that thou art a teacher come from God" is very close to the faith that Jesus asked from His listeners.

This courteous introductory remark was very unsatisfactory to Jesus, and it is not easy for us to see why. Nicodemus simply had noted Jesus' signs. Their miraculous nature had convinced him that Jesus was working with divine power. Jesus regretted all attention given to miracles. Perhaps if Nicodemus had said, "Rabbi, we know that thou art a teacher come from God, for no one can present teachings such as you present, except God be with him" Jesus might have been better pleased. In spite of his courtesy and sincerity, Jesus felt that Nicodemus was not in the Kingdom of God. But what is "the Kingdom of God"? In Jesus' mind it is simply the rule of God in men's hearts, a personal thing with no political connotations whatever.

One wonders at Jesus' use of this term, for after using the phrase "born of God" we would expect Him to speak of the "family of God." To the Jews "kingdom of God" meant a political state. Jesus gives it a new meaning. God was not in the first place King to Jesus. He is our Heavenly Father. God's kingdom is His family.

Jesus' reply seems brusque and discourteous to us. Evidently it seemed so to the disciples then, for this is one of the episodes that John recalled with great vividness many years later.

Jesus was facing a difficult task. Before Him was a splendid

Nicodemus saith unto him, How can a man be born when he is old? can he enter the second time into his mother's womb, and be born? Jesus answered, Verily, verily, I say unto thee, Except a man be born of water and *of* the Spirit, he cannot enter into the kingdom of God. That which is born of the flesh is flesh; and that which is born of the Spirit is Spirit. Marvel not that I said unto thee, Ye must be born again. The wind bloweth where it listeth, and thou hearest the sound thereof, but canst not tell whence it cometh, and whither it goeth: so is every one that is born of the Spirit.

---

example of what the old dispensation could produce. The law of Moses had rarely shown a finer worshipper.

The law of Moses was a perfect law. At least Nicodemus thought so. But the grace and truth which Jesus brought reached far beyond the law, and Nicodemus needed them, just as everyone does. His need for emancipation from the law was especially deep, for his very eminence in the old dispensation would make it hard for him to follow Jesus into the new. Jesus is not condemning Nicodemus. He is offering him something new. Those good deeds and this courtesy and kindness were outstanding, but they belonged to the old order. Jesus brought something better than Moses and his law, better than a political kingdom. He came to give men eternal life.

Perhaps nothing Jesus ever said cleared away so much underbrush of false and obsolete ideas as this bald and dreadful statement to Nicodemus. Nicodemus needed to be "born again." Many volumes can hardly explain what these few words imply.

John considered this interview important. It dealt with profound and fundamental things, not often touched on by Jesus. This topic — one of the most difficult of them all — Jesus took up with Nicodemus, not at all because of his position and reputation, but because of the qualities of mind and spirit Jesus saw in him.

Nicodemus stood at the top of his community. His learning and ability were great, and his personal character exemplary. The Jews of those days would point at him as an outstanding ornament of their nation and faith. What could be added to him by a new teaching?

Nicodemus answered and said unto him, How can these things be? Jesus answered and said unto him, Art thou a master of Israel, and knowest not these things?   Verily, verily, I say unto thee, We speak that we do know, and testify that we have seen; and ye receive not our witness. If I have told you earthly things, and ye believe not, how shall ye believe if I tell you *of* heavenly things?   And no man hath ascended up to heaven, but he that came down from heaven, *even* the Son of man which is in heaven.

Probably that is why this scene was chosen for preservation. Brushing aside his very real greatness, Jesus had for him the simple statement, "Except a man be born again, he cannot see the kingdom of God." This abruptness was no accident. Jesus was trying to bring Nicodemus into the Kingdom of God. This jarring introduction overrode Nicodemus' outer defenses, so that he had to consider Jesus' message. Jesus' approach to men was always shaped by His desire to save them. They all needed to be shown the way into the Kingdom of God. Reputation and position were irrelevancies which Jesus did not even see. What He wanted was to save Nicodemus.

Still, the more we study this reply, the more astonishing it seems. Nicodemus' blameless life, his good deeds for others — were they not in accordance with God's will? The courtesy which he had shown is surely what God wants us to show.

These difficulties are made worse by the fact that Nicodemus was not merely wise in the things of the world. He was wise in the books of God. From the days before he was ten, up to this interview when he was probably sixty, he had lived in the Old Testament. He could repeat long passages, probably whole books. He had earnestly studied it all his life. Every letter and syllable were to him divinely inspired. He had obeyed all the commands that he had found in his study.

It is terrifying to hear Jesus telling such a man that until he is born again he cannot see the Kingdom of God. God's will then does not become visible to us simply by studying the Scriptures. We must be born from above.

Whatever God's purpose was in giving men the Old Testament, the Pharisees of Jesus' time had so twisted and misinterpreted it, that its study gave them no foothold at all in God's Kingdom. Paul tells us that it was God's purpose that the law, that is, the Old Testament be observed "in the Spirit and not in the letter." The Pharisees, whom Jesus knew, would have been horrified at such blasphemy.

It seems remarkable that Jesus did not use the Old Testament to show Nicodemus the way back to God. He took a useful symbol from it, but nothing more. The immense wealth of Old Testament knowledge in Nicodemus' mind was passed by.

Jesus' method is worth studying. He gave Nicodemus a sort of shock treatment to get a closed door open. Jesus had to penetrate Nicodemus' indifference at least to the extent of having His initial statement understood, and His teaching removed from the realm of the grotesque and the indelicate.

Jesus was opening before Nicodemus a door into the Kingdom of God through which he could enter, right at this moment, just where he stood. Jesus did that for the woman of Samaria too. Probably He always did. Nicodemus understood very little of all this at the moment, but he remembered it, and eventually the seed germinated and brought forth fruit.

Once planted in men's minds Jesus' message grows with divine power. That night there were many onlookers. Who knows in how many hearts the miraculous seed was planted?

In this chapter Jesus has a remarkable pupil. Nicodemus also has a remarkable teacher. He carried Nicodemus easily from one step to the next, as He presented a difficult lesson. First, Nicodemus' need, a new birth. Second, how to gain this divine gift by means of faith put in terms so simple that a child cannot misunderstand it. He was to believe in the heavenly things that Jesus brought, or simpler still, in Jesus Himself.

But in the comment which follows the initial dialogue we are introduced to something deeper than this. This Gospel is a life of Jesus written from God's standpoint. It is the story of Jesus putting into the minds and hearts of limited men the unlimited truth of God. He was sent from His Heavenly Father to do just this.

In this evening visit Jesus saw the opportunity He had been waiting for, not merely to save Nicodemus, but to insert into a tiny human mind on this planet one of the infinite divine truths which He must put into our earthly, childish mentalities. In all his life Nicodemus had received no honor such as this, namely, that Jesus chose him as the vessel into which this wonderful teaching was poured. He did not understand it, did not even believe it at the time, but he was its necessary receptacle.

Into this great and magnificent mind Jesus poured the deepest and most difficult lesson which He had to give. We are to be made partakers of the divine nature, and this by means of a new birth. Every birth we know is a feeble and earthly copy of this eternal reality. Jesus had to find someone, somewhere, into whose mind this superb glimpse of reality could be placed.

Nicodemus' must have been the greatest mind that Jesus met down here. He asked no such tremendous feat of anyone else. Jesus did not explain this lesson. He did not defend it. It is not capable of either explanation or defense. It comes from God.

The Interview with Nicodemus

Jesus Teaching God's Love

And as Moses lifted up the serpent in the wilderness, even so must the Son of man be lifted up: That whosoever believeth in him should not perish, but have eternal life.

For God so loved the world, that he gave his only begotten Son, that whosoever believeth in him should not perish, but have everlasting life. For God sent not his Son into the world to condemn the world; but that the world through him might be saved.

He that believeth on him is not condemned: but he that believeth not is condemned already, because he hath not believed in the name of the only begotten Son of God. And this is the condemnation, that light is come into the world, and men loved darkness rather than light, because their deeds were evil. For every one that doeth evil hateth the light, neither cometh to the light, lest his deeds should be reproved. But he that doeth truth cometh to the light, that his deeds may be made manifest, that they are wrought in God.

Except a man be born from above, he cannot see the Kingdom of God.

We have studied the beginning of John's portrayal of Jesus' glory. Every subsequent episode will add to its beauty. Jesus' interview with Nicodemus is one of these pictures. Looking at it, we have already caught the outline of Jesus' teaching.

No doubt, the people of that time, by simply looking at Jesus and His life, had the supreme proof of His divine nature. But this Gospel appeared late among the Greek churches, and by that time surely it was Jesus' grace and truth which convinced the world that He was divine. The record of Jesus' teachings continues throughout the Gospel. It begins here with Nicodemus. It is the most important of all lessons because it is the foundation of all the rest.

The truths which Jesus was to introduce He called "words." These "words" from His Father He passed on to us. Once these truths were given, His task was finished.

Jesus' task was the more difficult because men's minds were dominated by mistaken and wrong ideas which He had to clear away. His teachings often roused bitter opposition.

Jesus had limitless faith in these "words." He poured them out into men's minds. His messages might not be understood, but they were remembered. Jesus knew that when God's truth is put into men's minds, it will fill and dominate them. It changes men eventually. The result is certain, for the message comes from God, and omnipotence is in it.

Our most careful study touches only the surface of these words, and conclusions must be stated with caution. But it would appear that the chapters in this Gospel have been arranged in their present order on the basis of the teaching which they contain. "Grace and truth came by Jesus Christ," so says the introduction, and grace and truth are what we find in Jesus' teaching. The two often overlap, and are intertwined, but meditation can usually separate them, at least partially. For far down underneath, God's grace is one thing, and His truth something else.

Jesus, or perhaps we should say John, usually presents the new vision of God's grace first, and that is what we have here. To Nicodemus with his unusual mind Jesus could give a view of this deep reality. All the infinite ramification of God's grace come from this fundamental gift.

Eternal life is the theme of the gospels. It is the theme of Paul. Here we begin to understand the nature and origin of Jesus' statement: "I came that they might have life." That life blossoms eventually into the fragrance and glory of the resurrection.

Jesus is going to abide in us. The Holy Spirit has taken His place and, fortified with divine omnipotence, we are to go out and do His work. "We rejoice in the hope of the glory of God." There is no limit to the development which we look forward to, now that we have been born again. The whole story of salvation, as the New Testament tells it, is founded on this "word" given to Nicodemus.

He did not understand it, and neither do we. We do not understand any of the things of God, but there is not one wonderful vision anywhere in the whole story of Jesus' life which does not spring from the lesson given to Nicodemus. It cannot be understood except in the light of that lesson.

Jesus was sent by God to accomplish a vast, well-nigh impossible task. He must put divine truth into human minds. That is like asking a teacher to put Einstein into the mind of a five-year-old boy. In this Gospel the high points of achievement are those mountain-top experiences where Jesus succeeds in getting one of these "words" lodged in men's minds. That is what He lived for.

John's was not a systematic mind. He put no convenient summary at the beginning of the Gospel, nor at its end. What a help such a summary would have been. We would understand Jesus better. Wrong, of course. Human systematizations of God's truth are very dangerous things as the history of the Church abundantly shows. They mix human limitations with the limitless Word of God.

The account of Jesus' teaching begins with this discussion between Nicodemus and Jesus. It is put first because it deals with the foundations. There is no more important lesson. We have here the recollections of John after many years. We read the passage in two minutes. It summarizes an evening's discussion which lasted as many hours.

We catch without difficulty the importance of this "word." It is our deepest view of God's redemptive thought. Apparently it was given only to Nicodemus. We have seen it already in the introduction, brought there, no doubt, from this interview.

"Except a man be born of God, he cannot see the kingdom of God." This then is salvation. Two life streams join, God's and our own. One pauses, almost afraid of this conception. It seems so far from our level and our possibilities.

It is an error to look on this as a figure or a symbol. Says Paul, "For this cause, I bow my knees unto the Father . . . from whom every fatherhood in heaven and on earth is named." Human fatherhood is merely an earthly parable, a small and human copy of a divine reality.

"Born again" is a conception we meet only in this talk with Nicodemus. "Eternal life" is the more frequent expression. The new birth is simply the beginning of that life. Jesus saw in Nicodemus the one man to whom he could give this beautiful and profound "word." It is our deepest view of divine grace, doubtless the deepest our human minds can reach.

Nicodemus should have been able to handle the phrase "born from above." It means, simply enough, "born of God." But the Greek word can mean "born again and Nicodemus took it that way. The difference in the spiritual level of the two men seems to be well indicated by the different meanings they gave to this word. Probably in this play on a double meaning of one word we are given the summary of a considerable discussion.

In this lesson to Nicodemus Jesus divides His thought into three fractions It is worth-while to give some attention to this, for it is an arrangement that recurs, and has significance. The first fraction is before us now, and we will cast it in the form of a paraphrase. This man came to Jesus by night, and said to Him, "We know that thou art a teacher come from God (that is, thou art a member of His kingdom), for no man can do the miracles that thou doest unless God is with him" (that is, ruling as king). Jesus answered him, "Verily, verily I say unto you, Unless a man is born of God, he cannot see the kingdom of God."

Whether we think of this as "born of God," or "born again," the significance of Jesus' terrifying reply cannot be missed. It is Jesus' statement of Nicodemus' personal need. No matter with whom He was dealing, Jesus tried to bring that man's personal need out into the open. John has recorded this interview for our instruction, but Jesus was not thinking of the centuries to come, ourselves included. He was thinking of Nicodemus.

We can be sure that this fragment has come down to us just as it passed between Jesus and his renowned visitor. The words were heard by all the onlookers, and Jesus' abrupt, almost discourteous, reply to the studied graciousness of Nicodemus remained vivid in their memories.

Jesus gets down to essentials, with no waste of time. In this first sentence Nicodemus learned just what he needed. Also in this first sentence, Jesus tells him that the Kingdom of God is simply the rule of God in men's hearts. An area of land has nothing to do with it.

Nicodemus did not protest against this. There were Jewish teachers in those days who understood the spiritual nature of God's Kingdom. He did not protest even against Jesus' assertion that he could not see that Kingdom. Probably Nicodemus came to Jesus because he realized that with all his attainments there was a spiritual Kingdom which he did not know. Like the woman at the well, he wanted it.

Nicodemus wanted to enter this spiritual Kingdom. That was a good desire, and Jesus accepted it. He used it as a level to lift Nicodemus up. "No one," Jesus explained, "can belong to this spiritual Kingdom, can have God as King, except he is born of God." Having God as King means two things. First, that we can see what God's will is, and, second, that once we see it, we will obey.

Of themselves men do not know what God wants them to do. Nicodemus had lived long enough to recognize the complete truth of that. A moment later Jesus tells Nicodemus that without this new birth no one can enter the Kingdom of God. Nothing could surpass the simplicity and clearness of this statement of Nicodemus' need. He must be born of God. Lacking that, his situation was hopeless.

This bald and rather awful statement of Nicodemus' need is followed by Jesus' explanation. That is the second fraction of the lesson. This was Jesus' plan — first a statement of a man's need, then an explanation which would make it possible to meet the situation.

Jesus explains His teaching so that Nicodemus will at least seriously consider it. He wants it removed from the realm of grotesque impossibility where Nicodemus was inclined to place it. We are working here with words of two meanings. The translators no doubt have done the best they could but much obscurity remains.

All three of these words, water, wind, and birth, carry ordinary earthly connotations, but also spiritual connotations. Wind and spirit are interchangeable translations for one Greek word. Sometimes it means the Spirit of God as is evident in this discussion. "Born of the Spirit" means "born of God."

"Water" is a more obscure term. John the Baptist used it as a symbol for repentance, and that is probably meant here. It is the human contribution to the new birth. The wind or spirit is God's contribution. This should not have disturbed Nicodemus. The Old Testament does not express the idea very clearly, but there are hints of it, and Jesus gently rebukes him for his failure to grasp it at all.

Nicodemus at the moment did not understand a great deal of what he heard. Jesus did not expect him to. But he would remember it and be guided by it later. The simple earthly things, water and wind, Jesus talked about, had been misunderstood. Jesus had talked about a new birth. That had been misunderstood, too.   But the trouble was not that Nicodemus failed to understand.   Where is the man, then or now, who understands these things?   Nicodemus had disbelieved.   That was serious, and the more so because every one of these things had a heavenly counterpart, and no one could tell Nicodemus these heavenly things except Jesus Himself. Moreover, these heavenly things must be believed.   It would be impossible to exaggerate the importance of that, for every man who believed these heavenly things would experience the new birth.

And so Jesus put visions in Nicodemus' mind which were one day to lead him to faith and the New Birth.   It is a fascinating exercise of the imagination to picture Nicodemus going home from that memorable evening and turning over in his mind the things he had heard.   He marvelled at this teaching.   In a perfectly "natural" but divinely beautiful way new life was brought into being.   And how simple was the path for the man who wanted it — just to believe the heavenly things Jesus taught. But Nicodemus was a man of discernment.   He knew, without being told, that believing Jesus' heavenly things meant thorns and trouble in the place of the rose-strewn path that had been his.

For God so loved the world, that he gave his only begotten Son, that whosoever believeth in him should not perish, but have everlasting life.

Now we are to see the base upon which this lesson is built, one of the foundation stones of God's universe of reality.   Is this a further statement from Jesus' own lips, or is it a comment by the author of the book?   We will treat it as coming directly from Jesus, principally because, if it is an inspired comment by John, it is doubtless something that He remembers Jesus saying, perhaps at a different time, but on the same subject.   Most likely of all is the supposition that it is a later part of the same discussion.

Jesus had outlined to Nicodemus the offer which God makes to him and to all men; nothing less, indeed, than membership in the family of God. We are to be born of God and be His children. How can God make such an incredible offer?   Here is the answer.

It is a matter of God's love. That we knew already. But it is also a matter of God's suffering and sacrifice, and that we did not know. We are simply defeated by this. Our minds cannot stretch that far. To the Mohammedan, the mere idea of God sacrificing Himself for men is impudent infidelity.

God "seeks and saves that which is lost." He does not wait for men to come to Him. He comes to us. Now Jesus is not with us bodily, but God's Holy Spirit is, and this is His constant work. He labors with undiscourageable patience to induce in men's hearts the attitude of faith.

God's contribution to this process goes further.   Jesus has come to earth so that we can see Him, and believe in the heavenly things which He brought. Faith is thus saved from spending itself on futilities and half truths. It is made comprehensible and available to all men, for its object is Jesus' own life.

This means that the stream of divine life which is joined to ours in making the new birth possible, is Jesus Himself. We believe what He says, and join ourselves to Him personally.

When men believe they have eternal life. That is to say, when faith emerges above the surface of human consciousness, we know that a child has been born. God's Spirit is the initiator, the agent. Our response to Him is probably simple repentance. John the Baptist uses the figure of water, as Jesus does here. Then faith emerges above the level of our consciousness. We do not feel the work of the Spirit. That is below the surface. But we depend on it, and without it every one of us would be helpless.

Thus we see that there is a human contribution to the New Birth. This interview is a good example. In Jesus, God was working in Nicodemus' heart. Every word and gesture and yearning was God's Spirit at work but He was defeated for the time being. Later Nicodemus' repentance was added to the divine effort, and he was born again, and entered the Kingdom of God.

It will be worth while to review at this point what we have learned of God's love, for a still deeper lesson lies ahead. God's Spirit works in men's hearts to induce in them an attitude of faith. Jesus brought a message from God, so that upon faith's emergence it could be furnished with the form and substance of reality, reflecting the mind of God Himself. Jesus told Nicodemus, in effect, that if he failed to accept His message, that is, the heavenly things He was anxious to tell him, valid faith would not be possible.

The acceptance of the heavenly things that Christ gives us means that to the limit of his tiny capacity the believer's attitudes and emotions and desires within, and his motives and objectives without, correspond to those of God. His will corresponds to God's will, for it is moulded by the message God sent.

God's Spirit then is at work in the depths of men's hearts leading them toward faith. Jesus brings them the message which gives that faith eternal reality. The divine effort does not stop at this point. As a part of the message, men are shown Christ as the object of faith. We can all see and understand that object. We no longer worship a far-off God, but Christ Himself, near at hand and sympathetic. Faith is no longer part of an abstruse divine philosophy. It is simple, warm-hearted loyalty to Christ. The incarnation with all of its wonder was the cost of making the message available to all.

By embodying the truth in a human life it was made universally comprehensible. It is thus the light for men everywhere, and by their reaction to it men are judged. By God sitting on high and assigning rewards and punishments? No. By rejecting the light men keep themselves out of God's family, away from all hope of gaining the eternal destiny that He wants them to enjoy.

We have already seen a wonderful vision of the omnipotent love of God establishing and maintaining the new order — His Spirit world in our sub-conscious minds. Faith is the result. In our conscious minds Christ's message works, and gives faith its eternal validity.

There is a further lesson here. Faith is brought into being. It is made genuine and true. Even so, it is a small human thing. Its only worthy element is that fraction of Christ's message which has been seen and followed. Nevertheless, with no additions or assistance whatever that faith, trivial as it is, has been made adequate for the believer's eternal redemption.

"Whosoever believeth . . . shall have eternal life," that is to say "shall be born again," for eternal life is simply the continuance of the new birth.

"God so loved the world, that he gave his only begotten Son." The accomplishment of this taxed the resources of omnipotence. For what purpose? Not in order to produce faith. That required no such unspeakable sacrifice. But the Son was given — not lent — to make faith, poor and insignificant as it is, adequate to eternal life, the life that makes us sons.

The height and depth of this tremendous accomplishment are far beyond our comprehension, but we can see something of its grandeur. Here God is proposing, in the words of Peter, to make us "partakers of the divine nature" to join His life with ours so that we might become His children.

And He proposes to do this for every man who believes, no matter how black his past or how full of wrongs done to others; no matter how foul his soul has been or how bound by the appetites of the flesh; no matter how meager his mental equipment or how twisted his psychology, faith opens the door to the inner circle of the family of God, and sets the believer within a destiny linked with that of God Himself.

Our minds stand dazed before the wonder of this achievement, but the deepest word of all remains to be spoken. Behind all of this is, "For God so loved the world." Here is our deepest truth. Love brings human births. It is no different with God.

This is the final word, the explanation of everything. Here, pictured for the mind of the smallest child, is the foundation of all our hopes. "For God so loved the world" is the beginning of the most important verse in the world. That is God's attitude toward us — love and nothing but love. There is no hate, here, no anger.

Human fathers love their children that way too, within the tiny dimensions that limit us. In our hearts too, there is no hate, and no selfish desire to vindicate our own honor. Nothing but love.

And whom did God love? The world. Not a few of them, and not even most of them, but all of them. All of them all the time. No Arab, and no Chinese, and no American, and no one else ever can or ever will get away from God's love. And does not the same lesson shine out of our imperfect hearts? What father stops loving his children even when they are in the penitentiary?

We reach our final mountain peak. How much does God love us? The words are so familiar that they have lost their impact. So much, that He gave us His only begotten Son. He does not loan us Jesus for thirty-three years nor for thirty-three million years. Jesus is speaking of an eternal gift, the Father giving away His son for all eternity.

Human comparisons are almost impossible here, but perhaps a real illustration is seen when a mother gives up her only daughter to become the wife of the young man of her choice. There is no rupture of the affection and regard between them, but it is a real gift and a permanent one. The empty place in the mother's heart is never filled.

Evidently such a sacrifice is the only way God can save us. So the Moravian mothers saved the West Indian slaves. Their sons sold themselves to go out to that evil land to die as slaves for the sake of slaves. They never came back. Real death, eternal death is separation from the Heavenly Father. Jesus' death delivers us from death. It means eternal life for us.

But what it means in the divine world, a later word in Hebrews shows. We see the cross, a beautiful and terrible picture of God's love. There Jesus accomplished His eternal sacrifice.

Just as real and far more terrible than our death, is Christ's death which, too, was a separation of the Father from the Son, and this for us, men, and for our sins. Here we gaze at the unbelievable love of God. There can be no measure of the extent and depth of God's grace, but it is easily believable after we have seen this.

For God sent not his Son into the world to condemn the world; but that the world through him might be saved.

He that believeth on him is not condemned: but he that believeth not is condemned already, because he hath not believed in the name of the only begotten Son of God. And this is the condemnation, that light is come into the world, and men loved darkness rather than light, because their deeds were evil. For every one that doeth evil hateth the light, neither cometh to the light, lest his deeds should be reproved. But he that doeth truth cometh to the light, that his deeds may be made manifest, that they are wrought in God.

This commentary on Jesus' visit is important. The visit was an act of pure love. It was not a method of subjecting the perishing world to further condemnation. It must be that in John's day this atrocious idea had gained a real vogue. It seems absurd to us, but perhaps it did not seem so to the convert from pantheistic Stoicism tempted to return to his hard and pitiless god.

Jesus' visit was necessary. Only so could the world be saved. If only men would believe the "heavenly things" that Jesus brought. No one else could bring them. Valid faith was made possible by His visit.

Hard questions emerge. What was there in Jesus' teaching, or life, that goes beyond the twenty-third Psalm? How sure can we be that Peter was a better man than Nicodemus?

These questions are not easy to answer. We can see one contribution that Jesus made. He brought us a new conception of God. Complete surrender to God and devotion to His service can be a road straight down to hell if our idea of God is wrong. The Pharisees served God with all their hearts, and crucified Jesus as part of that very sincere service.

It was Jesus' life that gave us the new picture, His human life which all could see. Once we realize that this human life of Jesus is a replica of God, then complete faith and devotion become safe. We climb upward toward God on that road.

After these things came Jesus and his disciples into the land of Judea; and there he tarried with them, and baptized.

And John also was baptizing in Enon near to Salim, because there was much water there: and they came, and were baptized. For John was not yet cast into prison.

Then there arose a question between some of John's disciples and the Jews about purifying. And they came unto John, and said unto him, Rabbi, he that was with thee beyond Jordan, to whom thou bearest witness, behold, the same baptizeth, and all men come to him. John answered and said, A man can receive nothing, except it be given him from heaven. Ye yourselves bear me witness, that I said, I am not the Christ, but that I am sent before him. He that hath the bride is the bridegroom: but the friend of the bridegroom, which standeth and heareth him, rejoiceth greatly because of the bridegroom's voice: this my joy therefore is fulfilled. He must increase, but I must decrease. He that cometh from above is above all: he that is of the earth is earthly, and speaketh of the earth: he that cometh from heaven is above all. And what he hath seen and heard, that he testifieth; and no man receiveth his testimony. He that hath received his testimony hath set to his seal that God is true. For he whom God hath sent speaketh the words of God: for God giveth not the Spirit by measure unto him. The Father loveth the Son, and hath given all things into his hand. He that believeth on the Son hath everlasting life: and he that believeth not the Son shall not see life; but the wrath of God abideth on him.

Men judge themselves by their reaction to the light, that is, by their reaction to this conception of God. Jesus at least does not sit in judgment over them.

And this visit of Jesus is no forlorn hope, doomed to eventual failure. God sent His Son into the world to accomplish something. Once we know that it is God's will that men be saved, once we see Him putting the resources of omnipotence into that effort, then we know that He will be completely successful. God's love and power are going to save the world that He loves so much. Not a fraction of it, but all of it.

We have here our last contact with John the Baptist. It seems a small and simple addition to his previous testimony, thus carrying out his own testimony, "He must increase, but I must decrease." The author closes the Baptist's story with a perfect ending.

As we have noted in the story of Jesus, here again it is difficult to know where the words of the Baptist end, and where comment on the part of the Gospel writer begins. But the whole
episode with Nicodemus seems to have been chosen to show the
divine foundation which underlies the New Order. This is its
final word. Christ has been "given" to us. "All things", that is,
the human race, have been given to Him. Christ has been given
to us, and we have been given to Him. For time and eternity we
belong to each other. He is our hope and we can have no other.

What then is the foundation underneath the new order? God's
love. He sends His Spirit to bring about in men's hearts the
attitude which we call faith. He sends His Son to bring men a
divine message which gives the form and substance of eternal
reality to faith when it appears. His Son took on human form
to make that message comprehensible and commanding to all
men, and so put valid faith within every man's reach. And,
finally, by the Father's eternal gift of His Son to men for that
purpose simple faith becomes adequate for our eternal life.

When therefore the Lord knew how the Pharisees had heard that Jesus made and baptized more disciples than John, (Though Jesus himself baptized not, but his disciples,) He left Judea, and departed again into Galilee. And he must needs go through Samaria. Then cometh he to a city of Samaria, which is called Sychar, near to the parcel of ground that Jacob gave to his son Joseph. Now Jacob's well was there. Jesus therefore, being wearied with his journey, sat thus on the well: and it was about the sixth hour. There cometh a woman of Samaria to draw water: Jesus saith unto her, Give me to drink. (For his disciples were gone away unto the city to buy meat.) Then saith the woman of Samaria unto him, How is it that thou, being a Jew, askest drink of me, which am a woman of Samaria? for the Jews have no dealings with the Samaritans. Jesus answered and said unto her, If thou knewest the gift of God, and who it is that saith to thee, Give me to drink; thou wouldest have asked of him, and he would have given thee living water. The woman saith unto him, Sir, thou hast nothing to draw with, and the well is deep: from whence then hast thou that living water? Art thou greater than our father Jacob, which gave us the well, and drank thereof himself, and his children, and his cattle? Jesus answered and said unto her, Whosoever drinketh of this water shall thirst again: But whosoever drinketh of the water that I shall give him shall never thirst; but the water that I shall give him shall be in him a well of water springing up into everlasting life. The woman saith unto him, Sir, give me this water, that I thirst not, neither come hither to draw. Jesus saith unto her, Go, call thy husband, and come hither. The woman answered and said, I have no husband. Jesus said unto her, Thou hast just said, I have no husband, For thou hast had five husbands; and he whom thou now hast is not thy husband: in that saidst thou

truly. The woman saith unto him, Sir, I perceive that thou art a prophet. Our fathers worshipped in this mountain; and ye say, that in Jerusalem is the place where men ought to worship. Jesus saith unto her, Woman, believe me, the hour cometh, when ye shall neither in this mountain, nor yet at Jerusalem worship the Father. Ye worship ye know not what: we know what we worship; for salvation is of the Jews. But the hour cometh, and now is, when the true worshippers shall worship the Father in spirit and in truth: for the Father seeketh such to worship him. God is a Spirit: and they that worship him must worship him in spirit and in truth. The woman saith unto him, I know that Messias cometh, which is called Christ: when he is come, he will tell us all things. Jesus saith unto her, I that speak unto thee am he.

And upon this came his disciples, and marvelled that he talked with the woman: yet no man said, What seekest thou? or, Why talkest thou with her? The woman then left her waterpot, and went her way into the city, and saith to the men, Come, see a man, which told me all things that ever I did: is not this the Christ? Then they went out of the city, and came unto him.

In the mean while his disciples prayed him, saying, Master, eat. But he said unto them, I have meat to eat that ye know not of. Therefore said the disciples one to another, Hath any man brought him aught to eat? Jesus saith unto them, My meat is to do the will of him that sent me, and to finish his work. Say not ye, There are yet four months, and then cometh harvest? behold, I say unto you, Lift up your eyes, and look on the fields; for they are white already to harvest. And he that reapeth receiveth wages, and gathereth fruit unto life eternal: that both he that soweth and he that reapeth may rejoice together. And herein is that saying true, one soweth, and another reapeth. I sent you to reap that whereon ye bestowed no labour: other men laboured, and ye are entered into their labours.

And many of the Samaritans of that city believed on him for the saying of the woman, which testified, He told me all that ever I did. So when the Samaritans were come unto him, they besought him that he would tarry with them: and he abode there two days. And many more believed because of his own words; And said unto the woman, Now we believe not because of thy saying: for we have heard him ourselves, and know that this is indeed the Christ, the Saviour of the world.

Now after two days he departed thence, and went into Galilee. For Jesus himself testified, that a prophet hath no honour in his own country. Then when he was come into Galilee, the Galileans received him, having seen all the things that he did at Jerusalem at the feast: for they also went unto the feast. So Jesus came again into Cana of Galilee, where he made the water wine. And there was a certain nobleman, whose son was sick at Capernaum. When he heard that Jesus was come out of Judea into Galilee, he went unto him, and besought him that he would come down, and heal his son: for he was at the point of death. Then said Jesus unto him, Except ye see signs and wonders, ye will not believe. The nobleman saith unto him, Sir, come down ere my child die. Jesus saith unto him, Go thy way; thy son liveth. And the man believed the word that Jesus had spoken unto him, and he went his way. And as he was now going down, his servants met him, and told him, saying, Thy son liveth. Then inquired he of them the hour when he began to amend. And they said unto him, Yesterday at the seventh hour the fever left him. So the father knew that it was at the same hour, in the which Jesus said unto him, Thy son liveth: and himself believed, and his whole house. This is again the second miracle that Jesus did, when he was come out of Galilee.

Chapter IV

THE SAMARITAN WOMAN

THE PICTURE

When therefore the Lord knew how the Pharisees had heard that Jesus made and baptized more disciples than John, (Though Jesus himself baptized not, but his disciples,) He left Judea, and departed again into Galilee. And he must needs go through Samaria. Then cometh he to a city of Samaria, which is called Sychar, near to the parcel of ground that Jacob gave to his son Joseph. Now Jacob's well was there. Jesus therefore, being wearied with his journey, sat thus on the well: and it was about the sixth hour. There cometh a woman of Samaria to draw water: Jesus saith unto her, Give me to drink.

Jesus' next mountain-top experience was in Samaria where He sat on a well and gave to a defeated village woman the word of God's grace.

Nicodemus had been told of the unbelievable love of God, of suffering and death which made possible the new birth into the family of God. That was truth. This is beauty.

(For his disciples were gone away unto the city to buy meat.)   Then
saith the woman of Samaria unto him, How is it that thou, being a Jew,
asketh drink of me, which am a woman of Samaria? for the Jews have
no dealings with the Samaritans.   Jesus answered and said unto her, If
thou knewest the gift of God, and who it is that saith to thee, Give me
to drink; thou wouldest have asked of him, and he would have given
thee living water.   The woman saith unto him, Sir, thou hast nothing
to draw with, and the well is deep: from whence then hast thou that
living water?   Art thou greater than our father Jacob, which gave us
the well, and drank thereof himself, and his children, and his cattle?
Jesus answered and said unto her, Whosoever drinketh of this water
shall thirst again:

God has one purpose, giving eternal life to the men and women
He has created. Here we learn how God can give such a gift to
limited and failing humans.

It is with real relief that we see God offering this as a pure
gift. We will never understand this, still less deserve or earn it.
Only as a gift could we possibly receive it.

Here we find contrast with the previous interview. Nicodemus
stood at the very top of the nation, most likely the most prominent
man Jesus ever taught. He was a Pharisee, the very type of
religious certainty. That certainty had ruled Nicodemus. His
self-satisfaction almost kept him out of the Kingdom of God in
spite of all Jesus did.

In the second interview Jesus is talking with a woman who is
at the bottom. Religious uncertainty had been her undoing. She
had lost her faith and then lacking any hold on God, she made a
shipwreck of her love life. There is nothing strange in either of
these histories. Society heaps its rewards on Nicodemus and his
sin. For the woman of Samaria it has ostracism, and poverty,
and public disgrace. In our day as well as then, it is bad for a
man's reputation to be seen talking with such a woman. The
disciples, naive reflectors of public opinion, they were, felt
strongly about this.

Jesus apparently knew about this woman. It is wiser not to
look for miraculous elements in the story unless we have to.
Jesus was extremely prudent in His use of the miraculous. The

But whosoever drinketh of the water that I shall give him shall never thirst; but the water that I shall give him shall be in him a well of water springing up into everlasting life. The woman saith unto him, Sir, give me this water, that I thirst not, neither come hither to draw. Jesus saith unto her, Go, call thy husband, and come hither. The woman answered and said, I have no husband. Jesus said unto her, Thou hast well said, I have no husband: For thou hast had five husbands; and he whom thou now hast is not thy husband: in that saidst thou truly. The woman saith unto him, Sir, I perceive that thou art a prophet. Our fathers worshipped in this mountain; and ye say, that in Jerusalem is the place where men ought to worship

---

woman's character was probably unconcealed and obvious. A prolonged *tete-a-tete* over the top of a well not more than four feet across constituted a public scandal. Moreover, she was unabashed in the presence of this strange Man, bold enough to argue with Him, with an easy effrontery indeed. That of itself told what manner of woman she was.

But in spite of her bad record and low reputation, she came to Jesus with an open mind, and was far quicker to respond than Nicodemus had been.

However, the real reason why we give special attention to this woman is that Jesus chose her as the recipient of His second great lesson. To us it may seem that the lesson to Nicodemus was deeper and more important. But we may be wrong there. We see a little of the very reality of God as we sit with Nicodemus in Jesus' *mejlis*.

Here we sit with Jesus at a party of two, and listen while He pours into the ears and the heart of an unlettered and defeated woman His deepest lesson, not for the mind, but this time a lesson about loves, and emotions, and gifts; His lesson for the heart. He saw in her a great opportunity, perhaps just as unique and important as His opportunity with Nicodemus. This story afford us a deep view into the pure grace of God, the God who gives.

This woman knew a good deal about giving. Five times in succession she had given herself to a husband. It is not likely that all of them had died. Perhaps none of them had. Each one

Jesus saith unto her, Woman, believe me, the hour cometh, when ye shall neither in this mountain, nor yet at Jerusalem, worship the Father. Ye worship ye know not what: we know what we worship; for salvation is of the Jews.   But the hour cometh, and now is, when the true worshippers shall worship the Father in spirit and in truth: for the Father seeketh such to worship him.   God is a Spirit: and they that worship him must worship him in spirit and in truth.   The woman saith unto him, I know that Messias cometh, which is called Christ: when he is come, he will tell us all things.   Jesus saith unto her, I that speak unto thee am he.

---

had left her when he was tired of her. And then, because she had to give herself to someone, she took another man. After a while she did not even insist on a marriage ceremony. There was great sin in this program, especially at its end, and we do not find it easy to believe that underneath such sin anything good is to be found. But Jesus was not much concerned with the repulsive surface that covered people's souls. As in so many other cases, He found under that surface something very beautiful indeed. A little of the fragrance of heaven was there. This time Jesus was telling of God's grace and that is simply God giving Himself. This woman had been giving herself through the years with pathetic completeness. There is no limit as to God's self-giving and no thought of any demand in return. So, however strange it may seem to us, Jesus chose this woman to be the recipient of His most profoundly beautiful teaching. None of the disciples could have understood this lesson, partly because there was no woman among them. This woman did not understand it either, at least not at the time. But it was not a thing to be understood. Gifts and loves and divine grace are to be accepted, not understood, and Jesus knew that she could embrace this lesson. She did not understand it but she remembered it, and most important of all, she accepted it.

There is one aspect in this interview which we of the West easily miss, because hospitality means so little to us. Jesus belonged to the kingdom of hospitality. He was King there. Hospitality is the foundation of every virtue in the Near East. In this episode Jesus entered the spiritual house of the woman as

And upon this came his disciples, and marvelled that he talked with the woman: yet no man said, What seekest thou? or, Why talkest thou with her? The woman then left her waterpot, and went her way into the city, and saith to the men, Come, see a man, which told me all things that ever I did: is not this the Christ? Then they went out of the city, and came unto him.

In the mean while his disciples prayed him, saying, Master, eat. But he said unto them, I have meat to eat that ye know not of. Therefore said the disciples one to another, Hath any man brought him aught to eat?

---

she stood beside the well. He entered as a guest and asked for a drink. In Arabia that is what an entering guest always asks for. It is a very beautiful thing to see the King take the place of a simple guest.

But this woman was timid about assuming the honored position of hostess, and the positions of host and guest are easily interchangeable. So Jesus assumed the position of host and the woman was His guest. No other relationship, then or now, could serve better as a framework for what He wanted to teach about the gifts of God, His divine grace. That is the essence of being a host. He gives gifts to his guest.

Jesus' assumption of the position of host to this guest who was in such deep trouble is particularly important, for He made it evident at once that it was simply a picture of God's hospitality. The gifts that He was anxious to give to this woman were gifts of God. "If thou knewest the gift of God . . . ," He said.

Jesus had an even deeper lesson than that for her as we shall see immediately. But this is an exquisitely beautiful beginning. God is our eternal Host, and we His sinful, shipwrecked guests. From this beginning, and in this atmosphere of pure gracious love, Jesus went on to give this woman one of the greatest lessons of the Gospel of John. Her respect for Christ showed itself almost at once. "Art thou greater than our father Jacob?" indicated such. "Our fathers worshipped in this mountain," etc. may have had in it an element of self-defense, as tending to precipitate theological controversy. But something else was in it too. Jesus saw real spiritual thirst in that reply, and we can almost

Jesus saith unto them, My meat is to do the will of him that sent me, and to finish his work. Say not ye, There are yet four months, and then cometh harvest? behold, I say unto you, Lift up your eyes, and look on the fields; for they are white already to harvest. And he that reapeth receiveth wages, and gathereth fruit unto life eternal: that both he that soweth and he that reapeth may rejoice together. And herein is that saying true, One soweth, and another reapeth. I sent you to reap that whereon ye bestowed no labour: other men laboured, and ye are entered into their labours.

---

feel His eagerness as He tried to make the truth clear to her. Jesus saw a soul of great beauty here, sincere, and honest, and humble — even in her sin.

In considering this chapter, our first necessity is a clear picture of the woman with whom Jesus was talking. But the picture of the woman is only incidental to our main quest. What we want is a vivid and genuine picture of Jesus. John evidently reckoned this episode at the well of Sychar as very important in his portrayal of Jesus' character. He gives us only two interviews with individuals and each affords an extremely vivid picture of Jesus. We have alrady noted how Jesus' brusqueness in dealing with Nicodemus made such an impression on the disciples that when this Gospel was written fifty years later, it could be recalled with the vividness of yesterday.

We see evidence of an equally vivid impression here — Jesus' exquisite courtesy and gentleness in dealing with a woman of this kind. His easy comradeship with her and His respect for her personality were as unexpected and shocking to the disciples as His brusqueness with Nicodemus had been. Jesus not only disregarded the low reputation of this woman, He put Himself under obligations to her, took the initiative and asked her for a drink, something that apparently surprised her as much as it did the disciples.

But Jesus Himself would quite surely have been very displeased with such a description of the occurrence. There was nothing surprising or worthy of comment in the way He treated her. It was the simplest sort of easy, natural equality. Sin had tripped her up badly, but her essential equality with others

was not in the slightest degree compromised. Without question
the conventions of His day were completely disregarded here, but
those conventions were simply one of the many varieties of human
pride and sin which Jesus met. They were always disregarded.

The conventions of our day, too. At this point we may well
ask ourselves some very radical questions. Have we been following the disciples, or Jesus, in our attitudes? Jesus here is not
endorsing her past acts. His mention of them constituted a
rebuke. But there is no demonstration of horror over her flagrant
and unrepented sin, no indignation over a broken divine law.
Jesus seemed not concerned to vindicate God's law. He did not
rebuke those who had broken it. He showed no anxiety to protect
society from the evil effect of such an example. What He wanted
was to put eternal life into the heart of this woman.

To accomplish this, Jesus did not simply treat her with courtesy,
He made Himself her comrade. He genuinely esteemed her
personality. The only rebuke Jesus wanted then and He wants
now, is the rebuke of our own revivified conscience.

In spite of her lack of education, and her meager and defective
background, Jesus did not prepare her for the truth by any
preliminary educational process. He did not send her to the genuine revelation of the Jews. He was able to make the truth comprehensible to her just where she stood, so she could without hesitation step into the Kingdom of God, if she chose.

For this purpose Jesus gave her the most luminous and profound truth. We cannot completely fathom it. She did not
understand it, but she remembered it. She accepted it and it
saved her.

Jesus did not drive this woman with threats, and He did not
draw here with rewards. He never did. As we look at this
picture, we are almost as much astonished as the disciples were.
We would probably have given her the message that Jesus gave
Nicodemus. Here was an outcast, floundering in repulsive sin.
Certainly she needed to be born again. No doubt she did need just
that, but Jesus put it another way.

As Jesus saw it, the important thing here was the fact that this woman felt a sharp spiritual thirst. Nicodemus failed. Jesus could not waken in him any such response. Once this woman took off her mask, so that her deep spiritual thirst was seen, there is something awe-inspiring in Jesus' reply. "Woman, believe me" shows a reaction very different from anything appearing in the talk with Nicodemus. This woman was not anxious to talk about the Kingdom of God. She wanted to enter it. Jesus' effort to make the road plain to her has given us the simplest and probably the most profound statement that we have of the requirements for those who wish to enter the Kingdom.

JESUS TEACHING THE GRACE OF GOD

When therefore the Lord knew how the Pharisees had heard that Jesus made and baptized more disciples than John, (though Jesus himself baptized not, but his disciples,) He left Judea, and departed again into Galilee. And he must needs go through Samaria.

We have been studying what the Samaritan woman said to Jesus. It is important. However, what Jesus said to her is much more important. "If you knew the gift of God and who it is that is saying to you, Give me a drink, you would have asked of him, and he would have given you living water"

We have already seen that God so loved the world that He sacrificed His Son for us. That was the first lesson. But love can be a far-away thing, and the great sacrifice made by that love is a stupendous mystery hidden in the deep counsels of God.

Jesus did not think of God in that vague way. We do not always notice Jesus' conception of God in His teaching. It is one of His most important contributions. In every lesson we study, underneath the truth which we see on the surface, there is a further contribution to our understanding of God, and often the deep lesson is more important than the surface one.

This is a good example. It is one of a series of new pictures of God. To see this completely, we will have to wait till the lesson is finished, but we will start with a preview, for what Jesus told this woman was very important indeed.

Then cometh he to a city of Samaria, which is called Sychar, near to the parcel of ground that Jacob gave to his son Joseph. Now Jacob's well was there. Jesus therefore, being wearied with his journey, sat thus on the well: and it was about the sixth hour. There cometh a woman to draw water: Jesus saith unto her, Give me to drink. (For his disciples were gone away unto the city to buy meat.) Then saith the woman of Samaria unto him, How is it that thou, being a Jew, askest drink of me, which am a woman of Samaria? for the Jews have no dealings with the Samaritans.

First, the hospitality of God. "If thou knewest the gift of God" puts the whole episode into the realm of hospitality. God is our host, as Jesus was host to this woman. We are guests, weak and sinful and ignorant guests. The very atmosphere is pure grace. What do hosts do? They give gifts, beautiful, lovely gifts, without limit and without return.

The second lesson is even more lovely — the Fatherhood of God. "The hour cometh, and now is, when the true worshippers shall worship the Father in spirit and truth." We do not bow before the Architect of the universe. We kneel before our Heavenly Father.

It is an immeasurable emancipation simply to realize that God is our Heavenly Father and not a far distant Judge, but the lesson which Jesus gave this woman goes farther than that. He offers her an immediate entrance into the heavenly Kingdom, if only she can worship the Father in spirit and truth. That runs down very deep. Eternal salvation was hers if she could worship in complete sincerity her Heavenly Father. She must see God as her Father, and even more difficult, she must see herself as His daughter.

And finally, the longing of God. "Such doth the Father seek to be His worshippers." Our Heavenly Father, too, "came to seek and to save that which is lost." Jesus is seeking the lost here. He was talking to one of God's daughters, whose soul had been bruised and soiled. She thirsted for the beauty that had once been hers, the beauty of holiness, though she could not have called it by that name. So Jesus said to her, "If you knew the gift of God, and knew that He who talks to you carries that gift in His hand, you might have asked from Him, and He would have given you all that you thirst for."

Jesus answered and said unto her, If thou knewest the gift of God, and who it is that saith to thee, Give me to drink; thou wouldest have asked of him, and he would have given thee living water. The woman saith unto him, Sir, thou hast nothing to draw with, and the well is deep: from whence then hast thou that living water?

This woman did not know anything about gifts from God. She knew of gifts to God. As far back in childhood as she could remember, her tiny pet lambs had been carried off as sacrifices and their throats cut, so that God would be satisfied. How many times she had cried over those little victims!

Jesus' teaching was not generally understood, neither was it here, but this woman knew that He was talking about something new and beautiful. It would take all her life to understand this little sentence, "If thou knewest the gift of God." But its deepest lesson, and its greatest, she did catch just because the sublimity of the lesson matched the simplicity of her mind. For the lesson of that sentence is its picture of God. God is a God of gifts, of fragrant, beautiful gifts. That is His nature. He wanted to give her every unbelievably beautiful thing that her inmost soul thirsted for, the opportunity and the power to love purely, the relaxed bliss of a pure and beautiful and forgiven soul that God Himself loves to look at, the ability to help others who had stumbled as she did.

All these things, and more, that her imagination could not even picture, God was holding out to her. She was His guest. How much did she understand of all this? Probably almost nothing, in precise detail. But instinctively, by seeing in Jesus' beautiful voice and manner, and above all in His eyes, the smile of a God who gives, and loves, and forgives, we can say that she caught it all.

For in spite of her past record and her present low position, God was offering her His very best gifts. She did not miss that.

And men have sat at her side from that day to this, to learn the same lesson. We do not deserve any of these things. They are a free gift. And that is the lesson taught at Jacob's well in Samaria, that God is a God of grace, of free, unmerited, saving grace. It is for all of those who must sit alongside of that troubled woman. Grace understood by none and deserved by none.

Art thou greater than our father Jacob, which gave us the well, and drank thereof himself, and his children, and his cattle? Jesus answered and said unto her, Whosoever drinketh of this water shall thirst again: But whosoever drinketh of the water that I shall give him shall never thirst; but the water that I shall give him shall be in him a well of water springing up into everlasting life.

Jesus might have used the figures of jewels or of flowers. This woman would have seen the beauty in such figures very easily indeed. But He chose something simpler; water for her thirst. Thirst is a subjective thing, and Jesus is thinking of subjective needs, our feelings of incompleteness and unrest, of desperate uncertainty, sin, and guilt. This woman was thirsty. Here was water to satisfy that thirst. Jesus had defined in, a clear statement Nicodemus' need. Here too, Jesus begins with a statement of this woman's need. She needed the gift of God and Jesus made it simpler than that. She needed living water. It would satisfy every thirst that her spirit felt, and make her an overflowing spring for others.

Jesus identifies this living water with Himself. "If thou knewest the gift of God and who it is that saith to thee, give me to drink, thou wouldest have asked of him." Jesus Himself is the living water. It was probably many years before the woman understood this. But everything that comes from Jesus is also living water — Jesus' example, His teaching, the total impression of His life upon us. Any or all of these can satisfy the dreadful thirst that sears our souls.

The woman saith unto him, Sir, give me this water, that I thirst not, neither come hither to draw. Jesus saith unto her, Go, call thy husband, and come hither. The woman answered and said, I have no husband. Jesus said unto her, Thou hast well said, I have no husband: For thou hast had five husbands; and he whom thou now hast is not thy husband: in that saidst thou truly.

As with Nicodemus so also here, Jesus' second effort is to show how this need can be met. Where and how can this woman get the living water? She must ask for it. Jesus does not pour it down any throat by force. He did not then, and He does not now. "Thou wouldest have asked of him." We must want this blessing. We must desire the imprint of Jesus on our life. And we must ask it from him, for it is available nowhere else. Every man may have it, even those at the very bottom. No one has to ask for it a second time.

But for both of us the second word is the difficult one. We must drink it. After water is drunk it is absorbed, and it becomes part and parcel of our physical body. That is an involuntary thing. It is God's work. But the drinking is our work,

Obviously, we must understand with some clarity just what it is that constitutes this living water, and precisely what we are to do with it. Jesus Himself and all the truth that comes from Him is the living water. That we understand. He presents Himself to each one of us. How does He present Himself? He uses a number of instruments. Our mothers, the Gospel account in which Jesus speaks to us directly, the fervent word of some evangelist. And there are those to whom Jesus comes in the beauty of nature, and in music. Indeed, where is the man who does not see Christ when he listens to the Hallelujah Chorus? Whenever Jesus presents Himself to a man, that presentation is the living water, which he must drink.

The woman saith unto him, Sir, I perceive that thou art a prophet. Our fathers worshipped in this mountain; and ye say, that in Jerusalem is the place where men ought to worship. Jesus saith unto her, Woman, believe me, the hour cometh, when ye shall neither in this mountain nor yet at Jerusalem, worship the Father. Ye worship ye know not what: we know what we worship: for salvation is of the Jews.

But what does it mean, then, to drink this living water? Doubtless it means complete acceptance. When a man swallows a drink of water, he accepts that water, completely and irrevocably. There are several corollaries. He must taste this water and enjoy

it. In dealing with Jesus, where is no such thing as swallowing
against our will and still tasting this living water. We can only
accept it if we enjoy it and rejoice in it. That is an essential part
of the acceptance, and it means that we must study Jesus' words
and works, until at least some part of them is clearly and deeply
comprehended. That much penetration into Jesus' real thought is
necessary before genuine acceptance is possible.

After meditation has made it possible for our imaginations to
hear Jesus Himself giving this teaching, and after careful thought
has made us understand what Jesus' thought really is, then, as the
delight of this teaching and insight glows in our soul, we accept it
with all our hearts. This means that to the limit of our tiny capacity we are going to do the works that Jesus did, and speak the
words that He spoke. And, as an Arab once said to me, even think
the thoughts that He thought. Above all things, it means that we
are going to desire the things that He desires, and love the things
that He loved. We also will grieve over the things that grieved
His heart.

But the hour cometh, and now is, when the true worshippers shall worship
the Father in spirit and in truth: for the Father seeketh such to worship
him. God is a Spirit: and they that worship him must worship him
in spirit and in truth. The woman saith unto him, I know that Messias
cometh, which is called Christ: when he is come, he will tell us all
things. Jesus saith unto her, I that speak unto thee am he.

The living water Jesus gives is a divine and wonderful thing.
Gods omnipotence is in it. Our acceptance of this gift is a poor,
human, defective thing, but if it is genuine, the living water trans-
forms us. We become overflowing springs of living water and
those around us can drink.

As with Nicodemus, so here, Jesus has a third lesson. He has
shown this woman her need, and He has shown her where to satisfy it, that is, where to get the living water she needs. Now He will
show her the great divine foundation upon which all this rests.
But in this case He has to do something else first. He is going to
show her not only where to secure that living water, but very
precisely for her own individual need, how to find it.

From a purely theoretical point of view, Jesus' discussion up to this point seems symmetrical and complete. We see God as the giver of gifts, Jesus as their purveyor, and the earnest suppliant as their receiver. What can be added to that? But from the woman's point of view it was very incomplete. Jesus had not given her yet anything that could be the living water for her. In all this discussion she probably saw nothing at all she could take hold of. Hers was a difficult situation. She was deep in sin, and she knew it. Where was the door for her so she could enter into the hospitality and grace of a loving and wonderful God?

This woman was different from Nicodemus. She did not want to talk about the Kingdom of God.

She wanted to enter it. The conversation continued with Jesus evidently trying to uncover some point at which spiritual need or spiritual aspiration or thirst of some sort was consciously felt. The search was soon rewarded. No sense of sin was uncovered, simply the thirst of a perplexed soul guided all her life from one futility to another. She wanted a real contact with God. Jesus reacted sharply to this discovery, much as a pearl diver does when searching through the day's catch of oysters, he suddenly comes on a pearl of great beauty. There was no demand that the woman recognize and repent of her sins. That subject was dropped. Jesus had found just what He wanted. He knew the water which would give her eternal life to be the contribution from Him that she needed.

This woman was deep in sin, and hers was a sin which we have all learned to fear. But Jesus was thinking of something else. She had tried to get the strength she needed from worship. She had tried two ways, but both were dead, so smothered with ritual, and so obscured by human agents, that everything else was crowded out. In her question she did not so much as mention God. Her search failed, and life became a more and more complete wreck. Nevertheless, Jesus saw that she was still pointed in the right direction, and all He told her was how to worship God.

Some profound questions arise here. A stern word after the fashion of the message to Nicodemus seems in order with this woman. No doubt we are wrong there. The crust of sin on the outside of her soul was unusually thick, and very repulsive, but that soul was pointed toward God. She was still trying to worship Him. She still believed that she belonged to God. What Jesus gave her was not even a better method of worship. He gave her simply a different conception of God.

Without doubt the woman understood only a small part of what Jesus wanted to teach her, but she caught enough of the wonder of it to see that Jesus was a prophet. His gentle rebuke to her previous manner of life seems to have had much to do with this conclusion. Here was a prophet, and all the thirst of her parched spirit comes to the surface. It was as if she said, "All these beautiful things that you have been telling of must come from God, or at least be connected in some way with Him. Where and how are we to worship God? His gifts surely will not be given to those who fail to worship Him acceptably." Jesus had spoken of eternal life. That of itself brought God into the discussion.

This woman had probably been trying all her life to worship God. Human leaders had led her badly. Perhaps she had finally given up the effort, and that was the reason why her life had become so tangled.

But she could remember when she worshipped God with great sincerity and with her whole soul. The student looking only at the surface can very easily say that all Jesus is doing here is to send her back to her former, sincere and wholehearted worship.

That is a great mistake, but it serves to introduce some very important questions. To worship God with our whole nature, and in complete, sincere devotion is not a rare thing in human history. But is it a good thing? That sort of complete, sincere devotion has been one of the blackest evils of humanity's past, witness the Inquisition of medieval Spain, or the Wahabees of our own time. The best example, of course, is the crucifixion of Jesus by the Pharisees. They worshipped God in earnest, and crucified Jesus as part of that worship.

Everything depends on the sort of God we worship. Jesus did not give this woman any new rules about how to worship, nor where. He abolished all the rules. He gave her a new God to worship, utterly and completely new, a Heavenly Father. In this Gospel John is building a new conception of God. In one sense that is all he is doing. It is a glorious picture. Nicodemus' lesson on the New Birth fits into this. They are great stones in the foundation of a divine cathedral. "True worshippers shall worship the Father." We caught the lovely colors of the dawn of this glorious vision, as the lesson opened, "If thou knewest the gifts of God." Fathers love to give gifts. And they give beautiful gifts, more beautiful by far than the children are wise enough to ask for.

With all her limitations this woman knew that any program of religious thought and expression must be built on a foundation of worship. She knew of two such foundations, the law of the Jews and the law of the Samaritans. There was the temple in Jerusalem, and there was the mountain nearby. Which was the right one?

We can feel Jesus' eagerness as He moves up to meet this question. The negative answer came first. Of these two laws, which? Neither. And in that answer is included every law of every sort whereby men try to guide and limit the religious life and worship and conceptions of their fellow-men.

There is a deep reason for this tremendous iconoclastic negative. We might have expected Jesus to tell her to go up into her mountain and worship the Father in spirit and truth there, or indeed, to go to Jerusalem. That would have built her new experience on her old one. We regard that as necessary. But Jesus knew better. Some idols have to be destroyed. Some sorts of error have to be cleared away to make real faith possible.

A matter of great importance is introduced here. We will meet it many times. No one can worship the Father in spirit and truth if he is bound by a law. Even on the human plane no one serves a father by means of laws. We approach our earthly father whenever we wish; not once a year after meticulous, ritual preparation; and we address him after the feelings in our hearts; not as some intermediary priest directs. A written law and ritual and sacrifices are simply absurd in such a setting.

With respect to our Heavenly Father this would be even worse. When men worship according to a law, completely false elements are put in. God becomes hard and rigid, with an insistence on ethical trifles which negates common intelligence. But the real trouble lies deeper. The law puts human religious leaders, an incredibly sacred written code, and a pompous and incomprehensible ritual of worship between the Heavenly Father and His worshippers. A Heavenly Father who talks to us, and leads us by the hand, is far removed from such a concept.

This lesson to the woman of Samaria has roots that run even deeper than this. It is not difficult to see what Jesus meant when He said that God is our Heavenly Father. The pure beauty of this picture is its authentication. But worshipping our Heavenly Father in spirit and truth takes hold of something else. We not only recognize God as our Heavenly Father, which is easy, but we recognize ourselves as His sons and daughters which is very difficult.

What was Jesus asking from this woman who was defeated, perplexed, cast out by her fellows and by her own conscience? He was asking her to go home and kneel down, and after focussing her mind on the love and forgiveness of her Heavenly Father and as His own daughter to worship her Father in spirit aud truth. Her sin had been great. Her separation from God and His truth had been dreadfully wide. Men had condemned her with great completeness. But all the repentance and restitution and faith that Jesus asked of her, was a simple return to her place as one of the daughters of God. And we must all sit next to this sincere and humble and unlettered woman if we are to enter our Father's Kingdom. This is the one place to go. Jesus demanded nothing from her in the way of intellectual apprehension of difficult things. It is a lesson for a child. How could Jesus open the door so widely to so weak and ignorant and sinful a woman? The cross is the answer to that question as it is to every question that our astonished unbelief asks regarding the incredible grace of God. But Jesus did not say anything about the cross. God's grace is not to be explained. It is to be accepted. This is a lesson for the primary class, the class for the children. We will squeeze up close to this dirty little girl from Samaria and remember that Jesus once said: "Except ye . . . become as little children, ye shall in no wise enter into the kingdom of heaven."

We are not quite finished even yet. What we have been considering is our loveliest picture of the grace of God. But now we are to see the foundation of all this. As with Nicodemus, so here, the lesson finishes with a view of the eternal reality of God which underlies this wonderful teaching. Grace and truth came by Jesus Christ. We find them together, almost always just as we do here. It is a new understanding of God we are learning to look for. Fundamentally, that is the only truth there is. And this picture of God's truth has the rose tints and the fragrance of the lesson on grace which preceded it.

Behind this picture of the unbelievable grace of God, who accepts us eternally as children, we catch the warmth and the fragrance of Heaven itself. "For such the Father seeks to be his worshippers." One is reminded of the mother searching through snow-covered streets, in one saloon after another, to beg one of those wanderers to come home and be her boy again.

This is our picture of the God of grace.

We can almost hear Jesus saying: "Your Heavenly Father longs for little girls like you who will recognize themselves as His daughters, for boys to be His sons." With them He finds companionship and association and love, which He desires and enjoys even as we do. He seeks long and finds few.

We will turn our eyes upward in pure gratitude for this addition to our understanding of God. No chains are on this picture Jesus gives us. This is the God of grace, the God who gives gifts. It is not a picture of a great, omnipotent Judge, but of a divinely gracious Host whose obligations and intentions are not to the smallest degree affected by the defects and sins of his guest. It is indeed infinitely more profound and beautiful than, that — nothing less than the concern of a Heavenly Father for His child.

And many of the Samaritans of that city believed on him for the saying of the woman, which testified, He told me all that ever I did. So when the Samaritans were come unto him, they besought him that he would tarry with them: and he abode there two days. And many more believed because of his own word; And said unto the woman, Now we believe, not because of thy saying: for we have heard him ourselves, and know that this is indeed the Christ, the Saviour of the world.

FURTHER EXPERIENCES

At this time, early in Christ's ministry, His disciples were actively engaged in baptizing large numbers of believers. We should like to know just who these believers were. So far as we can gather from the account, Christ continued this for only a short time. Later we hear nothing of it. What the purpose and significance of this baptism were would be interesting to learn.

By this time Christ was a wandering teacher with a company of disciples who followed Him wherever He went. This is a common thing in the East. In many ways Jesus was more an Easterner than a Westerner. Almost the first question arising in the materialistic Western mind is that of their support. Who provided for them? The Easterner would be surprised at such a question. They were religious mendicants, of course, living as religious teachers in the East usually do, as dependents on others. The idea is very repugnant to the Western mind. We think it a sort of crime. Paul working at his trade suits us better.

Hardly any individual except a religious teacher in the East could be so emancipated from concern over the needs of the body as the author of this Gospel represents Jesus to have been. He and His disciples seem never to have been hungry or thirsty,

Now after two days he departed thence, and went into Galilee. For Jesus himself testified, that a prophet hath no honour in his own country. Then when he was come into Galilee, the Galileans received him, having seen all the things that he did at Jerusalem at the feast: for they also went unto the feast. So Jesus came again into Cana of Galilee, where he made the water wine. And there was a certain nobleman, whose son was sick at Capernaum. When he heard that Jesus was come out of Judea into Galilee, he went unto him, and besought him that he would come down, and heal his son: for he was at the point of death.

---

never cold or hot. Jesus' being tired here is perhaps the only place where His physical limitations emerge into view.

If Jesus lacked a normal man's preoccupation with what he is going to eat, there are other lacks too, quite as notable. We see no signs of the powerful functioning of the human instincts. His whole attention and conscious desire were devoted to the things of the spirit.

But again this has to be modified, for certain elements of the life of the spirit, as we usually understand the term, are lacking. The eager investigation of the nature and behavior of our material environment, which is the peculiar glory of the Western mind, is not to be found, and even the quest of the beautiful which we call art, if present at all, is to be seen only in its most rudimentary and insignificant form. Christ was like the roving Bedouin of the desert. He found in this life only two things worthy of attention — sincere worship of God, and fraternal association with His fellow men.

Jesus put His best effort into training the disciples. They went with Him everywhere and were participants in practically everything He did. Even at this time He undoubtedly realized that it would soon be necessary to commit to them the message that He brought from God. So they shared with Him popularity and unpopularity, hunger and satisfaction. They found it very difficult to understand His teachings. They were loyal to Him, but His disregard of public opinion and His love for the ostracized and distressed was something they hardly accepted or even understood.

Then said Jesus unto him, Except ye see signs and wonders, ye will not believe. The nobleman saith unto him, Sir, come down ere my child die. Jesus saith unto him, Go thy way; thy son liveth. And the man believed the word that Jesus had spoken unto him, and he went his way. And as he was now going down, his servants met him, and told him, saying, Thy son liveth. Then inquired he of them the hour when he began to amend. And they said unto him, Yesterday at the seveneth hour the fever left him.

However, their stupidity and pride brought from Christ no burning rebuke. He met it with a vivid portrayal of the motive that dominated Him, and the great overwhelming objective that stretched out before Him. Christ did not expect that they would absorb this vision and be transformed by it at once. So far as immediate results were concerned, no doubt a burning rebuke would have been more effective. But Christ did not want men driven by a fear of His disapproval. He wanted them dominated by the same vision that ruled Him.

"My meat is to do the will of him that sent me, and to finish his work" is a vivid picture of Jesus' motive. It will bear study. The will of men and their praise and approbation count for nothing. Moreover, it is a picture of objective loyalty. Jesus is never heard expressing the hope that His love for the Father may be adequate, or congratulating Himself that it is. Doing the Father's will and accomplishing the Father's work occupied His whole attention. The self-consciousness, and the self-esteem that base our sense of sin and our feeling of spiritual achievement on our own mental states, our own feelings, were utterly foreign to Christ's mind. He did not find His motive in self-development or in any other form of camouflaged selfishness. He found it in the Father's will. He was not in the world for self-expression of whatever spiritual sort, but to execute a divine commission.

We have here two little pictures of Jesus, beautiful and illuminating. The Samaritans responded to His teachings as no one else did. So He stayed there two days. It seems surprising that He did not stay two months, or two years. Indeed, why did Jesus

So the father knew that it was at the same hour, in the which Jesus said unto him, Thy son liveth: and himself believed, and his whole house. This is again the second miracle that Jesus did, when he was come out of Judea into Galilee.

---

not make this city His headquarters? What success He might have enjoyed!

But Jesus was carrying out a divine plan. It was not utterly rigid. Two days could be found for an unexpected demand, but not two months. One wonders what became of these promising believers. They are not heard from again, but later it was a Samaritan whom Jesus made the hero of one of his most striking parables.

We see here another evidence that Jesus was working according to a definite long-range plan. He still had a long list of almost impossible profound and difficult teachings to give to men. That would not have been possible in Sychar. So He left that center of friendliness and faith, and took up again His ministry to the hostile world outside.

The problem of miracles comes up here. We shall meet it many times. Apparently Jesus performed this miracle to produce belief. In this it was almost unique, for that was not often His reason. Perhaps even here the motive of compassion was behind the actual healing as seems to have been the case always. It was the publicity that made this miracle effective in creating faith. That was unusual also, for Jesus more often discouraged publicity.

JOHN 5

After this there was a feast of the Jews; and Jesus went up to Jerusalem. Now there is at Jerusalem by the sheep market a pool, which is called in the Hebrew tongue Bethesda, having five porches. In these lay a great multitude of impotent folk of blind, halt, withered, waiting for the moving of the water. For an angel went down at a certain season into the pool, and troubled the water: whosoever then first after the troubling of the water stepped in was made whole of whatsoever disease he had. And a certain man was there, which had an infirmity thirty and eight years. When Jesus saw him lie, and knew that he had been now a long time in that case, he saith unto him, Wilt thou be made whole? The impotent man answered him, Sir, I have no man, when the water is troubled, to put me into the pool: but while I am coming, another steppeth down before me. Jesus saith unto him, Rise, take up thy bed, and walk. And immediately the man was made whole, and took up his bed, and walked: and on the same day was the sabbath.

The Jews therefore said unto him that was cured, It is the sabbath day: it is not lawful for thee to carry thy bed. He answered them, He that made me whole, the same said unto me, Take up thy bed, and walk. Then asked they him, What man is that which said unto thee, Take up thy bed, and walk? And he that was healed wist not who it was: for Jesus had conveyed himself away, a multitude being in that place. Afterward Jesus findeth him in the temple, and said unto him, Behold thou art made whole: sin no more, lest a worse thing come unto thee. The man departed, and told the Jews that it was Jesus, which had made him whole. And therefore did the Jews persecute Jesus, and sought to slay him, because he had done these things on the sabbath day.

But Jesus answered them, My Father worketh hitherto, and I work. Therefore the Jews sought the more to kill him, because he not only had broken the sabbath, but said also that God was his Father, making himself equal with God. Then answered Jesus and said unto them, Verily, verily, I say unto you, The Son can do nothing of himself, but what he seeth the Father do: for what things soever he doeth, these also doeth the Son likewise. For the Father loveth the Son, and sheweth him all things that himself doeth: and he will shew him greater works than these, that ye may marvel. For as the Father raiseth up the dead, and quickeneth them; even so the Son quickeneth whom he will. For the Father judgeth no man, but hath committed all judgment unto the Son: That all men should honour the Son, even as they honour the Father. He that honoureth not the Son honoureth not the Father which hath sent him. Verily, verily, I say unto you, He that heareth my word, and believeth on him that sent me, hath everlasting life, and shall not come into condemnation; but is passed from death unto life. Verily, verily, I say unto you, The hour is coming, and now is, when the dead shall hear the voice of the Son of God: and they that hear shall live. For as the Father hath life in himself; so hath he given to the Son to have life in himself; And hath given him authority to execute judgment also, because he is the Son of man. Marvel not at this: for the hour is coming, in the which all that are in the graves shall hear his voice, And shall come forth; they that have done good, unto the resurrection of life; and they that have done evil, unto the resurrection of damnation. I can of mine own self do nothing: as I hear, I judge: and my judgment is just; because I seek not mine own will, but the will of the Father which hath sent me. If I bear witness of myself, my witness is not true.

There is another that beareth witness of me; and I know that the witness which he witnesseth of me is true. Ye sent unto John, and he bare witness unto the truth. But I receive not testimony from man; but these things I say, that ye might be saved. He was a burning and a shining light: and ye were willing for a season to rejoice in his light.

But I have greater witness than that of John: for the works which the Father hath given me to finish, the same works that I do, bear witness of me, that the Father hath sent me. And the Father himself, which hath sent me, hath borne witness of me. Ye have neither heard his voice at any time, nor seen his shape. And ye have not his word abiding in you: for whom he hath sent, him ye believe not.

Search the Scriptures; for in them ye think ye have eternal life: and they are they which testify of me. And ye will not come to me that ye might have life. I receive not honour from men. But I know you, that ye have not the love of God in you. I am come in my Father's name, and ye receive me not: if another shall come in his own name, him ye will receive. How can ye believe, which receive honour one of another, and seek not the honour that cometh from God only? Do not think that I will accuse you to the Father: there is one that accuseth you, even Moses, in whom ye trust. For had ye believed Moses, ye would have believed me: for he wrote of me. But if ye believe not his writings, how shall ye believe my words?

Chapter V

JESUS' PORTRAIT

After this there was a feast of the Jews; and Jesus went up to Jerusalem. Now there is at Jerusalem by the sheep market a pool, which is called in the Hebrew tongue Bethesda, having five porches. In these lay a great multitude of impotent folk of blind, halt, withered, waiting for the moving of the water. For an angel went down at a certain season into the pool, and troubled the water: whosoever then first after the troubling of the water stepped in was made whole of whatsoever disease he had. And a certain man was there, which had an infirmity thirty and eight years.

In this chapter John continues his task of painting Jesus' portrait, and recording what He taught. There is little or no chronological connection with what precedes. This episode was a dramatic and vivid affair, and it is not surprising that its details remained in the disciples' minds with great distinctness. The account is a model of condensation. It is extraordinary how much the writer gets into a mere handful of words.

Here, as in many other places, the account revolves around a miracle. The miracle itself was unusual. Jesus, for reasons which we are not told, went to the pool of Bethesda. Dozens, indeed perhaps hundreds, were waiting for healing in the porches around this pool. The ruins of those porches can be seen to this

When Jesus saw him lie, and knew that he had been now a long time
in that case, he saith unto him, Wilt thou be made whole? The
impotent man answered him, Sir, I have no man, when the water is
troubled, to put me into the pool: but while I am coming, another
steppeth down before me. Jesus saith unto him, Rise, take up thy
bed, and walk. And immediately the man was made whole, and took
up his bed, and walked: and on the same day was the sabbath.

---

day. They could accommodate a large number. One of the
unfortunates lying there caught Jesus' eye. We are not told the
reason for that either. Apparently he did not ask Jesus for help.
But he had been there a long time, and it was natural that Jesus
should sympathize with him. By inquiry, probably, Jesus learned
that he had been there for thirty-eight years, and that is a long
time by any standard. Most likely he was generally known, and
any bystander could tell Jesus about him.

When a man has been begging for thirty-eight years we expect
a very twisted character, and this man showed himself to be just
such a case. But once His sympathies were aroused, Jesus tried
hard to do something for him. Jesus picked this man out and
healed him although he had shown no faith nor even asked for
help. The man himself was probably more surprised than any-
body else.

The healing itself was a singularly beautiful, unforced bit of
kindness. It would be pleasant to let our imagination believe
that in it the man felt the impact of Jesus' personality quite as
vividly as Nicodemus, or even the woman at the well.

All three were changed probably quite as much by their mere
contact with Jesus as by any teaching that He gave them. So far
as we can judge from the account, Jesus' teaching was hardly
ever understood at once. It was like leaven, or like a seed which
must be given time to germinate and grow.

But such an easy and beautiful reading of this incident is, to
say the least, incomplete if not fundamentally wrong. For Jesus
did this act of kindness on the Sabbath. Jesus once healed a man
with a withered hand on the Sabbath, and from the account it is

The Jews therefore said unto him that was cured, It is the sabbath day: it is not lawful for thee to carry thy bed. He answered them, He that made me whole, the same said unto me, Take up thy bed, and walk.   Then asked they him, What man is that which said unto thee, Take up thy bed and walk?   And he that was healed wist not who it was: for Jesus had conveyed himself away, a multitude being in that place.

---

evident that the simple act of healing on that day laid Jesus open to criticism. However, in the discussion which followed that act of mercy, He was able to justify Himself, at least to some of His critics. On a first reading one marvels that this miracle of healing, where a multitude of other unfortunate people could look on, was not followed by a wild riot of requests asking for similar help. It was the Sabbath and they did not want it.

The miracle by itself could not have stirred up the wild scenes that followed. Such an act of mercy on the Sabbath was not sufficient to precipitate a conflict with the religious leaders. Although the Pharisees are not mentioned by name, it is their spirit that we see here, and no doubt this large crowd included many of them. Jesus added a second feature to this healing which could not fail to stir things up. He did not say, "Rise up and walk," but rather, "Rise, pick up your bed, and go home with it." The thin mattress-like pallet upon which he had been lying was rolled up into a large cylinder-shaped burden, and carried on his head. The place was crowded. Hundreds were there waiting for healing, and Sabbath crowds of onlookers were giving alms. A more public demonstration of Sabbath-breaking could hardly be imagined.

The more this act of Jesus is considered, the more surprising it appears. Why not leave the little bed in place till sundown when the Sabbath ended! Any neighbor would have kept it for him, and he could have come back for it in the evening. That would have avoided all the trouble. We would surely have told him to leave it there, and come and follow Jesus quietly, carefully keeping the law, as good citizens do.

Afterward Jesus findeth him in the temple, and said unto him, Behold, thou art made whole: sin no more, lest a worse thing come unto thee. The man departed, and told the Jews that it was Jesus, which had made him whole. And therefore did the Jews persecute Jesus, and sought to slay him, because he had done these things on the sabbath day.

It is impossible to suppose that Jesus forgot that it was the Sabbath and equally impossible to suppose that He did not know what the result of breaking the Sabbath would be. He "broke" the Sabbath intentionally, or, rather, He told the man to do it. It is a little surprising that the man obeyed Jesus and carried his bed on his head in full view of the crowd. His unexpected healing must have left him a little dazed. He did not get very far, probably not a hundred feet and then someone with a little religious authority stepped imperiously in front of him and ended it.

Some very difficult questions arise here. Why did Jesus want to have the Sabbath broken? No doubt the Pharisees had added to the divine commands of the Old Testament a multitude of the most trifling regulations which Jesus' followers could not be expected to keep. But these regulations had behind them the force of community sentiment and of wise law-givers. Surely no one is greatly injured by keeping the Sabbath even in excessive detail. At least, we might suppose that he had better avoid breaking it publicly. The Christian missionary in a Mohammedan country is careful during the fast month of Ramadhan not to eat anything in public. Would it not have been better for Jesus to teach this man and His disciples to follow the Pharisees' commands at least as far as they reasonably could?

But perhaps we are wrong there. Perhaps a man is injured, or, rather, wrecked by unquestioning obedience to a dead law. At least men are wrecked by supposing that God is interested in that sort of thing, or that He corresponds in any way to the legalistic idol of the Pharisees' imagination.

Whatever Jesus' underlying thought, He decided to seize this opportunity to renounce the Pharisees and all their works. They were the religious leaders of society, and their power over the common people was unlimited. But undoubtedly Jesus' first pur-

But Jesus answered them, My father worketh hitherto, and I work. Therefore the Jews sought the more to kill him, because he not only had broken the sabbath, but said also that God was his Father, making himself equal with God.   Then answered Jesus and said unto them, Verily, verily, I say unto you, The Son can do nothing of himself, but what he seeth the Father do: for what things soever he doeth, these also doeth the Son likewise.

For the Father loveth the Son, and sheweth him all things that himself doeth: and he will shew him greater works than these, that ye may marvel.   For as the Father raiseth up the dead, and quickeneth them; even so the Son quickeneth whom he will.   For the Father judgeth no man, but hath committed all judgment unto the Son:

---

pose in stirring this conflict up was the salvation of the man He healed. He hoped that the conflict with the religious authorities would break him away from them, so personal discipleship would become possible.

This was a plan that worked well in the case of the man born blind. We have that record in chapter 9. Here, as there, before the man could come into a personal relationship with Jesus, he would have to break away from the enormously strong legalistic system which enmeshed him. That would not be easy, but gratitude for his healing, and the personal impression that Jesus had made on him, would help very powerfully indeed. The man born blind came out of just such a conflict magnificently, but this man was made of weaker stuff. He slipped away from the conflict, the hands of his enemies, at the first opportunity. The man escaped easily but Jesus was at once in danger of His life.

Jesus did not resent this. He probably expected it, and in a way welcomed it. His attitude here surprises us at first. These men were His bitter enemies, trying at the moment to kill Him, but He taught them with undisturbed self-composure. More than that, He seemed to see in this situation a great opportunity. Scarcely anything in Jesus' whole life is more surprising than the teaching He gave to this terrifying mob of bitter enemies.

We must proceed cautiously in any attempt to penetrate Jesus' mind, but the account has been given us for just that purpose, so with a prayer for the Spirit's guidance, we will try to understand

That all men should honour the Son, even as they honour the Father. He that honoureth not the Son honoureth not the Father which hath sent him. Verily, verily. I say unto you, He that heareth my word, and believeth on him that sent me, hath everlasting life, and shall not come into condemnation; but is passed from death unto life. Verily, verily, I say unto you, The hour is coming, and now is, when the dead shall hear the voice of the Son of God: and they that hear shall live.

Jesus here. We know that Jesus had at least three things to do on earth. First of all, He had to die on the cross. Second, He had to give us in His life an adequate picture of God, His Heavenly Father. Finally, there were a certain number of teachings which He had to give to men. He called them "words." "The words that the Father hath given me, I have given unto them." His work would not be finished till they were all given. Here an opportunity was held out to Him by the Father for the presentation of one of His most difficult and profound "words." The depth and beauty of this message reach far beyond our understanding.

In the series of pictures which this chapter contains, we have now observed with some care the first picture. Jesus healed a man waiting at the pool, and broke the Sabbath as He did it. We come now to the second picture. This act of healing precipitated a conflict with the Pharisees, and the conflict was immediately a roaring conflagration. The leaders were anxious to murder Him. It was to be a year, or even more, before they succeeded, but their hearts were full of murder now. The Pharisees hated Jesus with a cold, deliberate hatred. This hatred is the most awful thing in the New Testament. Nor is this an isolated example of human depravity. It is a typical example of legalism versus the grace of God. The Wahabees of Central Arabia, and doubtless the inquisitionists of medieval Spain could sit for this portrait to the last detail.

What is there in such devotion to law, that is so appallingly dangerous? Jesus met Roman officials who were known for their cruelty. He met women who had fallen into adultery. But these unfortunates did not hate Him. Only the devotees of legalistic religion were able to do that.

For as the Father hath life in himself; so hath he given to the Son
to have life in himself; And hath given him authority to execute judgment
also, because he is the Son of man.   Marvel not at this: for the hour
is coming, in the which all that are in the graves shall hear his voice,
And shall come forth; they that have done good, unto the resurrection of
life; and they that have done evil, unto the resurrection of damnation.

It is not easy to put our finger on the exact reason for this. As
we see them here, the Pharises were characterized by a dreadful
devotion to the Sabbath, ready indeed to murder anyone under-
mining it.   One thinks of the Wahabees who used to kill people
who smoked tobacco. But such manifestations are only indications of the deep and strong currents of evil underneath.

No doubt Jesus' difference to their rules for Sabbath-keeping
endangered their own position. But that is not the deep explanation. Iconoclasts are often murdered, and the destroyers of the
legalist's idols most of all. We need to understand the exact nature
of the idols Jesus was destroying.

This is one of our easy introductions to the Pharisees. We are
to meet them many times in the Gospel of John. Indeed we have
met them already as we saw Jesus cleansing the temple. Human
sin, in meeting and opposing and eventually murdering Jesus,
did not take the form of drunkenness and adultery, nor of covet-
ousness and avarice. When Jesus met human sin, it fought back
in the form of self-satisfaction and pride, the hatred and callous
cruelty of the Pharisees.

We pass to the third picture, the most remarkable of all. Jesus
is teaching this wild mob of murderers. The fact that He taught
them at all is remarkable enough. He was able and willing to
teach such men. But the teaching He gave them is simply unbelievable.

Evidently the pedagogical problem that Jesus faced was extremely difficult. His, at the moment, was the task of transmitting
to men the most difficult teaching that the Father had given Him.
Jesus did not have to reply to His enemies, "My Father worketh
even until now, and I work." When He healed the man with the

I can of mine own self do nothing: as I hear, I judge: and my judgment is just; because I seek not mine own will, but the will of the Father
which hath sent me.   If I bear witness of myself, my witness is not
true.

There is another that beareth witness of me; and I know that the
witness which he witnesseth of me is true.   Ye sent unto John, and
he bare witness unto the truth.   But I receive not testimony from man:
but these things I say, that ye might be saved.

---

withered hand on the Sabbath, His defense that He was doing
good on the Sabbath would have been adequate here.

But Jesus saw before Him a great opportunity. His audience
was apparently made up largely of Pharisees. So He did not
justify His good deed simply on the basis of the benefit it
brought to the man himself. He dug down deeper, much deeper,
and put the discussion on a completely new plane. "My Father
worketh even until now, and I work." There was more than one
thing here to which the Pharisees could have taken exception.
God, His Heavenly Father, did not observe any Sabbath, at
least not one of complete inactivity. That point was bad enough,
but the point which they picked up without a moment's delay,
just as Jesus knew they would, was far more serious. Jesus was
calling God His own Father, making Himself equal with God.

Of all the teachings which Jesus had to give, this was the farthest outside of any possible human comprehension. It is supremely important, for man's salvation depends on it. But then
as now it could only be seen by men who have a deep understanding of the nature of God, as far as that is possible to feeble
men. Somewhere along the road of His earthly life, Jesus knew
that He must leave this teaching that the omnipotent Creator is
our Heavenly Father and that Jesus is His human Son, His equal,
His comrade, His collaborator.

Jesus' disciples could not reach the first rung of this mental
ladder, but the mob, raging against Jesus and thirsting for His
blood, did understand what He was trying to tell them about
God, and about Himself. They repudiated it with fury. The
notion that God was like Jesus was to them the blackest blas-

He was a burning and a shining light: and ye were willing for a season to rejoice in his light.

But I have greater witness than that of John: for the works which the Father hath given me to finish, the same works that I do, bear witness of me, that the Father hath sent me.

---

phemy. They crucified Jesus eventually just because of this. But they understood it. "But now," said Jesus, "have they both seen and hated both me and my Father." Only men of the profoundest theological training, and stirred to their depths by violent emotion, could see this. And because his enemies saw it, eventually the disciples understood it too. But they had not caught the vision then, and it is doubtful if we in our day see it as clearly and well as those Pharisees did when they rejected it and raged against it.

To those men who saw and repudiated God the Father and God the Son, Jesus went on to complete the picture. We would not have supposed that such a vision could legitimately be given to murderers like these. But Jesus knew better. He knew that some of those men would remember the lesson, and its beauty and truth would eventually capture them. They would remember it with some degree of adequacy just because their fierce repudiation of its every element, and because their rage at its preposterous blasphemy gave them a real penetration into its nature and depth.

As the picture ends, Jesus is trying with great patience and courage to show His enemies a rational path to faith and discipleship. This is the dominant theme is Jesus' consciousness of His mission. "The Father who sent me" was in His mind always, and most of all here. That was all that He expected men to understand about Him and believe of Him. He did not explain nor even assert any theological rank. Wherever we meet Him, we find this on the very surface of His consciousness, that He came from the Father, to do the work of His Heavenly Father, and to speak the words the Heavenly Father had given Him.

In dealing with Nicodemus and with the woman of Samaria, Jesus began with a discussion of their personal need, and from that proceeded to more general things. This time the profound

And the Father himself, which hath sent me, hath borne witness of me. Ye have neither heard his voice at any time, nor seen his shape. And ye have not his word abiding in you: for whom he hath sent, him ye believe not.

Search the Scriptures; for in them ye think ye have eternal life: and they are they which testify of me. And ye will not come to me, that ye might have life. I receive not honour from men. But I know you, that ye have not the love of God in you. I am come in my Father's name, and ye receive me not: if another shall come in his own name, him ye will receive.

---

discussion of deep divine things came first. But eventually Jesus was able to get to the personal need of these men. The atmosphere was so very hostile that to us the effort looks utterly futile. We are wrong there, of course. Like the rest of the discussion, this was not understood at the time but it was remembered, and it produced its fruit later.

This latter part of Jesus' discussion is not theological. It is personal. It has to do with men's personal needs and how God wants to meet them. This, too, was met with resentment and opposition, though the tone is not so bitter as in the earlier discussion.

But Jesus' claims here are as overwhelming as ever. Men could only have eternal life by coming to Him. His listeners were rejecting these claims with scorn. They demanded evidence to support such incredible statements.

Jesus did not resent this. On the contrary, He welcomed it. As far as it went it was the reaction He wanted, and He entered upon an effort to meet it. The necessary evidence could not come from men, He said. Such testimony He did not accept under any circumstances. This should not surprise us, for in the nature of the case no man can testify regarding Jesus' rank or position. Faith in Him must rest on two lines of evidence, that of the Scriptures, in which men can hear the voice of God, and upon Jesus' works by which He meant quite certainly all that He said and did.

Jesus considered this sufficient. He offered nothing further. Nevertheless His listeners did not believe. They were well

How can ye believe which receive honour one of another, and seek not the honour that cometh from God only?   Do not think that I will accuse you to the Father: there is one that accuseth you, even Moses, in whom ye trust.   For had ye believed Moses, ye would have believed me: for he wrote of me.   But if ye believe not his writings, how shall ye believe my words?

---

acquainted with both lines of evidence. The Scriptures had been their study since childhood, and Jesus' deeds and teachings had been open and public and constantly under the scrutiny of these men. Far from believing, they reached toward Jesus with greater and fiercer hostility. Jesus gives a surprising explanation of this. "How can ye believe who receive glory one of another, and the glory that cometh from the only God, ye seek not." That is to say, receiving glory one of another, enjoying each other's praise makes faith in Jesus impossible. It is not the praise of bad men that Jesus discusses here, but human praise of any sort.

A moment later Jesus adds another surprising statement. "If ye believed Moses, ye would believe me." These men then did not believe Moses. They had spent their lives studying Moses. Their confidence in the divine inspiration of his writing could not have been surpassed. They believed that God wrote it all, that every word was absolutely true and divinely authoritative. Nevertheless, Jesus, who saw ultimate reality, assured these men that they did not believe Moses. What then is belief? In Jesus' mind it must mean a penetration below the surface of the words to a comprehension of the teaching underneath. It means more — a complete surrender to the truth which God breathes into His messages. His teaching must be allowed to dominate our lives if Jesus is to reckon us believers.

One point here we must not fail to realize: that Jesus identified Himself completely with Moses' teaching and message. We may say that Jesus regarded Himself as the embodiment of God's word as given through Moses. Perhaps we, too, need to study Moses more and understand him better.

JESUS' TEACHING

The man departed and told the Jews that it was Jesus, which had
made him whole. And therefore did the Jews persecute Jesus, and
sought to slay him, because he had done these things on the sabbath
day.

But Jesus answered them, My Father worketh hitherto, and I work.

The writer of this Gospel chose certain occurrences in Jesus'
life and recorded them for us, not primarily because of the
episodes themselves, but because of the teaching that we gain
from them. Neither Nicodemus nor the woman at the well had
great significance for the writer, but the teaching that Jesus gave
these two people had very great significance indeed.

The same is true here in chapter 5. A beautiful miracle of
healing is recorded, but its significance lies in the teaching that
flows from it, and the picture of Jesus that it affords. This time
it is the truth Jesus brought which is presented to us first. The
chapter's new revelation of God's grace comes afterwards.

The miracle itself was remarkable enough. Jesus healed a man
who had not asked for it, and He seized the opportunity to
publicly break the Sabbath. This precipitated such a controversy
with the Pharisees as we have not seen before. The bitterness
they showed was extreme. They wanted to murder Him. There
is food for thought in this dreadful picture. We see men, the
best brains that the Jewish nation possessed and who devoted their
whole lives to the study of the Old Testament, ending up literally
as sons of the Devil, hating with a dreadful hatred the embodied
mercy and grace of God as He stood before them. As John
develops the theme of this Gospel, this is our first introduction
to the bitter opposition from the Pharisees which played such a
large part in Jesus' life.

But it is Jesus' teaching that we are to study. We are interested in the Pharisees and their hatred only because in this way
we understand the audience to whom Jesus gave His wonderful
teaching, a teaching so profound and beautiful that we follow
it with difficulty after centuries of Christian thinking.

Therefore the Jews sought to kill him, because he not only had broken the sabbath, but said also that God was his Father, making himself equal with God. Then answered Jesus and said unto them, Verily, verily, I say unto you, The Son can do nothing of himself, but what he seeth the Father do: for what things soever he doeth, these also doeth the Son likewise.

We can see three divisions in this teaching. First, Jesus gives His hearers a new and striking picture of God. Second, He tells them about Himself and His relationship with His Heavenly Father. Here we are taken deeper into the infinite mysteries of God's nature than anywhere else in the whole New Testament. And, finally, Jesus shows how all this works out to the salvation of men.

"My Father worketh even until now, and I work." This was given as an explanation of why Jesus worked on the Sabbath. Jesus' audience paid no attention to that angle. They saw in it the assertion of equality with God, and as such it was the starting point for a long discussion. But from the writer's standpoint and from ours, we will do well to take this fresh revelation of the nature of God and study it carefully. We have already seen the God of sacrifice, who has given His Son for us, and the God of grace who gives gifts to us. Here we see the God who works. His divine and omnipotent energy and His equally divine and omnipotent love are actively exerted, unhasting and unresting, for the accomplishment of His will. That is why His Son worked, and that is why all His sons must work.

God the Father is at work then. So far as men are concerned, He works through the Son. The divine omnipotence is unceasingly exerted for the redemption of men through Christ. He is the embodiment of the energies of God, a radiant light drawing men to the truth and to eternal life. He is far more. He is the divine power energizing the New Order. For the New Order is no mere rearrangement of human society. It is an illimitable outpouring of divine energy in a tremendous, almost fierce effort to save mankind.

For the Father loveth the Son, and sheweth him all things that himself doeth: and he will shew him greater works than these, that ye may marvel. For as the Father raiseth up the dead, and quickeneth them; even so the Son quickeneth whom he will. For the Father judgeth no man, but hath committed all judgment unto the Son: That all men should honour the Son, even as they honour the Father. He that honoureth not the Son honoureth not the Father which hath sent him.

God worked in the Old Order, too. "My Father worketh even until now," but in Jesus He can work to better advantage. In this new day suffering and love are added to simple power. When we are working to save men, that is a very great addition.

This statement of Jesus gave great offense to the Pharisees and those under their influence. They regarded it as an assertion on Jesus' part that He was equal to God. They were correct in this, and Jesus followed their thought in the discussion that followed. Evidently this was what He wanted.

But we must not forget that Jesus made this statement to explain His working on the Sabbath. It raises the question whether in Jesus' mind there is any significant difference between the Sabbath and the other days in the week. In the work of every day it is the will of our Heavenly Father that we follow Him. The Father works and we work just as Jesus said, and to the limit of our infinitesimal capacity our work must be a reflexion of the Father's work in the activities of every day.

Is there, then, any difference between the Sabbath and other days? Yes, there is, but it is a matter of individual judgment. We are always to do God's will and there is no activity that is proper at any time, that is not proper on the Sabbath, if it is needed. But a weekly day of rest is of great benefit to us. That we know from experience. And we know, too, that a day devoted to the worship and service of God is perhaps even more important. The other days we serve men and earn our living, and most emphatically that is God's will. The Sabbath was instituted for the purpose of worship and rest. They are our deepest needs. Only we must be careful not to put this under law, for then one man will be telling another what God's will is.

But for the moment His listeners were not interested in the Sabbath. They insisted on making the discussion a controversial theological one. Jesus probably expected this. He *was* making Himself equal with God. But it would seem that beneath this very extreme surface reaction there was a semi-instinctive feeling which took subconsciously account of deeper implications.

The God of the legalist, whether Jewish or Mohammedan, or indeed Christian, is a static God, and such a God demands a deistic universe with laws established for the governance of the universe, God standing to one side without touching things. From these laws men get their daily guidance. Unfortunately, they really get it from the mouths of priestly interpreters. This is inevitable, for there never can be a law which applies to daily life without interpretation.

Jesus here shows us a new kind of God. He is working daily in men's hearts, guiding them and leading them toward Himself, and toward every good thing in human association. The official interpreter of the law disappears. Even the law itself has only a secondary authority. God's voice in man's hearts is supreme.

These Jews, the Pharisees, were bitterly repudiating not so much a divine God-like Jesus, as a Jesus-like God. It was recorded by Luke and not John, but we can gain light here from Jesus' statement to Zacheus, "The Son of man came to seek and to save that which is lost." Here through clouds of fog, we catch a glimpse of a very high mountain. "My Father worketh even until now" and this is what He is working at. Like Jesus, God is seeking and saving those who are lost. He has always been working for that.

It is an enterprise of the greatest difficulty, for the world that God loves is made up of men and women who are dead, and out among these dead men Jesus goes armed with all the forces of omnipotence. And the errand is no forlorn hope. "The hour cometh and now is, when the dead shall hear the voice of the Son of God, and they that hear shall live."

Our first impression is that here we have a superb and beautiful teaching which will be welcomed by everyone. The fragrance of Heaven is in it. That God speaks directly to our hearts is one of the most important and beautiful things that Jesus ever taught. It is a shock to discover what bitter opposition it stirs up in the

legalistic mind. Every missionary to Mohammedans has many
opportunities to meditate on the intensity of hatred which this
teaching produces.

There is a reason for this. Every legalist believes that God
worked once. He gave men a sacred and final law. Men get their
guidance from that law, and they get it through necessary human
interpreters. This is precisely where the Pharisees of Jesus' time
stood. They were the necessary interpreters.

Jesus flatly contradicts this view. God is working now, every
day and every hour in our hearts and in the world. The road to
salvation is not keeping the law. We must learn the will of the
living God every day and do it.

To this new conception of God, Jesus went on to add a wonderful discussion of His relationship as Son to His Heavenly Father.
It is a picture of beautiful personal relationships raised to the
level of the divine. Whether Christ presented the material thus in
the first place, or whether it simply represents the writer's mind,
the argument is put in a form that seems inverted to us. Arranged
after a Western order it would run like this:

The Father loveth the Son and showeth Him all things
that Himself doeth
     therefore
What things soever He doeth, these the Son also doeth
in like manner
     therefore
The Son can do nothing of Himself, but what He seeth
the Father doing.

"The Father loveth the Son," the current of life and mutual
exchange between them is pure love and nothing but love. It is
John who says later in an epistle, "God is love." It is a revelation of the Father's unlimited love and a revelation, too, of the
Son's divine capacity. "All things that Himself doeth" means all
the Father's works, what He has done in the past, and what He is
doing now. It means His will too, that is, what He will do in the
future. It is a vision of the complete mind of God.

"What things soever He doeth, these the Son also doeth in like manner." That is to say, a perfect vision of God's power and will gives the capacity to do His work. Jesus was no doubt thinking especially of divine power transforming men into the divine image. We have no record of His ever discussing physical power, or even mentioning it.

At least one other thing is suggested. "What things soever He doeth, these the Son also doeth in like manner." Jesus did not mean to assert that every activity of the Father is duplicated with scrupulous fidelity by the Son. Quite surely the meaning runs deeper than that. Everything the Father does is done also by the Son. This pictures a mutual effort. It is done by the Son as far as the human aspect is concerned, but by the Father when considered from the divine aspect. Regarding Christ's work for men we know that this is so. "No man can come to me except the Father that sent me draw him."

Therefore, "the Son can do nothing of Himself but what He seeth the Father doing." "Can" means perhaps that the only possible response of filial love to so complete and divine a paternal love is absolute loyalty. Doubtless it means, too, that the one work which Christ was anxious to do, that is, the work of transforming men by giving them eternal life, was not possible even to one of His power, except as it was a reflection in activity and conscious effort of His personal vision of the Father's character and will.

"Of myself," says Christ, "I can do nothing." A wonderful list of Christ's activities precedes this statement. He gives life. He raises the dead. Our judgment, our eternal destiny is in His hands. In spite of it all He says that of Himself He can do nothing, and apparently the meaning is real inability. It was His connection with His Father that made them all possible.

In this discussion we find no mention of God's physical power. On the other hand, changing men, bringing them out of death into life called for the utmost of divine power. However, by the united efforts of the Father and the Son it is accomplished.

In this account only a brief space is devoted by Jesus to His relation as Son to His Heavenly Father. We pass on to the more extended discussion of how this divine power and love work out to human salvation. We have just seen what the life of God is. It is love pure and divine, uniting the different Persons of the Godhead. We are to see a new thing now, new and beautiful. Men are to have this life of God, eternal life. That is what their salvation consists of. And the life of God is simply the love that flows between the Father and the Son. It flows into us, His children, too. Love for the world, love for our enemies, perhaps most important of all love for each other — it is all God's love, His life flowing into us.

If we lack this love we are dead. That is practically what Jesus said to Nicodemus. When we are born from above, it is eternal life that is born in our souls, the divine love which is God's life. And Jesus does not forget the negative aspect of this. We are not to come into judgment. Doubtless that is also an essential part of our salvation.

Verily, verily, I say unto you, He that heareth my word, and believeth on him that sent me, hath everlasting life, and shall not come into condemnation; but is passed from death unto life. Verily, verily, I say unto you, The hour is coming, and now is, when the dead shall hear the voice of the Son of God: and they that hear shall live.

To Nicodemus Jesus showed the love and the sacrifice of God. To the woman of Samaria He showed the pure grace of God. In this chapter we see the omnipotent energy of God. "My Father worketh even until now" not at trifling physical things such as atom bombs. He works at the hard task of changing men from dead, futile things to live, vibrant projections of His own energy.

God is a God of life and energy. His world is a dead world filled with dead men. The God of omnipotent energy goes out to change those dead men by putting eternal life into them. The voice of the Son of God is the instrument. That voice finds its way into the ears and the comprehension of men as a pure divine agency.

This is a very striking picture of God's salvation. We see no reference to sin, nor to repentance; not even to faith. Human agency has disappeared. Perhaps this affords real light as to the nature of salvation. The Son of God on the cross tasted of death for every man. The voice of the Son of God changes the dead men of this dead world into members of the Kingdom of God with eternal life in their souls.

For as the Father hath life in himself; so hath he given to the Son to have life in himself; And hath given him authority to execute judgment also, because he is the Son of man. Marvel not at this: for the hour is coming, in the which all that are in the graves shall hear his voice, And shall come forth; they that have done good, unto the resurrection of life; and they that have done evil, unto the resurrection of damnation.

Jesus goes to great lengths in this chapter to tell these people how the power of God comes down to needy men. It is through Him and not otherwise that men are to gain eternal life. Eternal life is in the Father. It is the Father's life. But it has been given to the Son now and we are to gain life through Him. The Son giveth life to whom He will.

And the reverse image of this teaching is true, too. All judgment has been given to the Son. One wonders how much of this was understood at the time. Probably very little. Indeed to this day we are unable to follow it at all. Life as opposed to Judgment is an antithesis that seems strange and poorly fitted. That, of course, is a reflection on us, not on the antithesis. Perhaps judgment is synonymous with death. Then it would mean simply separation from God.

But Jesus did not develop this idea, and so we cannot either. He was anxious to emphasize His own position, and the importance of faith in Him. So He goes on to say that men must honor Him as they honor the Father. This is perhaps the only time when Jesus demanded honor of this sort from men. It comes as a surprise for it seems inconsistent with His usual spirit. But it was a necessary addition. The entrance of His listeners into eternal life depended completely on their learning to honor Jesus in this way. At the moment they contemptuously rejected any

41793

such idea. But they remembered it, and no doubt it saved some of them.

I can of mine own self do nothing: as I hear, I judge: and my judgment is just; because I seek not mine own will, but the will of the Father which hath sent me. If I bear witness of myself, my witness is not true.

There is another that beareth witness of me; and I know that the witness which he witnesseth of me is true.

It is not entirely clear just how Jesus and His Father wish to be honored. By obedience, no doubt. Empty phrases from disobedient lips are not wanted. The honor of sincere worship is principally in Christ's mind. That is our road to eternal life.

Here the omnipotent energy of the living God is at work. Into the voice of the Son of God He has put His whole divine power. From one end of the world to the other, from one millennium to the next, Christ is calling men. He called them with His own lips. He called them through the disciples. He is calling them now through His servants, the world over. Always and everywhere it is Christ who takes the initiative. He is not waiting for men to come and drink the living water from His hand. He is the driving power of a great aggressive effort to bring men into the Kingdom of God. "And the hour cometh, and now is, when the dead are hearing the voice of the Son of God," in America and India and China and Arabia, and they that hear, live.

We gain additional light here on the nature of the response which opens for men the door of the New Order. Every man who hears the voice of the Son of God lives. He has to listen, so to speak. But it is the voice of the omnipotent Christ that accomplishes this, and the man who hears that voice does not stop with the satisfaction of his own thirst. He goes out to share in the work and the sacrifice and the glory of Christ in redeeming others.

For eternal life is no easy and comfortable thing. The man who hears the voice of the Son of God thereafter sees the world through Christ's eyes. Some fraction of the plan and will of God becomes to him luminous and beautiful and divine, and life thereafter is one long, unresting, undiscourageable effort to objectify the heavenly vision. That is what life is, pure energy, and the life of God which Jesus puts into our hearts is a vivid and active, unresting thing. The voice of the Son of God has sent men to the depths of Africa to die there in the murderous forests as they bring Christ to the men there. It has burned men out in the effort to abolish human slavery, a task even yet incomplete. It has sent men to prison as pacifists and to the stake as martyrs. Every man who hears the voice of the Son of God gains eternal life and fares forth into the great stagnant world of dead men to be a source of divine life and energy and light. He has passed out of death into life.

And it is the voice of the Son of God that they hear. People can listen to Jesus with admiration, and even make an effort to follow, but if all they hear is the voice of a strikingly good man, the core of the matter is missed. We have to hear His word and to believe on Him who sent Jesus, that is to say, we have to see our Heavenly Father as the God who sent Jesus. If we hear Jesus' voice in that way, we are hearing the voice of the Son of God. That re-defines Jesus. He is the Son of God. It re-defines God. He is like Jesus.

Why is that necessary? Probably we will never completely understand. We are dealing with life here, God's life, divine life, eternal life. It is God's purpose to give us that life, to make us sons. If only we hear the voice of the Son of God. He can do it.

Ye sent unto John, and he bare witness unto the truth. But I receive not testimony from man: but these things I say, that ye might be saved. He was a burning and a shining light: and ye were willing for a season to rejoice in his light.

As we come to the end of this discussion, it is evident that Jesus' aim has changed. He is trying to reach these men personally. The debate about the nature of God is finished. Now He is trying to show His listeners the path by which they can enter the Kingdom of God.

Jesus was talking to a sharply defined class. They are with us still. They were not indifferent to religion. They were fanatically devoted to it. Perhaps no section in this entire Gospel is more important than this one. In spite of a profound sincerity in their search for God, and in spite of a life-long devotion to the book that God had given them, these men were going astray, and worse than that, they were leading the people whom they guided, straight down to hell.

At first we are surprised that Jesus should make any effort to justify Himself and His teaching to these men. They had never heard the voice of God and were complete enemies. But Jesus did not respond with irritation and repudiation to hostility of this sort. These men, like everybody else, could be saved only by adopting toward Him an attitude of confidence and faith. On that day maybe no one believed, but they remembered what He said, and who can say how much fruit the seed that Jesus planted in their hearts bore eventually?

Jesus' negative teaching is easy to catch. We do not gain eternal life just from studying the Scriptures. These men were devotees of Moses, but they had not found God through Moses. Jesus said they did not believe Moses. We do not find eternal life that way.

But I have greater witness than that of John: for the works which the Father hath given me to finish, the same works that I do, bear witness of me, that the Father hath sent me. And the Father himself, which hath sent me, hath borne witness of me. Ye have neither heard his voice at any time, nor seen his shape. And ye have not his word abiding in you: for whom he hath sent, him ye believe not.

This is an extremely disturbing teaching. As Jesus stood before them, there was a sharp and unmistakable contrast between the books that Moses had left, and Jesus in person teaching them. Jesus is not here now, and we are back in the Pharisees' position. All we have is a book which records for us the character and teachings of Jesus. The Holy Spirit interprets it for us. But we, too, must come to Jesus. If we do, we will find life in Him and we must use our book only as a means to that end.

We see Jesus here making a careful effort to satisfy the demand of His listeners for evidence. His claims are very great indeed, and no one can believe Jesus' claims or anyone else's, except as the evidence bears them out. Probably, as a matter of theological theory, these men could have opened their hearts, and heard the voice of God through Moses. Certainly that would have been possible once. But it was not possible for these men. They would have to come to Jesus if they were to receive life.

A very difficult question emerges here. Just what is the relationship between the word of God through Moses, and His word through Jesus? Certainly in the earlier dispensation men found their way to God through Moses. But now that Jesus had come, that was apparently no longer possible. Jesus did not send them back to a better and more intelligent use of Moses. Their only hope was to come to Him.

> Search the Scriptures; for in them ye think ye have eternal life: and they are they which testify of me. And ye will not come to me, that ye might have life. I receive not honour from men. But I know you, that ye have not the love of God in you. I am come in my Father's name, and ye receive me not: if another shall come in his own name, him ye will receive.

Jesus was greatly concerned to show the evidence that was available to those men. The evidence of John the Baptist, Jesus said, was valid, but He gave it a low rating. We would have supposed that to these fanatical devotees of Moses the evidence of John the Baptist would have been very valuable indeed.

But Jesus did not care for the evidence of any man, not even the Baptist who came as a fulfillment of Old Testament prophecy. It was His own works, the works that the Father had given Him to accomplish, which constituted Jesus' major evidence. This answer does not help us much. Indeed it rather adds to our difficulties. At this moment, with His listeners in a mood of sharp hostility, this line of evidence must have seemed feeble indeed. Jesus' works showed the love and the grace and the beauty of God, but they did not convince those critics.

We can see that God's power is shown above all things in giving life to dead men, in changing them "from death into life." But here, too, God's power was only indifferently revealed by Jesus, for His success in changing men was very slight. God in the Scriptures is Jesus' second witness and that undoubtedly added to the difficulties of His listeners for they had studied the Scriptures all their lives, and had not found anything there which even pointed toward this Jesus.

But with this company of listeners Jesus was not aiming at the sort of belief and acceptance which they had in mind. They wanted a politically-minded Messiah. All that Jesus was trying to prove was that "the Father hath sent me." That meant two things, that God is our Heavenly Father, and that He had sent Jesus to represent Him perfectly down here among men. They may not look to us like a very impressive body of proof, but it was what Jesus wanted.

How can ye believe, which receive honour one of another, and seek not the honour that cometh from God only? Do not think that I will accuse you to the Father: there is one that accuseth you, even Moses, in whom ye trust. For had ye believed Moses, ye would have believed me: for he wrote of me. But if ye believe not his writings, how shall ye believe my words?

Jesus adds a further explanation as to why these men did not believe. So often our perplexity increases. These men did not believe because they had failed to find the testimony which is in the Scriptures. They failed because they had never heard the voice of God. And finally, Jesus said they could not believe because they received glory one of another, and the glory that comes from the only God they did not seek.

It would have been impossible to phrase a statement more completely at variance with His listeners' view of the situation. They had been labouring since they could talk, to gain the glory that comes from the only God. They had written out God's laws in the most meticulous details. They knew just how many steps a man might take on the Sabbath. Then, they were despised Jews. The glory that comes from men they could not have in any case.

But Jesus' word is the important thing. We must come to Jesus. We will find life in Him. No mere book entered into this teaching at all, and it must not with us. We have in this Gospel of John and in the whole New Testament material which will

help. No doubt these New Testament books are essential to our
search. But it is a perilous path that we enter here. Devotion to
Moses had led straight to the bottomless pit. These devotees of
Moses did not simply reject Jesus, they hated Him, they were
hating Him savagely as He talked with them, and just as soon as
they could compass it, they murdered Him. The trouble was that
Jesus had come in His Father's name. He was re-defining God.
These same works done in His own name as a great prophet would
have aroused the greatest enthusiasm.

We wish, with a very great desire indeed, that Jesus had
elaborated a little on this theme. Just how do men come to Him
and find life? But Jesus left this undeveloped. It is a lesson for
the fanatical legalist. All the zeal that he had spent on this law,
his code, his book, he must now spend on a new quest, that of
finding the actual living Jesus, in this twentieth century, and
coming to Him, and following Him, and receiving life from Him.

JOHN 6

After these things Jesus went over the sea of Galilee, which is the sea of Tiberias. And a great multitude followed him, because they saw his miracles which he did on them that were diseased. And Jesus went up into a mountain, and there he sat with his disciples. And the passover, a feast of the Jews, was nigh.

When Jesus then lifted up his eyes, and saw a great company come unto him, he saith unto Philip, Whence shall we buy bread, that these may eat? And this he said to prove him: for he himself knew what he would do. Philip answered him, Two hundred pennyworth of bread is not sufficient for them, that every one of them may take a little. One of his disciples, Andrew, Simon Peter's brother, saith unto him, There is a lad here, which hath five barley loaves, and two small fishes: but what are they among so many? And Jesus said, Make the men sit down. Now there was much grass in the place. So the men sat down, in number about five thousand. And Jesus took the loaves: and when he had given thanks, he distributed to the disciples, and the disciples to them that were set down; and likewise of the fishes as much as they would. When they were filled, he said unto his disciples, Gather up the fragments that remain, that nothing be lost. Therefore they gathered them together, and filled twelve baskets with the fragments of the five barley loaves, which remained over and above unto them that had eaten. Then those men, when they had seen the miracle that Jesus did, said, This is of a truth that Prophet that should come into the world.

When Jesus therefore perceived that they would come and take him by force, to make him a king, he departed again into a mountain himself alone. And when even was now come, his disciples went down unto the sea, And entered into a ship, and went over the sea toward Capernaum. And it was now dark, and Jesus was not come to them.

And the sea arose by reason of a great wind that blew. So when they had rowed about five and twenty or thirty furlongs, they see Jesus walking on the sea, and drawing nigh unto the ship: and they were afraid. But he saith unto them, It is I; be not afraid. Then they willingly received him into the ship: and immediately the ship was at the land whither they went.

The day following, when the people, which stood on the other side of the sea, saw that there was none other boat there, save that one whereinto his disciples were entered, and that Jesus went not with his disciples into the boat, but that his disciples were gone away alone; Howbeit there came other boats from Tiberias nigh unto the place where they did eat bread, after that the Lord had given thanks: When the people therefore saw that Jesus was not there, neither his disciples, they also took shipping, and came to Capernaum, seeking for Jesus. And when they had found him on the other side of the sea, they said unto him, Rabbi, when camest thou hither? Jesus answered them and said, Verily, verily, I say unto you, Ye seek me, not because ye saw the miracles, but because ye did eat of the loaves, and were filled. Labour not for the meat which perisheth, but for that meat which endureth unto everlasting life, which the Son of man shall give unto you: for him hath God the Father sealed.

Then said they unto him, What shall we do, that we might work the works of God? Jesus answered and said unto them, This is the work of God, and ye believe on him whom he hath sent. They said therefore unto him, What sign shewest thou then, that we may see, and believe thee? what dost thou work? Our fathers did eat manna in the desert; as it is written, He gave them bread from heaven to eat. Then Jesus said unto them, Verily, verily, I say unto you, Moses gave you not that bread from heaven; but my Father giveth you the true bread from heaven. For the bread of God is he which cometh down from heaven, and giveth life unto the world. Then said they unto him, Lord, evermore give us this bread. And Jesus said unto them, I am the bread of life; he that cometh to me shall never hunger; and he that believeth on me shall never thirst. But I said unto you, That ye also have seen me, and believe not. All that the Father giveth me shall come to me; and him that cometh to me I will in no wise cast out. For I came down from heaven, not to do mine own will, but the will of him that sent me. And this is the Father's will which hath sent me, that of all which he hath given me I should lose nothing, but should raise it up again at the last day. And this is the will of him that sent me, that every one which seeth the Son, and believeth on him, may have everlasting life: and I will raise him up at the last day. The Jews then murmured at him, because he said, I am the bread which came down from heaven. And they said, Is not this Jesus, the son of Joseph, whose father and mother we know? how is it then that he saith, I came down from heaven? Jesus therefore answered and said unto them, Murmur not among yourselves. No man can come to me, except the Father which hath sent me draw him, and I will raise him up at the last day. It is written in the prophets, And they shall be taught of God. Every man therefore that hath heard, and hath seen the Father, cometh unto me. Not that any man hath seen the Father, save he which is of God, he hath seen the Father. Verily, verily, I say unto you, He that believeth on me hath everlasting life. I am that bread of life. Your fathers did eat manna in the wilderness, and are dead. This is the bread which cometh down from heaven, that a man may eat thereof, and not die. I am the living bread which came down from heaven: if any man eat of this bread, he shall live for ever: and the bread that I will give for the life of the world. The Jews therefore strove among themselves, saying, How can this man give us his flesh to eat? Then Jesus said unto them, Verily, verily, I say unto you, Except ye eat the flesh of the Son of man, and drink his blood, ye have no life in you. Whoso eateth my flesh, and drinketh my blood, hath eternal life; and I will raise him up at the last day. For my flesh is meat indeed, and my blood is drink indeed. He that eateth my flesh, and drinketh my blood, dwelleth in me, and I in him. As the living Father hath sent me, and I live by the Father; so he that eateth me, even he shall live by me. This is that bread which came down from heaven; not as your fathers did eat manna, and are dead: he that eateth of this bread shall live for ever. These things said he in the synagogue, as he taught in Capernaum. Many therefore of his disciples, when they had heard this, said, This is a hard saying; who can hear it? When Jesus knew in himself that his disciples murmured at it, he said unto them, Doth this offend you? What and if ye shall see the Son of man ascend up where he was before? It is the Spirit that quickeneth; the flesh profiteth nothing: the words that I speak unto you, they are spirit, and they are life. But there are some of you that believe not. For Jesus knew from the beginning who they were that believed not, and who should betray him. And he said, Therefore said I unto you, that no man can come unto me, except it were given unto him of my father.

From that time many of his disciples went back, and walked no more with him. Then said Jesus unto the twelve, Will ye also go away? Then Simon Peter answered him, Lord, to whom shall we go? thou hast the words of eternal life. And we believe and are sure that thou art that Christ, the Son of the living God. Jesus answered them, Have not I chosen you twelve, and one of you is a devil? He spake of Judas Iscariot the son of Simon: for he it was that should betray him, being one of the twelve.

Chapter VI

THE PICTURE

After these things Jesus went over the sea of Galilee, which is the sea of Tiberias. And a great multitude followed him, because they saw his miracles which he did on them that were diseased. And Jesus went up into a mountain, and there he sat with his disciples. And the passover, a feast of the Jews, was nigh.

When Jesus then lifted up his eyes, and saw a great company come unto him, he saith unto Philip, Whence shall we buy bread, that these may eat? And this he said to prove him: for he himself knew what he would do. Philip answered him, Two hundred pennyworth of bread is not sufficient for them, that every one of them may take a little.

In this chapter we have four scenes to observe and study. As before, Jesus is dealing with a crowd. These men are fishermen and artisans, ordinary people. We see no religious fanatics.

Vividness is added to the picture when we read the story in the other Gospels. It is found in all of them. Evidently the events of this chapter stood out in the disciples' memories as great peaks.

The disciples needed a rest, and Jesus arranged to take them to a deserted spot along the shore opposite Capernaum. But there was no rest on this trip. Pilgrims were on their way to the Passover. From half a million to a million went up each year to this feast.

It is not surprising that a crowd of thousands surrounded Jesus, for to the pilgrims turning aside from their journey were added large numbers of local Galileans who came to be healed or to listen to Jesus' teachings or, most commonly of all, from simple curiosity. After all, a good deal happened wherever Jesus went.

The people of the East were evidently as improvident and happy-go-lucky then as they are now. They had been listening all day long, as Jesus healed and taught. It had been an interesting day, but now as the evening drew on, they were without food, and there was no town within reach where some might be bought.

Jesus' was the soul of hospitality. He entertained five thousand guests that afternoon. To the Oriental this is the supreme virtue. We do not see it often in Jesus' life, for He was a wanderer and poor.

One of his disciples, Andrew, Simon Peter's brother, saith unto him, There is a lad here, which hath five barley loaves, and two small fishes: but what are they among so many?   And Jesus said, Make the men sit down. Now there was much grass in the place.   So the men sat down, in number about five thousand.   And Jesus took the loaves; and when he had given thanks, he distributed to the disciples, and the disciples to them that were set down; and likewise of the fishes as much as they would.   When they were filled, he said unto his disciples, Gather up the fragments that remain, that nothing be lost.   Therefore they gathered them together, and filled twelve baskets with the fragments of the five barley loaves, which remained over and above unto them that had eaten. Then those men, when they had seen the miracle that Jesus did, said, This is of a truth that Prophet that should come into the world.

When Jesus therefore perceived that they would come and take him by force, to make him a king, he departed again into a mountain himself alone.   And when even was now come, his disciples went down unto the sea, And entered into a ship, and went over the sea toward Capernaum.   And it was now dark, and Jesus was not come to them. And the sea arose by reason of a great wind that blew.   So when they had rowed about five and twenty or thirty furlongs, they see Jesus walking on the sea, and drawing nigh unto the ship: and they were afraid.   But he saith unto them, It is I; be not afraid.   Then they willingly received him into the ship: and immediately the ship was at the land whither they went.

This is hospitality at its best.   Severely simple, it was free from any taint of payment or reward, as indeed in the East it always is.   A boy's lunch gave a delightful element of cooperation, gracious hospitality for five thousand people, the simple entertainment of one neighbor by another. Barley bread and roasted fish, the food of the artisan, the fisherman, and the farmer, a good balanced meal. It was what they ate every day.

But if adornment and luxury were completely absent, the quantity was extravagantly abundant, and that is Oriental too. After a long day outdoors men can eat a great deal, if it is offered. That afternoon it was, and they ate all they could hold.

But in spite of the abundance, thrifty economy was the word, and twelve baskets were filled with the fragments which remained, food for the disciples for a day or two at least.

The people were tremendously impressed. Divine power was in their midst. Their reaction was a very natural one. They would make Jesus king, by force if necessary. The situation came close to getting out of hand, an unusual thing in Jesus' life. Evening was coming on. Jesus took His disciples to the water's edge and sent them across to Capernaum at once.

It is not difficult to see what was in the disciples' minds. The golden dream of centuries shone before their eyes. The Kingdom of God was about to be set up. With the people Jesus had less difficulty. He simply dismissed them.

Then He went up into the mountain to pray, to fight back Satan and his glittering temptation.

Why did Jesus resist this temptation so desperately, that is to say, why was it a temptation? Why not a superb opportunity? "The Kingdom of God is at hand" was His message. Why not accept kingship at the hands of these men? They would have been glad to accept any possible teaching, and to carry out any command. He could have organized them into a veritable city of God. St. Augustine's dream and Calvin's. But Jesus saw here the deadliest poison of the Satanic serpent. One remembers His fierce reaction in cleansing the temple of abuses that seem to us trivial, but which He reckoned as straight from the bottomless pit. Even now, with centuries of Christian thinking behind us, we find it hard to see the evil in this situation. But evil was there in that offer to make Him king, and it was so glitteringly attractive that He fled almost in terror to the throne of God for help. What did He pray for? Discernment to see the dreadfully faint line of divine will and duty, or fortitude to follow it? Both probably.

John is a dramatist. One day Jesus faces a crowd of fanatics anxious to murder Him. Here we see a company of every-day people who want to take him by force and make Him king. Jesus was much more troubled by this second reaction. Satan reached out and almost touched His soul. Sometimes friendship is worse than enmity. The fierce murderous hostility of the fanatics did not disturb Jesus at all. In it He felt no temptation worthy the name.

The day following, when the people, which stood on the other side of the sea, saw that there was none other boat there, save that one whereinto his disciples were entered, and that Jesus went not with his disciples into the boat, but that his disciples were gone away alone; Howbeit there came other boats from Tiberias nigh unto the place where they did eat bread, after that the Lord had given thanks: When the people therefore saw that Jesus was not there, neither his disciples, they also took shipping, and came to Capernaum, seeking for Jesus.   And when they had found him on the other side of the sea, they said unto him, Rabbi, when camest thou hither?   Jesus answered them and said, Verily, verily, I say unto you, Ye seek me, not because ye saw the miracles, but because ye did eat of the loaves, and were filled.   Labour not for the meat which perisheth, but for that meat which endureth unto everlasting life, which the Son of man shall give you: for him hath God the Father sealed.   Then said they unto him, What shall we do, that we might work the Works of God?

Jesus answered and said unto them, This is the work of God, that ye believe on him whom he hath sent.   They said therefore unto him, What sign shewest thou then, that we may see, and believe thee? what dost thou work?   Our fathers did eat manna in the desert: as it is written, He gave them bread from heaven to eat.   Then Jesus said unto them, Verily, verily, I say unto you, Moses gave you not that bread from heaven; but my Father giveth you the true bread from heaven.   For the bread of God is he which cometh down from heaven, and giveth life unto the world.   Then said they unto him, Lord, evermore give us this bread.   And Jesus said unto them, I am the bread of life: he that cometh to me shall never hunger; and he that believeth on me shall never thirst.

And like a dissolving picture on the screen, it gives way to another. To our limited minds, this is the most gratuitous of all Jesus' miracles. The disciples torn by force from their beloved dream were struggling with an impossible sea. Sudden and severe storms characterize the Sea of Galilee to this day. In the region of Capernaum the sea is about four miles across. It was the fourth quarter of the night, and they had not yet made land. How long Jesus spent walking on that rough sea before He overtook them, we are not told. The waves must have smoothed themselves down in front of Him to make any walking possible, and if they did, an hour would have been sufficient.

But I said unto you, That ye also have seen me, and believe not. All
that the Father giveth me shall come to me; and him that cometh to
me I will in no wise cast out. For I came down from heaven, not to
do mine own will, but the will of him that sent me. And this is
the Father's will which hath sent me, that of all which he hath given me
I should lose nothing, but should raise it up again at the last day.
And this is the will of him that sent me, that every one which seeth the
Son, and believeth on him, may have everlasting life: and I will raise
him up at the last day. The Jews then murmured at him, because he
said, I am the bread which came down from heaven. And they said,
Is not this Jesus, the son of Joseph, whose father and mother we
know? how is it then that he saith, I came down from heaven?

The miracle was for the benefit of the disciples. No one else
saw it. Their loyalty had been badly shaken. This reinforced
them. Jesus did a great deal for His disciples. Their training was
always on His mind. Evidences of this are seen everywhere once
our attention is called to it.

For some reason John does not mention the dramatic episode
with Peter. The big fisherman came forward with his usual im-
pulsiveness. Jesus welcomed it. Peter attained to great faith
here. No doubt he could swim well, but even so, stepping over
the side of the boat into that raging sea was a great deed. When
his eyes were on Jesus all went well, but when he put his attention
on the big waves and the howling wind he began to sink. As a
demonstration of the nature and power of faith that lesson has
never been surpassed, and it is just as valid for us now as it was
for the disciples then.

The picture changes again. Jesus is teaching a crowd of people.
Yesterday He fed them. Theirs was the simplest conclusion in
the world. "He can feed us again." But this time Jesus was
giving them a lesson in self-respect. No more free food. He had
a definite message for this company. It was built on yesterday's
miracle.

He knew just what He wanted to tell them. Their preoccupation with their stomachs did not deflect Him a hair's breadth.
Probably three or four thousand were listening, and no doubt
such a crowd always does contain some sincere seekers. But the

Jesus therefore answered and said unto them, Murmur not among yourselves. No man can come to me, except the Father which hath sent me draw him: and I will raise him up at the last day.   It is written in the prophets, And they shall be all taught of God. Every man therefore that hath heard, and hath learned of the Father, cometh unto me.   Not that any man hath seen the Father, save he which is of God, he hath seen the Father.   Verily, verily, I say unto you, He that believeth on me hath everlasting life.   I am that bread of life.   Your fathers did eat manna in the wilderness and are dead.   This is the bread which cometh down from heaven, that a man may eat thereof, and not die.

---

drive and precision of Jesus' teaching seem to rest on something beyond that.   Few of His listeners understood Him; indeed, probably none of them did. But it was understood eventually, for it was so phrased that it could not be forgotten. Ten years later, every man there remembered the vivid little sentence, "I am the bread of life." They could not forget that and it was all they needed to remember.

Jesus had an immeasurable faith in the teaching God gave Him.   He knew that once these divine seeds were put into men's hearts, they could not be kept from growing into genuine faith and so into eternal life.

There is a tremendous thrill in this picture of Jesus teaching the crowds.   Some of those crowds were hostile and wanted to murder Him.   Some were frivolous, incapable of one serious thought.   This crowd was thinking about some more free bread and it did not want to think about anything else.   Poised and confident and happy, facing thousands of people, we see Him putting God's miraculous seeds into the hearts of the tired, hungry men and women who sat before Him.

We must note with some care one or two of these crowds. One crowd (the one mentioned in chapter 5) was dominated by the Pharisees. They did not suffer from a lack of religion. They had too much. Their lives were full of religion, utterly dominated by the legalistic system which the Pharisees had developed from the law of Moses. Theirs was a dreadful sin. They wanted to dominate their fellows. This type of pride and selfishness was very

I am the living bread which came down from heaven: if any man eat of this bread, he shall live for ever: and the bread that I will give is my flesh, which I will give for the life of the world. The Jews therefore strove among themselves saying, How can this man give us his flesh to eat? Then Jesus said unto them, Verily, verily, I say unto you, Except ye eat the flesh of the Son of man, and drink his blood, ye have no life in you. Whoso eateth my flesh, and drinketh my blood, hath eternal life; and I will raise him up at the last day. For my flesh is meat indeed, and my blood is drink indeed. He that eateth my flesh, and drinketh my blood, dwelleth in me, and I in him.

---

repulsive to Jesus, hence they hated Jesus and on His own authority, they hated God.

Jesus gave carefully chosen, incredibly beautiful and profound teaching to that company that hated Him. It fitted those minds which long study had developed so well and which sin had warped so dreadfully, fitted them with beautiful exactness like a key which a carpenter (in the Near East) fashions for a special lock. They wanted to know how Jesus in His humanity could be divine. It was the question of an educated mind. Jesus told them how this impossible thing could be. It was the divine answer. Jesus did not allow the murderous hate of His listeners to distort by a hair the beautiful key He was making for that particular lock.

But the crowd we are observing here knew nothing about the sin of the Pharisees. They worked hard all day and most of the night to keep body and soul together. Their sin was not the desire to dominate over others, but rather the sin of indifference. How many times a month did they think about God? Hungry men think about their next meal.

Jesus was from their own number. For years He had worked as a carpenter. How beautifully He fashioned a key for their lock. We may be inclined to think that He gave a more profound lesson to the Pharisees. But as far as we are concerned we owe more to this lesson for everyday people with their earthly-mindedness and their preoccupation with simple hunger: "I am the bread of life." How beautifully that key fitted its lock.

As the living Father hath sent me, and I live by the Father; so he that eateth me, even he shall live by me. This is that bread which came down from heaven; not as your fathers did eat manna, and are dead: he that eateth of this bread shall live for ever. These things said he in the synagogue, as he taught in Capernaum. Many therefore of his disciples, when they had heard this, said, This is a hard saying; who can hear it? When Jesus knew in himself that his disciples murmured at it, he said unto them, Doth this offend you? What and if ye shall see the Son of man ascend up where he was before? It is the Spirit that quickeneth; the flesh profiteth nothing: the words that I speak unto you, they are spirit, and they are life.

We may get a great thrill from this view of Jesus the teacher. His listeners did not. More disappointing, His disciples did not. It had not been an easy time. A hard day of healing and teaching was capped by a tremendous miracle. And when the gales of omnipotence swept through that limited human frame it was evidently a very exhausting experience. But He came back from His night prayers with His mind clear and His message for those men sharp and definite.

The next day again was very taxing. Jesus took the healing and the teaching, and the tremendous feeding of five thousand men, and compressed it all into unforgettable sentences that could not be misunderstood. All day long He framed the divine thoughts which contained the omnipotence, and the wisdom and the grace of God. He inserted them by the pure force of His personality into the dull, resisting, dead minds before Him. He must have regarded His work with something of the same satisfaction as a surgeon who has accomplished an extremely difficult operation. We knew that He did the work well, for the centuries since have stood gazing on that day's work with speechless admiration.

But many of His disciples did not. They left Him in a body. The original twelve remained but their enthusiasm was down. However, they came through, and with Peter as their spokesman, we see that their loyalty was unbroken.

No doubt Jesus was disappointed over these promising beginners who had left. He made no effort to persuade them to stay. If what they had seen and heard did not hold them, He preferred

But there are some of you that believe not. For Jesus knew from the beginning who they were that believed not, and who should betray him. And he said, Therefore said I unto you, that no man can come unto me except it were given unto him of my Father.

From that time many of his disciples went back, and walked no more with him. Then said Jesus unto the twelve, Will ye also go away? Then Simon Peter answered him, Lord, to whom shall we go? thou hast the words of eternal life. And we believe and are sure that thou art that Christ, the Son of the living God. Jesus answered them, Have not I chosen you twelve, and one of you is a devil? He spake of Judas Iscariot the son of Simon: for he it was that should betray him, being one of the twelve.

---

that they leave. His personal influence and persuasion probably could have brought them back but He did not want them if they had to be won that way. What, then, did Jesus want men to follow? Himself to be sure, but not as Hitler was followed. Jesus wanted no man's loyalty unless they saw the love and truth of the Heavenly Father in Him.

The love and loyalty between Jesus and the disciples was very deep by this time. There was one exception. Judas was an evil influence in the ranks, and a traitor. He was not dismissed. No doubt we would have promptly removed such a contamination from the inner circle. Jesus knew better. The man born blind was saved not by separating him from temptation and persecution, but by immersing him in them. The mission field teaches the same lesson every day.

The interests of the disciples were not sacrificed for Judas' sake. It would be nearer the truth to say that the interests of Judas were sacrificed for the disciples' sake, for it would have been better for Judas to have been dismissed from the group before his sin had reached such proportions. But the question runs deeper than that. Judas no doubt was anxious to stay, and Jesus tried hard to win him.

As the little company wandered through the country and visited the towns, there is no effort on Jesus' part to shield them from the temptations of the flesh, or from the urge toward avarice which proved the undoing of Judas. If His own example and personal

influence could not save those men and keep them, Jesus had no
further resources to utilize toward that end.

The number of the disciples was greatly reduced now. Apparently only the twelve were left. Why did so many leave?
Because they failed to understand Jesus? Just the opposite.
Previous to this tremendous episode they had indeed failed to
understand Him. Now for the first time they did, but they did not
want the real Jesus and the real message.

Jesus' Teaching

And when they had found him on the other side of the sea, they said
unto him, Rabbi, when camest thou hither? Jesus answered them and
said, Verily, verily, I say unto you, Ye seek me, not because ye did
eat of the loaves, and were filled. Labour not for the meat which
perisheth, but for that meat which endureth unto everlasting life, which
the Son of man shall give unto you: for him hath God the Father sealed.

Here again Jesus is talking to a crowd. The people are friendly,
but in no mood for things of the Spirit. Nevertheless, Jesus gave
them a wonderful message. Its depths will remain unplumbed
until we sit at His feet in the Father's mansions. It is simple,
childlike indeed. Surely, the Kingdom of God belongs to the
children.

And these children of hard work and meager living Jesus
taught. He told them about the life that the New Order brings.
That was always Jesus' message. He told men about the grace of
God, that is, the eternal life which is God's gift. Nicodemus was
told about the new birth which is the beginning of eternal
life, and the woman of Samaria about the water which Jesus
gave, and which resulted in eternal life. Here we hear Jesus tell
His listeners that He is the bread of life, eternal life.

"Work not," Jesus said, "for the food that perisheth, but for
the food that abideth unto eternal life." Jesus knew all about
the hard work by which those men earned their daily bread.
Nevertheless, food is not worth the supreme place in our minds.
That place is for eternal things. We have to work for eternal life,
indeed give it the supreme place in our program.

The next question was obvious enough. "What must we do that we may work the works of God?" Jesus' reply was prompt and simple. "This is the work of God that ye believe on Him whom He hath sent." God works among men by sending messengers. We must receive them and listen to them. God worked thus in the days of the Old Testament. All that we can do for God is to receive His messengers and listen to them.

Then said they unto him, What shall we do, that we might work the works of God? Jesus answered and said unto them, This is the work of God, that ye believe on him whom he hath sent. They said therefore unto him, What sign shewest thou then, that we may see, and believe thee? what dost thou work? Our fathers did eat manna in the desert; as it is written, He gave them bread from heaven to eat. Then Jesus said unto them, Verily, verily, I say unto you, Moses gave you not that bread from heaven; but my Father giveth you the true bread from heaven.

This sense of having been sent by God was a very important element in Jesus' life. It appears in all His activities. The words He spoke and the works He did were given Him by the Father. Of Himself He did nothing.

"This is the work of God that ye believe on him whom he hath sent," was a simple lesson. They could have understood it, but what they wanted was something to eat. They were hungry. Jesus had fed them only yesterday. How ready people are to rely on charitable support. Jesus knew that He must not feed them again. He continued His explanation in the face of their desire to eat. "I am the bread of life: He that cometh to me shall not hunger, and he that believeth on me shall never thirst."

For the bread of God is he which cometh down from heaven, and giveth life unto the world. Then said they unto him, Lord, evermore give us this bread. And Jesus said unto them, I am the bread of life: he that cometh to me shall never hunger; and he that believeth on me shall never thirst. But I said unto you, That ye also have seen me, and believe not. All that the Father giveth me shall come to me; and him that cometh to me I will in no wise cast out. For I came down from heaven, not to do mine own will, but the will of him that sent me.

This little sentence: "I am the bread of life" is one of the most profound and wonderful things Jesus ever said. Its truth stretches out in many directions and runs very deep. His whole message from the Heavenly Father is in it. It is beautifully suited to the hungry people that heard it. Jesus came from this type of people and with them He was perfectly at home. To them bread and life were two aspects of the same thing. He had lived that meager, hungry life too. Jesus presented a message perfectly fitted to its audience.

And just because bread as the embodiment of life was so vividly real to them, the deep lesson of getting spiritual bread and eating it was bound to be difficult. Everyday bread is a simple matter. The fisherman catches a fish, the carpenter makes a bench. They sell their products in the market and bread is bought with the proceeds. What is the corresponding process with this heavenly bread?

Everything men may want is in this bread from heaven, but the important question for imperfect and stupid men is how they can get it and eat it. In the discussion that follows Jesus answers just that question. The simplest listener must learn this answer. Jesus was not a philosopher. He was an evangelist. His purpose was to save men and to bring them into the Kingdom. Faith on their part was the one thing needed. The first necessity is making the road plain.

And this is the Father's will which hath sent me, that of all which he hath given me I should lose nothing, but should raise up again at the last day. And this is the will of him that sent me, that every one which seeth the Son, and believeth on him, may have everlasting life: and I will raise him up at the last day. The Jews then murmured at him, because he said, I am the bread which came down from heaven. And they said, Is not this Jesus the son of Joseph, whose father and mother we know? how is it then that he saith, I came down from heaven?

One special point must be noted here. "This is the work of God that ye believe on him whom he hath sent" brings into clear focus a point of great importance. We get this bread of life from Jesus. There is no reference to their own religious faith, or their own Scriptures, and none to social improvement, or better education. Jesus is the bread of life and there is no other.

Jesus analyzes this further. "Every one who beholds the Son and believes on him has eternal life." We must see Jesus first. Then we can believe on Him. This is not as simple as it sounds. The Pharisees saw Jesus and they hated Him. But they did not see the real Jesus. We must see Jesus as He is. "Every one who beholds *the Son*" is the way He puts it. This is a little surprising. To these men of labor and want, He gave His deepest truth. To the bitter and murderous Pharisee He simply said, "The Father hath sent me." Two ways, no doubt, of saying the same thing. We in our day must meditate on Jesus until we see that He came from the Father, and that He is the Son. Then we hold the Bread of Life in our hands to eat it and live.

Jesus therefore answered and said unto them, Murmur not among yourselves. No man can come to me, except the Father which hath sent me draw him: and I will raise him up at the last day. It is written in the prophets, And they shall be all taught of God. Every man therefore that hath heard, and hath learned of the Father, cometh unto me. Not that any man hath seen the Father, save he which is of God, he hath seen the Father. Verily, verily, I say unto you, He that believeth on me hath everlasting life. I am that bread of life. Your fathers did eat manna in the wilderness, and are dead.

"No man can come to me, except the Father that sent me draw him." The Heavenly Father then is working continually to draw men toward Jesus, and without His help coming is impossible. The implication is that God draws us by showing us Jesus in this profound way. Unless we see Jesus as He is, we will not be drawn to Him. Here Jesus corrects a possible mistake. No man fails to come because God did not draw him. We have all been taught of God, Jesus says, but not all of us have learned. Those who learned, come.

His listeners murmured against this, which is hardly surprising. Men have to be taught of God to enjoy this sort of thing. Moreover, Jesus had not given them a bite to eat. But we feel grateful to the critics because Jesus met them with a further explanation, and an important one.

"The bread which I will give," said Jesus, "is my flesh for the life of the world." To His listeners this was completely absurd.

What is Jesus' "flesh"?   "The Word became flesh and dwelt among us," so says the introduction.   Jesus was not talking about His eternal co-existence with the Father.   He lived here on earth in His flesh for about thirty-three years.   Everything His flesh embodied came to visibility then, so we can see it is His flesh. Only about three and a half years of the thirty-three have been preserved for us.   That is the bread which we are to eat.   Eternal life is in it.

This is the bread which cometh from heaven, that a man may eat thereof and not die.   I am the living bread which came down from heaven: if any man eat of this bread, he shall live for ever: and the bread that I will give is my flesh, which I will give for the life of the world.   The Jews therefore strove among themselves, saying, How can this man give us his flesh to eat?   Then Jesus said unto them, Verily, verily, I say unto you, Except ye eat the flesh of the Son of man, and drink his blood, ye have no life in you.   Whoso eateth my flesh, and drinketh my blood, hath eternal life; and I will raise him up at the last day.

Jesus' statement that we are to eat His flesh and drink His blood was a shock to His hearers.   It is to us, too.   Paul makes "flesh" almost synonymous with sin.   Here it denotes simply Jesus' humanity.   It was not the seat of sin but it was the seat of suffering.   Jesus assumed our flesh so that He could suffer and die. "My flesh I will give for the life of the world."

Does this refer to the cross?   Probably not.   These were simple untheological people and Jesus did not discuss the cross even with His disciples.   It was His flesh as He walked up and down the paths and roads of Judaea and Galilee which His listeners were to eat.   His final explanation makes things clear.   The words that He spoke unto them were spirit and life.   The flesh was only a more or less unprofitable figure.   When we obey Jesus' words then we have eaten His flesh.   When we eat His flesh, Jesus abides in us.   We would not have dared to carry the parable so far, if Jesus had not done it for us.   When flesh is eaten it becomes an integral part of our body.

For my flesh is meat indeed, and my blood is drink indeed.   He that eateth my flesh, and drinketh my blood, dwelleth in me, and I in him.

As the living Father hath sent me, and I live by the Father; so he that eateth me, even he shall live by me. This is that bread which came down from heaven; not as your fathers did eat manna, and are dead: he that eateth of this bread shall live for ever. These things said he in the synagogue, as he taught in Capernaum.

And in the same way, Jesus, when He is eaten, becomes part of our inner being, mentally and spiritually, artistically and emotionally. He abides in us. He that eats this food and drinks this drink, lives forever, and it could not be otherwise. They are absolute, infinite things, as are all things connected with God.

Jesus abides in us, that is, lives within us. This is difficult to realize for we cannot feel His presence. And seeing our sinfulness and futility and littleness, it almost terrifies us. We would not dare even to wish for it. It was difficult for the disciples, looking at Jesus as He spoke, but what of us, two thousand years later? How can we eat His flesh and drink His blood? All that is left of that wonderful life is a meager record.

Our four Gospels have been kept for us with divine care. In them we can see Jesus' attitudes, His motives, His teaching, His love. We surely have an evidence here of God's hand in men's affairs. It is not simply the preservation of the records through the centuries, but even more the vividness of the picture of Jesus which those records give us.

The bread of life is the human life of Jesus. Just what does this life show? What is Jesus? He is an example. We are to "follow in His steps."

Many therefore of his disciples, when they had heard this, said, This is a hard saying; who can hear it? When Jesus knew in himself that his disciples murmured at it, he said unto them, Doth this offend you? What and if ye shall see the Son of man ascend up where he was before? It is the Spirit that quickeneth; the flesh profiteth nothing: the words that I speak unto you, they are spirit, and they are life. But there are some of you that believe not. For Jesus knew from the beginning who they were that believed not, and who should betray him.

Also, Jesus came to bring God's truth. His principal activity was teaching, passing on to men the "words" which God had sent. Without those "words" we will never know the path to God, or to genuine human comradeship. And Jesus came as the culmination of God's plan of redemption. Jesus died on the cross. On that death the whole plan of redemption is built. The "unsearchable riches of Christ" are far beyond our comprehension.

This unsearchable Christ is the bread of life. No one single attribute or single gift is so designated. He applies the term to Himself in all His divine totality. "He that eateth of this bread shall live forever." It does not say, "He that eats all of it," or even "he that eats a great deal of it." Every man who eats of this bread, even though he eats only a small fragment, shall live forever. And of the searchable riches no man eats more than a mere crumb. So we need not wonder that different men gain eternal life through the apprehension and acceptance of different aspects of Jesus and His life.

There are millions who have found life through Christ their Savior, the one in whom they find forgiveness of sins. No genuine Christian faith is without this. This has been the dominant note in the Christian experience of the West for centuries. Many have found life by listening to Jesus' voice calling them out of selfishness and worldliness and laziness into the sacrifice and service and toil of the Cross. The missionaries of the Church include many such men and women. Some of the most beautiful approximations to Jesus' own purity and holiness have found their entrance into real life in the hope of our Lord's return. Strong men have found their eternal life in Jesus' call to social service from the day of St. Francis to the present. Every man who really touches Jesus, who is dominated by something he has seen there, receives eternal life into his soul.

And he said, Therefore said I unto you, that no man can come unto me, except it were given him of my Father.

For Jesus' life is a variegated picture. Every man's earnest study discovers something, but no two of us see quite the same thing as we worship and follow Him. It is like a table set with many dishes. One man lives by Jesus' example, another by Jesus' teachings, a third by imitating His love for all sorts and conditions of men.

Now we know what the bread of life is — Jesus Himself. He is for us to see and to adore and imitate. Each seeker finds something that fills his deepest need. Moreover, we know just where to get it. There lying on our study table are all His words.

There is one question still. How do we eat this bread? First of all by complete acceptance of course. But we must study this a little. Admiration comes first. We cannot accept Jesus unless we admire Him. We may admire His example, or His teaching, or His love. Indeed, every man seeing Jesus admires all of these.

After admiration comes understanding. It takes reading and meditation nad hard mental effort to understand Jesus. And let no man deceive himself. He will not understand all. But some feature of that wonderful life will become luminous and commanding, and at some point, be it ever so small, he will understand it in a profound way which is the foundation of acceptance.

Jesus astonishing word to the Pharisees: "If ye believed Moses, ye would believe me," is also a word for us. Nothing could surpass their belief in Moses. Their confidence in the divine inspiration and authority of his writings was fathomless. But Jesus says that they did not believe Moses. Listen to what Hebrews says: "Beware, lest there be in any one of you an evil heart of unbelief."

And after admiration and understanding follows complete acceptance. This is the supremely important matter. It is nothing less, indeed, than eating the bread of life. To see bread and say that it is excellent food is not the same thing as eating it. It is the man who eats, even a little, who gains eternal life. Nothing interested Jesus less than a tepid acquiescence in the philosophical system which He brought. Men must catch a glimpse of one of the "words" that He brought and be completely dominated by that vision.

We still have the mountain top of this wonderful lesson to climb. Bread, when it is eaten, is assimilated, and we know its material atoms help constitute our body. We are made of that bread. When Jesus is eaten, His Saviorhood His example, His teaching, is taken into the inner constitution of our spirits. He abides in us. We are partakers of the divine nature.

"He that cometh unto me I will in no wise cast out." Divine yearning and human energy are both needed before this can take place. What is it to come to Jesus? The Greek preposition means "toward" rather than "to." But all notion of physical distance is pure metaphor. The Roman soldiers were closer to Jesus on the cross than the disciples were. It is a matter of our minds and hearts, of our souls. Our soul must come to Jesus' soul. This looks like a preliminary thing, but to Jesus it was final. The figure comes from Jesus and His circle of disciples. When men were drawn into that circle they gained eternal life.

Jesus adds a last word: "It is the spirit that giveth life, the flesh profiteth nothing: the words that I have spoken unto you are spirit, and are life." These are the omnipotent "words" that He brought from His Heavenly Father. Now we know just what we are to eat, and just where we can get it. We know just how to eat it. May God grant that we all do.

On this mountain peak we have gained a better understanding of faith. Now, for the first time we reach some insight into the nature of eternal life, and was dazed, almost overpowered, by this vision — "the riches of the glory of this mystery which is Christ in you the hope of glory." This is journey's end for the reverent seeker. Like a diver coming up from his deepest dive, our spirits come back with the pearl of great price in their hands.

Ultimately men are not saved by faith, but by the eternal life which God gives them as soon as their faith makes the gift possible. We are children of the living God. This means companionship with Jesus, but it is far more. He lives in us and we become like Him for He is a constituent element of our very souls.

This is frightening and unbelievable. The idea of Jesus living every day within us, is a strange, heavenly teaching. It seems out of place on this earthly planet, and most of all in our soiled and imperfect souls.

Jesus goes on to make it still more beautiful and heavenly and heavenly and forbidding. God Himself comes down into the realm of companionship with us. "As the living Father sent me, and I live because of the Father so he that eateth me shall live because of me. "Most of us would like to run away from this, at least at first, for we feel impure and unworthy and trivial. Jesus will have to purify and remake us. None but He can do such a thing.

JOHN 7

After these things Jesus walked in Galilee: for he would not walk in Jewry, because the Jews sought to kill him. Now the Jews' feast of tabernacles was at hand. His brethren therefore said unto him, Depart hence, and go into Judea, that thy disciples also may see the works that thou doest. For there is no man that doeth any thing in secret, and he himself seeketh to be known openly. If thou do these things, shew thyself to the world. For neither did his brethren believe in him. Then Jesus said unto them, My time is not yet come: but your time is always ready. The world cannot hate you; but me it hateth, because I testify of it, that the works thereof are evil. Go ye unto this feast: I go not up yet unto this feast; for my time is not yet full come. When he had said these words unto them, he abode still in Galilee.

But when his brethren were gone up, then went he also up unto the feast, not openly, but as it were in secret. Then the Jews sought him at the feast, and said, Where is he? And there was much murmuring among the people concerning him: for some said, He is a good man: others said, Nay; but he deceiveth the people. Howbeit no man spake openly of him for fear of the Jews.

Now about the midst of the feast Jesus went up into the temple, and taught. And the Jews marvelled saying, How knoweth this man letters, having never learned? Jesus answered them, and said, My doctrine is not mine, but his that sent me. If any man will do his will, he shall know of the doctrine, whether it be of God, or whether I speak of myself. He that speaketh of himself seeketh his own glory: but he that seeketh his glory that sent him, the same is true, and no unrighteousness is in him. Did not Moses give you the law, and yet none of you keepeth the law? Why go ye about to kill me? The people answered and said, Thou hast a devil: who goeth about to kill thee? Jesus answered and said unto

them, I have done one work, and ye all marvel. Moses therefore gave unto you circumcision; (not because it is of Moses, but of the fathers;) and ye on the sabbath day circumcise a man. If a man on the sabbath day receive circumcision, that the law of Moses should not be broken; are ye angry at me, because I have made a man every whit whole on the sabbath day? Judge not according to the appearance, but judge righteous judgment. Then said some of them of Jerusalem, Is not this he, whom they seek to kill? But, lo, he speaketh boldly, and they say nothing unto him. Do the rulers know indeed that this is the very Christ? Howbeit we know this man whence he is: but when Christ cometh, no man knoweth whence he is. Then cried Jesus in the temple as he taught, saying, Ye both know me, and ye know whence I am: and I am not come myself, but he that sent me is true, whom ye know not. But I know him; for I am from him, and he hath sent me. Then they sought to take him: but no man laid hands on him, because his hour was not yet come. And many of the people believed on him, and said, When Christ cometh, will he do more miracles than these which this man hath done?

The Pharisees heard that the people murmured such things concerning him; and the Pharisees and the chief priests sent officers to take him. Then said Jesus unto them, Yet a little while am I with you, and then I go unto him that sent me. Ye shall seek me, and shall not find me: and where I am, thither ye cannot come. Then said the Jews among themselves, Whither will he go, that we shall not find him? will he go unto the dispersed among the Gentiles, and teach the Gentiles? What manner of saying is this that he said, Ye shall seek me, and shall not find me: and where I am, thither ye cannot come? In the last day, that great day of the feast, Jesus stood and cried, saying, If any man thirst, let him come unto me, and drink. He that believeth on me, as the Scripture hath said, out of his belly shall flow rivers of living water. (But this spake he of the Spirit, which they that believe on him should receive: for the Holy Ghost was not yet given; because that Jesus was not yet glorified.)

Many of the people therefore, when they heard this saying, said, Of a truth this is the Prophet. Others said, This is the Christ. But some said, Shall Christ come out of Galilee? Hath not the Scripture said, That Christ cometh of the seed of David, and out of the town of Bethlehem, where David was? So there was a division among the people because of him. And some of them would have taken him; but no man laid hands on him.

Then came the officers to the chief priests and Pharisees; and they said unto them, Why have ye not brought him? The officers answered, Never man spake like this man. Then answered them the Pharisees, Are ye also deceived? Have any of the rulers or of the Pharisees believed him? But this people who knoweth not the law are cursed. Nicodemus saith unto them, (he that came to Jesus by night, being one of them,) Doth our law judge any man, before it hear him, and know what he doeth? They answered and said unto him, Art thou also of Galilee? Search, and look: for out of Galilee ariseth no prophet. And every man went unto his own house.

Chapter VII

THE PICTURE

After these things Jesus walked in Galilee: for he would not walk in Jewry, because the Jews sought to kill him. Now the Jews' feast of tabernacles was at hand.

This is another of the episodes where Jesus deals with crowds. The feast of Tabernacles was being celebrated in Jerusalem, and the people had gathered in great numbers. Many of the incidents John records took place in connection with feasts to which great crowds came. Nicodemus and the woman at the well had individual interviews with Jesus, but these were exceptions. The Gospel of John is for the greatest part made up of addresses and debates which developed as Jesus taught the feast crowds.

The feast of Tabernacles was not an intensely religious occasion like the Passover. It was more like our Thanksgiving made eight days long, and, as might be expected, Jesus met a good natured, frivolous crowd, unwilling to give serious thought to anything. He took them as they were. Their lightmindedness did not disturb Him.

In chapters 5 and 6 we have already seen Jesus' dealing with crowds. Those were sharply individualized groups, with much unity of viewpoint. In chapter 5 Jesus met intellectual and the-

His brethren therefore said unto him, Depart hence, and go into Judea, that thy disciples also may see the works that thou doest. For there is no man that doeth any thing in secret, and he himself seeketh to be known openly. If thou do these things, shew thyself to the world. For neither did his brethren believe in him.

Then Jesus said unto them, My time is not yet come: but your time is always ready. The world cannot hate you; but me it hateth, because I testify of it, that the works thereof are evil. Go ye up unto this feast: I go not up yet unto this feast: for my time is not yet full come. When he had said these words unto them, he abode still in Galilee.

---

ological Judaism. There we find His message to the educated man with his trained mind, and his sin of pride and intolerance. In chapter 6 Jesus talked to everyday humanity. It is His message to the common man, with his indifference to God and his preoccupation with the necessities of life.

Here in chapter 7 we have a still different crowd. They had heard a good deal about Jesus. Some had begun to believe on Him. Some saw in Him a menace to the nation. Jesus wanted to minister to them all. Nothing was more important to Him than this, for Jesus' one purpose was to save men. And He knew only one way for men to be saved. They must believe on Him. This transfer of men from the ranks of His critics and enemies to the company of His friends and believers was His constant purpose.

In this chapter we come to a new section in John's Gospel. Jesus is in contact with "the world." This is a new concept. Jesus, to be sure, lived in the world and was immersed in it, like everybody else. But to Jesus the world is more than a mere environment in within which every man is placed. His listeners once their preference was aroused, could not simply start from where they were and follow. They were members of a close-knit community, stones set in concrete. Only by breaking away from the world could they come to Him. Their social organization bound them with chains. It was not easy to follow Jesus.

Jesus' world was made up mostly of Jews, but in His mind it was not so limited. He looked on humanity as constituting a unit, and in this "world" all were included.

But when his brethren were gone up, then went he also up unto the feast, not openly, but as it were in secret. Then the Jews sought him at the feast, and said, Where is he? And there was much murmuring among the people concerning him: for some said, He is a good man others said, Nay; but he deceiveth the people. Howbeit no man spake openly of him for fear of the Jews.

Men can be considered as members of political states, or of guilds and trades in the business world. There is also the world of learning and of the mind. Jesus looked on men from none of these aspects. His "world" was a religious world. He regarded men from the viewpoint of their relations to God.

This religious world was made up of two classes, the leaders, that is, the Pharisees, and the people whom the Pharisees led. No doubt there were Sadducees too, but in this Gospel we see little of them.

This "world" was bound by a dreadful legalism. To the law given by Moses the Pharisees had added an incredible mass of details and regulations which hedged in the whole of life. As is always the case in legalistic systems, a special point was chosen for emphasis, in this case the Sabbath.

As illogical as it seems to us, breaking the Sabbath was an adequate cause for killing a man. In central Arabia smoking tobacco used to be a capital crime. Pride and intolerance marked the Pharisees. If needed to stop and silence a dissenter they did not shrink from murder.

Under this system the common people fared badly. They were shut away from contact with God. Their contact was with the Pharisees. Among the rank and file there was little rebellion. There was little genuine worship of God but much perplexity or indifference.

The "world" was a hostile world. It still is. "The friendship of the world is enmity against God," James said. "The world cannot hate you, but me it hateth." This is a dreadful statement, coming from Jesus' own lips. From now on "the world" is to receive much attention in Jesus' teaching. "But now have they

But when it was now the midst of the feast Jesus went up into the temple and taught. The Jews therefore marvelled saying, how knoweth this man letters, having never learned.

Jesus therefore answered them, and said, My teaching is not mine, but his that sent me. If any man willeth to do his will, he shall know of the teaching, whether it is of God or whether I speak from myself. He that speaketh from himself seeketh his own glory, but he that seeketh the glory of him that sent him, the same is true and no unrighteousness is in him.

---

both seen and hated both me and my Father" was His estimate of the situation.

In the society around Him Jesus saw three classes of people. There were men and women who hated Him. There was a growing number who were followers. And finally there were many not yet definitely associated with either group.

All of us are born into the world. A transfer is necessary if we are to enter the Kingdom. All of us are born under one or another religious law. In order to be united with Jesus we must die to the law and be released from it.

And God so loved the world, this hostile, evil world, that He gave His Son to die for it. Release from the world and entrance into the Kingdom is made possible by that death. But here we are told nothing about the cross. Jesus' death was still in the future when these words were spoken. That sacrifice makes our transfer possible, but evidently it is not necessary that it be known or understood at the time.

Jesus says that the works of the world are evil. Difficult questions emerge. Are all the works of the world evil? Some of them look very good. The world is very sure that its works are good. Usually they aim to benefit a certain group. Within the family, those done for children are surely good. Years ago Kropotkin showed us that nature, far from being universally "red in tooth and claw," is filled with mutual aid.

But these works are done independently of God and His guidance. Does that make them evil? Jesus does not say so. He testified thus against the Pharisees but against no one else. They seem to be the only class that hated Jesus. Those who hate Him are members of the world. Perhaps we are safe in limiting our category of evil works to those who hate Jesus. He did not say that an Arab mother loving her baby is doing an evil work.

Jesus once said, "He that is not with me is against me" and that would seem to put every man not in the Kingdom squarely in the world. But Jesus also said, "He that is not against us is for us. It is not difficult to get Jesus' mind here. The "world" is made up of those who hate Him. There is active intensity in the word.

There is also a group which loves Jesus. They belong to the Kingdom. There is intensity to this response too, and the indifferent are not included. Where then are the indifferent classified. One day we hope that they will belong to God.

At this feast the common people in their perplexity and frivolity and indifference were not hostile. They were friends. Here and in the feasts that follow, the people listening to Jesus divided themselves into two fractions. Some were favourably impressed and of these some went on to belief. Another fraction definitely rejected what they heard. Most of the listeners made no decision at all.

It is interesting that in this story we catch no glimpse of the disciples. Jesus was dealing with a great company and He evidently regarded it as an important occasion. We should have supposed that the presence of the disciples might have been a real reinforcement. For some reason Jesus did not want them.

His message was simple too — Jesus healed no one. He fed no one. A word from God, unadorned, unexplained, undefended was all He offered. We may well meditate on this for a moment. for we are in precisely the same situation. The temptation to fall back on the reputation of a great man or the impressiveness of an erudite philosophy is very great sometimes. No doubt it was very great here but Jesus did not yield to it.

Jesus made no effort to water His message down, neither for enemies nor for friends. He did not try to show its connection with His hearers' stock of religious ideas. He was not anxious to

Did not Moses give you the law, and yet none of you keepeth the law? Why go ye about to kill me? The people answered and said, Thou hast a devil: who goeth about to kill thee? Jesus answered and said unto them, I have done one work, and ye all marvel. Moses therefore gave unto you circumcision; (not because it is of Moses, but of the fathers;) and ye on the sabbath day circumcise a man. If a man on the sabbath day receive circumcision, that the law of Moses should not be broken; are ye angry at me, because I have made a man every whit whole on the sabbath day? Judge not according to the appearance, but judge righteous judgment.

---

make it comprehensible. He did not explain it. He never defended it. It was a divine word direct from God, and Jesus had complete confidence in its ability once it was accepted to capture the most hostile, and to save men no matter what their condition.

Here we see a radical contrast. On the one side, Jesus' divine message which could not be added to nor subtracted from, or changed in any way whatever. On the other side, the law of Moses "You break the Sabbath to save the law of Moses, surely it is proper for me to bread the Sabbath to make a man whole" is the way Jesus' argument runs. A man then is more important than the Sabbath, and more important than the law of Moses. If this refers to the miracle of chapter 5, as certainly seems to be the case it is the physical man which Jesus considers so important. That ungrateful betrayer of his benefactor certainly was not made whole spiritually.

"The Faith of Jesus" would be a good title for this chapter. It stands out, impressive and wonderful, like a mountain peak, or rather like a whole range of mountains; His faith in God, who could put omnipotence into His human words, His faith in the message, His faith in the men who were listening. In spite of the stupidity and sin that He saw there, and in spite of what He suffered at their hands Jesus knew that the possibility for eternal life was there, once the miraculous little seeds that He brought from God were put in their hearts. And finally faith in Himself as the embodiment of the eternal God saving the world, that hostile, pharisaical, devilish world.

Then said some of them of Jerusalem, Is not this he, whom they seek
to kill?   But, lo, he speaketh boldly, and they say nothing unto him.
Do the rulers know indeed that this is the very Christ?   Howbeit we
know this man whence he is: but when Christ cometh, no man knoweth
whence he is.

This picture of the "world" and Jesus' relation to it, begins
with a scene where Jesus is talking with His brethren. There are
several stages in the attitude of the world toward Jesus. His
brethren were in the first stage. They did not hate Him as the
Pharisees did, but they did not believe on Him either, and their
rejection was definite and complete. Why did they not believe?
The essence of that terrible mystery is beyond us. Perhaps it
always will be. They had seen Jesus' life, indeed who better
than they? His teachings they knew. The beauty of that soul
they had lived with. But they rejected Him, rejected Him utterly,
with their insincere advice to go back to Judea where enemies
were lying in wait to imprison and murder Him. Nor were the
brethren ignorant of these things, though they may not have
appreciated the bitterness of the Jerusalem hostility, and we will
not number them at the moment with Jesus' murderers.

But this pitiful evidence of sin and treachery and rejection
gives us a message of hope, for we know that later they did
accept Him. Time for the seed to grow is one of the important
elements which we must keep in mind as we study the transfer of
men from the realm of the world to the realm of life in Jesus.
And if men who have shown this degree of treachery and sin can
eventually yield to the voice of Jesus in their hearts, then surely
there is hope for anyone.

Jesus was entirely undisturbed by this treachery. With the
greatest care He gave His brethren the message they needed, and
remained behind to go up by Himself to the feast later. "My hour
is not yet come," He said. John is the one Gospel writer who
penetrates deeply enough into Jesus' mind to catch His view of a
world ordered by God. Not only did Jesus move and teach as
God directed, but all other things in the world moved that way

Then cried Jesus in the temple as he taught, saying, Ye both know me, and ye know whence I am: and I am not come of myself, but he that sent me is true, whom ye know not. But I know him; for I am from him, and he hath sent me. Then they sought to take him: but no man laid hands on him, because his hour was not yet come.

And many of the people believed on him, and said, When Christ cometh, will he do more miracles than these which this man hath done?

The Pharisees heard that the people murmured such things concerning him; and the Pharisees and the chief priests sent officers to take him.

---

too. "The hour cometh and now is," said Jesus to the Samaritan woman. Jesus lived in an orderly, God-directed world.

Once in Jerusalem, Jesus found a great multitude waiting for Him. They were not rejecting Him as His brethren had done. They were in what we call the second stage of the world's reaction to Jesus. They had heard a good deal about Him and, in this indirect way, had given a good deal of attention to Him and His message. Some regarded Him as a good man. Some said that He was leading the people astray. Perhaps their initial reaction had been hostile, as Jesus suggests in His talk to His brethren. But at least some of them had changed. This change toward friendship and approval had resulted simply from additional attention to Jesus and His message. It was not a response to a promotional campaign. Jesus never made such an effort with anyone.

It took real courage to go up alone into this mixed and dangerous situation. Jesus, however, seemed completely immune to fear. He had the feeling which strong men often show, that, God having entrusted Him with a definite errand, nothing was to be feared from any source till that errand was done.

As a matter of fact, the situation did not prove especially difficult. His enemies were there, but the people were His friends, so His enemies could not arrest Him and put Him to death. To this mixed company, some friendly some hostile, Jesus addressed Himself with great earnestness and depth. His whole purpose and drive were toward those who were favorably inclined and not a word of rebuke was pointed toward those who hated Him.

In addressing these beginners Jesus read into their attitude more than we would have dared to do. He saw that at least some of them wanted to do God's will. This means far more than appears on the surface. Every Pharisee wanted to do God's will, just as the fanatical Wahabees of Central Arabia want to do God's will now. It all depends on what sort of God is in men's minds when they say that. But when a man wants to do the will of God who sent Jesus, the God whom He represented, such a man is a long distance on the way toward genuine faith.

This is a part of Jesus' faith. We may call it faith in the growing seed. Once the divine seed is sown in man's hearts, Jesus can wait with complete confidence for the result. It is here that we find the explanation for His attitude of complete and even satisfied composure when men were rejecting Him and His message. He knew that it would be rejected, He knew indeed that such a rejection was inevitable at first. And once the miraculous seed has found lodgment in men's minds, its slow development is part of God's own purpose.

But Jesus did not hesitate to demand and accept complete faith when the time came. He pressed His absolute claims on the human will as soon as men had progressed to a point where they could entertain such demands. This feast offered Him a good opportunity for all these things. The division in sentiment among the people grew more and more intense. "This is of a truth the prophet," "this is the Christ' came from one section of the crowd. On the other hand, some wanted to take Him and put Him to death. And to these men whose minds had progressed so far, Jesus stood and cried, "If any man thirst, let him come unto me and drink." The exclusiveness of that invitation is complete. There were plenty of others to whom they could go. The Pharisees were themselves listening to the invitation. They wanted men to come to them and drink. Their response was to send a band of the temple police to arrest Jesus so He could be killed. Jesus was undisturbed. He knew that this would happen eventually, but it was still in the future.

Then said Jesus unto them, Yet a little while am I with you, and then I go unto him that sent me. Ye shall seek me, and shall not find me: and where I am, thither ye cannot come. Then said the Jews among themselves, Whither will he go, that we shall not find him? will he go unto the dispersed among the Gentiles, and teach the Gentiles? What manner of saying is this that he said, Ye shall seek me, and shall not find me: and where I am, thither ye cannot come?

In the last day, that great day of the feast, Jesus stood and cried, saying, If any man thirst, let him come unto me, and drink. He that believeth on me, as the Scripture hath said, out of his belly shall flow rivers of living water. (But this spake he of the Spirit, which they that believe on him should receive: for the Holy Ghost was not yet given; because that Jesus was not yet glorified.)

This chapter is perhaps our best study of the sin of rejecting the message, and the Christ, and the salvation of God. What was the trouble with the Pharisees? Why had they sunk so low that they supposed that by hating Jesus they were serving and pleasing God? John draws a vivid picture of the Pharisees. The Jews held in their hands a divine revelation of great beauty and power, as, for instance, Psalm 23, "The Lord is my shepherd, I shall not want." The best brains of the nation were devoted to its study and interpretation. But these religious leaders, immersed in that revelation since babyhood, were so filled with arrogant pride, and so pitiless in their intolerance, that they have stood as the classical examples of those sins ever since. Mohammedanism itself has produced nothing worse. We see them here plotting Jesus' death with a cold hatred, which reveals the lowest point that human nature can reach.

In the case of the Pharisees, the initial hatred for Jesus and His teachings had persisted and grown. Jesus is not shocked by this, neither than nor now. It is his hope that men will center their attention on Him with some persistence, and then many who hate Him, will change and regard Him as a good man. Most people do get as far as that. Pharisees as in Jesus' day are a small number. Men who look on Jesus as a "good man" have made a very great step forward. Once such a man is brought into contact with Jesus' teachings, and sees that those teachings

Many of the people therefore, when they heard this saying, said, Of a truth this is the Prophet. Others said, This is the Christ. But some said, Shall Christ come out of Galilee? Hath not the Scripture said, That Christ cometh of the seed of David, and out of the town of Bethlehem, where David was? So there was a division among the people because of him. And some of them would have taken him; but no man laid hands on him.

Then came the officers to the chief priests and Pharisees; and they said unto them, Why have ye not brought him? The officers answered, Never man spake like this man. Then answered them the Pharisees, Are ye also deceived? Have any of the rulers or of the Pharisees believed on him? But this people who knoweth not the law are cursed. Nicodemus saith unto them, (he that came to Jesus by night, being one of them,) Doth our law judge any man, before it hear him, and know what he doeth? They answered and said unto him, Art thou also of Galilee? Search, and look: for out of Galilee ariseth no prophet. And every man went unto his own house.

---

come from God, the road to complete surrender and faith is wide open.

One of our great failures is here, Jesus was willing to wait for months and years for the first reaction to grow into the second, and the second into the third, and for the seed to grow up into the complete flower of faith.

The writer takes this opportunity to give us another illuminating glimpse of the Pharisees. He has an eye for the dramatic, even the ludicrous. The Pharisees sent the temple police to arrest Jesus, but they came back empty handed. The Pharisees' desire to commit murder as only a little delayed, but they were extremely annoyed. Jesus had captured the ear of the people for the time being so the arrest could not be made. Jerusalem was full of visitors from Galilee, and they were a firy group who did not easily subject themselves to anyone.

"This multitude which knoweth not the law is accursed" is a very illuminating statement. In the uninhibited annoyance of the moment, these men told lots of truth. According to their religious convictions, men were good or bad, accepted or ostracised, according to their knowledge of the law. They believed in all sincerity that God felt the same way. The blasphemy of entertaining such a notion of God was the root of all their sin, God was simply an idol shaped after their own unsavory likeness. What could better express their pride and hardness of heart than these words: "This multitude that knoweth not the law is accursed."

Jesus' Teaching

The teaching of Jesus in this chapter is fragmentary and disconnected. It has new and unexpected features in it. For the first time we see Jesus teaching about the "world." We have listened as He taught Nicodemus of the relations of individual men to God. We learned there of God's desire that men should be born again and become partakers of eternal life. There we saw, too. the unbelievable sacrifice which makes this possible.

At the well of Samaria we learned that God is the God of grace, that eternal life is a pure gift to unworthy and helpless men. We learned, too, about the human response which makes our entrance into the new order possible.

The sins of the intellect, the pride and love of domination which trip up leaders of society are shown in chapter 5 in a group-reaction of extraordinary virulence and hatred. It may be mixed with religion but then it is worse than ever. The crowd that Jesus was teaching wanted to kill Him.

The sins of the body which made the woman of Samaria stumble are expanded in chapter 6 to a group reaction. Preoccupation with bodily appetites was the undoing of those hard-working men and women, though in their case was a very legitimate desire for something to eat. They did not want to kill Jesus. They wanted to make Him king. Jesus was harder pressed by this temptation than by anything which sprang from the bitterness dealt with in chapter 5.

But up till now, we have not realized that the "world" has any connection with this, or that it was an entity of itself in Jesus' mind. Here in chapter 7 Jesus shows the road that men must travel if they are to leave the world and enter His kingdom. No subject is more important than this, for Jesus' purpose was to lead men into God's Kingdom, and they all come from the world. We all start there.

Many difficult questions arise here. Why is "the world" that way? We are all born into it. Why is it an area of sin, and opposition to God?

His brethren therefore said unto him, Depart hence, and go into Judea, that thy disciples also may see the works that thou doest. For there is no man that doeth any thing in secret, and he himself seeketh to be known openly. If thou do these things, shew thyself to the world. For neither did his brethren believe in him.

The lesson opens with a conversation between Jesus and His brethren. They did not believe on Him, which is something of a surprise. They were in possession of all the evidence. They had watched His work, and listened to His teachings. But Jesus was not surprised. No doubt He knew what they thought of Him. The point of importance for us here is that He took their attitude as representing the attitude of the world. "My time is not yet come, but your time is always ready." This is not the way we should have begun the discussion, and it is a little puzzling at first. But what Jesus had in mind is made clear by His later remarks. He is stating the difference between the life of the Kingdom and the life of the world, that is, the difference, between His own life and that of His brethren, who were members of the world.

Jesus was guided always by the Father's will. His brethren, on the contrary, as members of the world, were guided by their own wills. Their time was always ready. In Jesus' mind this is the fundamental difference between the world and God's Kingdom. Members of God's Kingdom live a God-directed life. Jesus had not yet received guidance to go up to this feast. Here is the essence of sin and the essence of righteousness. The self-directed life is sin. The God-directed life is righteousness.

The teaching which follows is still more surprising. "The world cannot hate you, but me it hateth, because I testify of it that its works are evil." Now as a matter of fact we see plenty of sharp dislike and conflict between different members of the world, and often enough real hatred. Jesus meant by this word just what

we do. He does not say that members of the world cannot hate
each other. Jesus' brethren must have been of an inoffensive
type which stirred up no reaction vivid enough to be called hate.
Their lives testified to no one that his works were evil. Most of
the time the conformists of this world escape unpopularity and
hatred. The important point here is that the world does hate
Jesus.

Then Jesus said unto them, My time is not yet come: but your time is
always ready. The world cannot hate you; but me it hateth, because
I testify of it, that the works thereof are evil. Go ye up unto this feast:
I go not up yet unto this feast; for my time is not yet full come.
When he had said these words unto them, he abode still in Galilee.

It is a terrifying statement, for, apparently, it is a universal rule.
When Jesus comes into contact with the world, this will be the
result. They will hate Jesus. This is not always permanent. Most
men go on to a different reaction later. Then they are no longer
members of the world. But the statement stands. When the world
is brought into a real contact with Jesus it reacts with hatred.

Jesus tells us the reason. The world hates Him because He
testifies of it that its works are evil. How? Not by His words.
Such testimony would not carry conviction and, moreover, barring
the Pharisees, Jesus scarcely touched such a topic in anything He
said. The God-directed life of Jesus testified to the world that its
works are evil. We are not dealing here with mere words, but
with Jesus' whole life. That life carried an extremely unwelcome
conviction into men's hearts. Hatred resulted because the men
of the world were convinced that Jesus' testimony was true and
that their works *were* evil.

We enter here a very interesting field. All of us know from
experience that members of the world insist that their works
are good. They are proud of them. A criminal boasts of loyalty
to his comrades, and a covetous millionaire of his thrift and
management. These works are sincerely considered to be good;
they are performed with a genuine intent to make them so, sometimes with real sacrifice. It is well to give a moment's attention
to this feeling on the part of the world, for later developments of

the theme depend on it. This pride in our good works is a very powerful thing. They aim at the good of men, usually the good of a particular group, and at obedience to law, which in a blind sort of way is devotion to God.

The hatred of Jesus which results from His testimony is simply a measure of this desire to do good works. To show that their goodness is a myth, that they are, in fact, evil, is sure to stir up hatred. This is inevitable and in a way desirable as a step to something better. No, doubt that is why Jesus was so completely undisturbed by it, as it recurred repeatedly in His life. If the men of the world had been anxious to do bad works, Jesus' demonstration that they were bad would simply have made Him popular.

The writer makes haste to show that this reaction is not permanent, at least not for most people. When Jesus went up to the feast He did not find the multitude at the feast hating Him. They had heard a good deal about Him and knew something of His teaching. As is inevitable if people will continue to keep Him before their attention, most of Jesus' listeners had changed their original reaction of hatred to a more favorable attitude. They considered Jesus a good man.

Now about the midst of the feast Jesus went up into the temple, and taught. And the Jews marvelled, saying, How knoweth this man letters, having never learned? Jesus answered them, and said, My doctrine is not mine, but his that sent me. If any man will do his will, he shall know of the doctrine, whether it be of God, or whether I speak of myself. He that speaketh of himself seeketh his own glory: but he that seeketh his glory that sent him, the same is true, and no unrighteousness is in him.

We might not think that this attitude indicates much progress toward God, but Jesus evidently estimated it highly. There is a vast difference between the reaction of hatred, and regarding Jesus as a "good man." These men had not chosen the God-directed life for themselves, but they admired it in Jesus.

So to these men Jesus said, "My teaching is not mine but His that sent me. If any man willeth to do his will, he shall know of the teaching, whether it is from God, or whether I speak from myself. These men had given attention to Jesus' works, and they realized that His God-directed life was a good life. They admired it, and we still take Jesus' estimate and say that in their hearts they wanted it.

What Jesus asked from them now was a little further attention, this time to His teachings. If they only would study His teachings they were sure to arrive at a clear conviction that these teachings are from God. For such a man the road to complete faith is open. The emphasis is on Jesus' teachings. Probably the men to whom Jesus was speaking had noted very little about Jesus except his more conspicuous miracles. The next step, and a supremely important one, is to realize that Jesus' works and His teachings were not merely good, but that they came from God. Fundamentally what Jesus wanted here was to bring about a complete change in their conception of God. God is good. Far more than that, He is like Jesus. From the standpoint of philosophy, this is the core of Jesus' entire message.

Did not Moses give you the law, and yet none of you keepeth the law? Why go ye about to kill me? The people answered and said, Thou hast a devil: who goeth about to kill thee? Jesus answered and said unto them, I have done one work, and ye all marvel. Moses therefore gave unto you circumcision; (not because it is of Moses, but of the fathers;) and ye on the sabbath day circumcise a man. If a man on the sabbath day receive circumcision, that the law of Moses should not be broken; are ye angry at me, because I have made a man every whit whole on the sabbath day? Judge not according to the appearance, but judge righteous judgment.

Jesus turns the argument aside at this point to an iconoclastic paragraph of refutation. Its connection with what He had been saying is not at once evident. That connection is underneath where we deal with men's understanding of God. In the minds of the men some extremely high and difficult mountains stood in the way of accepting Jesus' teaching, most of all accepting it as from God.

Perhaps hostile questions started this discussion, but we gain the impression that Jesus Himself points the argument in this direction. In a sense the Pharisees were behind the attitude of mind we see here, but it is not really the hand of the Pharisees but rather the whole legalistic system which held the community in its iron grip. The Sabbath, the God-instituted Sabbath had been broken. That rankled in their minds. How could they suppose that He came from God? This put the debate precisely where Jesus wanted it. The real issue is the nature and character of God.

But there was a second question, and one of importance. The religious leaders had taught them that certain things would characterize the Messiah when He appeared, and Jesus did not correspond with these specifications.

Jesus moved out against these objections from an anti-legalistic platform that must have seemed utterly subversive. "Judge not according to appearance," He said, "but judge righteous judgment." That is to say, It is right for you to judge on these religious questions. You must judge, but do not judge according to appearance, nor according to the opinions of your leaders, nor according to a superficial reading of the Scriptures. "Judge righteous judgment." That means judgment that corresponds with the sense of justice which each man has in his own soul. We are to judge according to our own moral sense and discrimination.

Then said some of them of Jerusalem, Is not this he, whom they seek to kill? But, lo, he speaketh boldly, and they say nothing unto him. Do the rulers know indeed that this is the very Christ? Howbeit we know this man whence he is: but when Christ cometh, no man knoweth whence he is. Then cried Jesus in the temple as he taught, saying, Ye both know me, and ye know whence I am: and I am not come of myself, but he that sent me is true, whom ye know not. But I know him; for I am from him, and he hath sent me. Then they sought to take him: but no man laid hands on him: because his hour was not yet come.

Jesus' argument in followng up this initial statement takes our breath away too. "You have broken one law to keep another," said He. "I have broken a law to heal a man's body." God is interested in His children. Even their physical bodies are precious to Him. Laws are very secondary affairs.

Jesus' second refutation is just as subversive to the legalists. His listeners did not know their prophecies well. Some had listened to statements that when the Messiah appeared, no one would know where He came from. They thought they knew that Jesus came from Galilee. Some knew of the prophecy that He was to be born in Bethlehem. We would have expected Jesus to welcome this, for it was correct. It should make accepting Jesus easier.

But apparently we are wrong. Jesus did not want that sort of acceptance. To follow Him because He corresponded with the prophecies of the Old Testament, would be of no help at all in entering God's Kingdom. To the Pharisees and their devotees it would be a hindrance, for it would make almost impossible any personal surrender. These prophecies were tied up in Jesus' day, with a completely wrong idea of God. It was necessary then, as it is now, for men to accept Jesus on His own account, because of what they see in Him, not on some information about Him gathered from their Scriptures.

And many of the people believed on him, and said, When Christ cometh, will he do more miracles than these which this man hath done?
The Pharisees heard that the people murmured such things concerning him; and the Pharisees and the chief priests sent officers to take him. Then said Jesus unto them, Yet a little while am I with you, and then I go unto him that sent me. Ye shall seek me, and shall not find me: and where I am, thither ye cannot come.

Thus the seed begins to grow. Men see Jesus. They continue to think about Him. Sooner or later they follow. Their Scriptures and the opinions of religious leaders have little to do with it. Jesus' attitude here is not as new as it seems. Paul, in writing to the Romans, roundly asserts that it was God's purpose, even in the days of the Old Testament, that the law be observed "in the spirit, not in the letter."

We will give a moments thought to this paragraph. Jesus is showing how men can be transferred from the world to the Kingdom. Nothing is more important than this. Those men must get rid of their old conception of a legalistic God. They must also get rid of the influence of the legalistic priests who had guided them away from God. Only when we realize that His words are not simply true in the sense of nonfalse, but

in the sense of coming from God and not from men, can
we follow Jesus here. His teachings and His works, coming
from above, establishing a new concepton of God, and only from
that platform can we come to Jesus, and receive from Him whatever our thirst asks for.

In the last day, that great day of the feast, Jesus stood and cried, saying,
If any man thirst, let him come unto me, and drink. He that believeth
on me, as the Scripture hath said, out of his belly shall flow rivers of
living water. (But this spake he of the Spirit, which they that believe
on him should receive: for the Holy Ghost was not yet given; because
that Jesus was not yet glorified.)

As we come to the final step in men's journey from the world
to the Kingdom, it will be worth our while to spend a moment
in observing carefully just how far we have travelled. Jesus has
been observed. His works and His whole life have been recognized
as good. More than this, we have seen that He represents God.
There is a vast emancipation even in this. The old slavery to a
legalistically conceived God is gone. Such a man can be a real
soldier of the common good. Missionaries to Mohammedans see
such cases, not many perhaps, but still a fair number. These
people have seen Jesus' life and teachings, sometimes by direct
study, far oftener by acquaintance with Christians. Jesus has
emancipated these men, and given them a new conception of God.
Ther intolerance is gone. Efforts for community uplift and relief
have their support. They help build Mission hospitals sometimes.
It is a pleasure to have them as friends. Bin Sulaim, the governor of Kateef, was one of the finest friends that I have ever had.

But Jesus wanted more than this. It was "the last day, the
great day of the feast." Discussions had continued through the
eight days. Jesus had been present for more than half of that
time. The crowd had moved on to sharper and more adequate
ideas about Jesus. "This is of a truth the prophet," "this is the
Christ." And those who rejected Him, rejected Him more completely and bitterly. Some were anxious to have Him arrested
and killed. The men who thought He was the Christ were accept-

ing Him as from God. It was a very complete understanding of His nature and mission.

To these men Jesus presented His ultimate message. He opened before them the door to the Kingdom of God; more than that — to the family of God. All that He has taught up till now is a preparation for this final invitation. "If any man thirst, let him come unto me and drink." It comes as the climax of a fragmentary and disconnected account. Real meditation is needed to understand it. But surely, there are bad desires and good desires, bad thirsts and good ones. Jesus does not agree with that. There are good and bad ways of gratifying our thirst. God our Creator put that thirst there.

"Whatever your thirst is," says Jesus, "come to me and drink." Are there no illegitimate thirsts? In the movies and in real life, the desire to be a "big shot" leads to dreadful crime. William Booth took his thirst to Jesus and drank and became one of the greatest leaders the armies of God ever had.

And the acquisitve instinct? We are afraid of that. But George Müller took that thirst to Jesus and drank, and the millions of dollars he collected and cared for in the most meticulous way, took care of thousands of orphans. This gave such a demonstration of the existence and power and love of God as confounds atheists to this day.

Both Kagawa and Hitler thirsted to lead men, and to lead their nations to places of preeminence. Hitler satisfied his thirst at the most evil fountains of the bottomless pit. Kagawa came to Jesus to drink and has led his friends to the new birth and eternal life, and is in a fair way to bring his whole nation into the Kingdom of God.

There are three things men must do. In the first place, they must thirst. Moreover, they must thirst hard. Not every man who has been emancipated from legalism and pride and intolerance wants to climb to a higher life. Not every man with a genuine thirst is willing to pay the price of drinking at Jesus hand, the price of unremitting work and abstinence from time-wasting pleasures, the price of perpetual servitude.

Most men prefer to remain below, because, it is not an unattractive plain where they live comfortably and well. There is freedom and humanitarian service. But if they continue to meditate on Jesus and in this way associate with Him, they will receive the better hope which, Hebrews tells us, is the first part of salvation. This hope, this thirst for a real membership in God's family is the first necessity.

This thirst is a development and growth of the desire to do good works as we noticed when the discussion began. The good works which the world is anxious to do, and of which they are so proud, are considered good largely as they gain men's approval. The thirst which Jesus is talking about is pointed upward. It desires God's approval.

However, that of itself means very little. Our conception of God may be so defective and bad that thirst to do His will pulls us deeper and deeper into pride and intolerance and sin. Probably it was *not the Pharisees* that Jesus said, "If *any man* thirst, let him come unto me and drink." It is very much a question whether the Pharisees could have come to Jesus.

But when men have come to recognize that Jesus' teachings are from God, when they realize that God is like Jesus, then, if they will drop their effort to gain men's approval, they can bring their thirst for divine approval to Jesus, and be God's children with eternal life in their souls.

The motive which Jesus holds out to such men is unusual. Not their own good but the good of others is the reason for coming. "Out of him shall flow rivers of living water." That is pure unselfishness. This may have been a frivolous crowd without a serious thought, but it was here that Jesus saw His opportunity. He presented a new aspect of the Kingdom. Men are offered salvation not on the basis of benefits that will come to them, but because of the blessing they will be to others.

When men thirst for the living God, for their Heavenly Father, they will come to Jesus. There are many other voices calling, many who want to act as introducers of Jesus, His interpreters. We must pass them all by. "Let him come into me." There is a complete exclusiveness in that statement. Jesus knew of no road to God except Himself.

Jesus probably had more trouble making this clear to the men of His own time, than the Spirit has in making it clear to us. But it is not easy with us either. The material, the four Gospels, we easily hold in one hand, but it is adequate. Through it we can enter the actual circle of Jesus' mind and attitude, but it is a matter of thought and effort and meditation. It takes time. Without a deep understanding we cannot come to Jesus, no matter what our desires are. We must take the picture in the Gospels and look at it long, earnestly, and reverently, every man for himself. From others we can accept unthinkingly a picture of Jesus that is as false as the Pharisees notion of God.

"And drink." This is the supreme surrender. Drink what? Drink, what our thirst calls for: Drink what Jesus gives us when we come to Him. Different comers are given different things to drink. Jesus does not give us all exactly the same picture to look at, nor precisely the same things to do. We all drink His teaching and His example, and so in a sense we all drink the same thing, but following Him, each receives his own drink. He tells us the work we are to do, and shows us, the things we are to believe and to admire. Here is the supreme lesson, the lesson of complete surrender. His work we do, His teachings we follow, His example we imitate.

And the result is far more than the good works we dreamed of, even at their idealized best. From within us shall flow rivers of living water, because God works through us. If in Jesus we align ourselves with God, He aligns Himself with us.

JOHN 8

Jesus went unto the mount of Olives. And early in the morning he came again into the temple, and all the people came unto him; and he sat down, and taught them. And the scribes and Pharisees brought unto him a woman taken in adultery; and when they had set her in the midst, They say unto him, Master, this woman was taken in adultery, in the very act. Now Moses in the law commanded us, that such should be stoned: but what sayest thou? This they said, tempting him, that they might have to accuse him. But Jesus stooped down, and with his finger wrote on the ground, as though he heard them not. So when they continued asking him, he lifted up himself, and said unto them, He that is without sin among you, let him first cast a stone at her. And again he stooped down, and wrote on the ground. And they which heard it, being convicted by their own conscience, went out one by one, beginning at the eldest, even unto the last: and Jesus was left alone, and the woman standing in the midst. When Jesus had lifted up himself, and saw none but the woman, he said unto her, Woman, where are those thine accusers? hath no man condemned thee? She said, No man, Lord. And Jesus said unto her, Neither do I condemn thee: go, and sin no more.

Then spake Jesus again unto them, saying, I am the light of the world: he that followeth me shall not walk in darkness, but shall have the light of life. The Pharisees therefore said unto him, Thou bearest record of thyself; thy record is not true. Jesus answered and said unto them, Though I bear record of myself, yet my record is true; for I know whence I came, and whither I go; but ye cannot tell whence I come, and whither I go. Ye judge after the flesh; I judge no man. And yet if I judge, my judgment is true: for I am not alone, but I and the Father that sent me. It is also written in your law, that the testimony of two men is true. I am one that bear witness of myself, and the Father that sent me beareth witness of me. Then said they unto him, Where is thy Father? Jesus answered, Ye neither know me, nor my Father: if ye had known me, ye should have known my Father also. These words spake Jesus in the treasury, as he taught in the temple: and no man laid hands on him; for his hour was not yet come. Then said Jesus again unto them, I go my way, and ye shall seek me, and shall die in your sins: whither I go, ye cannot come. Then said the Jews, Will he kill himself? because he saith, Whither I go, ye cannot come. And he said unto them, Ye are from beneath; I am from above: ye are of this world; I am not of this world. And I said therefore unto you, that ye shall die in your sins: for if ye believe not that I am he, ye shall die in your sins. Then said they unto him, Who art thou? And Jesus saith unto them, Even the same that I said unto you from the beginning. I have many things to say and to judge of you: but he that sent me is true; and I speak to the world those things which I have heard of him. They understood not that he spake to them of the Father. Then said Jesus unto them, When ye have lifted up the Son of man, then shall ye know that I am he, and that I do nothing of myself; but as my Father hath taught me, I speak these things. And he that sent me is with me: the Father hath not left me alone; for I do always those things that please him. As he spake these words, many believed on him. Then said Jesus to those Jews which believed on him, If ye continue in my word, then are ye my disciples indeed; And ye shall know the truth, and the truth shall make you free.

They answered him, We be Abraham's seed, and were never in bondage to any man: how sayest thou, Ye shall be made free? Jesus answered them, Verily, verily, I say unto you, Whosoever committeth sin is the servant of sin. And the servant abideth not in the house for ever: but the Son abideth ever. If the Son therefore shall make you free, ye shall be free indeed. I know that ye are Abraham's seed; but ye seek to kill me, because my word hath no place in you. I speak that which I have seen with my Father: and ye do that which ye have seen with your father. They answered and said unto him, Abraham is our father. Jesus saith unto them, If ye were Abraham's children, ye would do the works of Abraham. But now ye seek to kill me, a man that hath told you the truth, which I have heard of God: this did not Abraham. Ye do the deeds of your father. Then said they to him, We be not born of fornication; we have one Father, even God. Jesus said unto them, If God were your father, ye would love me: for I proceeded forth and came from God; neither came I of myself, but he sent me. Why do ye not understand my speech? even because ye cannot hear my word. Ye are of your father the devil, and the lusts of your father ye will do: he was a murderer from the beginning, and abode not in the truth, because there is no truth in him. When he speaketh a lie, he speaketh of his own: for he is a liar, and the father of it. And because I tell you the truth, ye believe me not. Which of you convinceth me of sin? And if I say the truth, why do ye not believe me? He that is of God heareth God's words: ye therefore hear them not, because ye are not of God. Then answered the Jews, and said unto him, Say we not well that thou art a Samaritan and hast a devil? Jesus answered, I have not a devil; but I honour my Father, and ye do dishonour me. And I seek not mine own glory: there is one that seeketh and judgeth. Verily, verily, I say unto you, If a man keep my saying, he shall never see death. Then said the Jews unto him, Now we know that thou hast a devil. Abraham is dead, and the prophets; and thou sayest, If a man keep my saying, he shall never taste of death. Art thou greater than our father Abraham, which is dead? and the prophets are dead: whom makest thou thyself? Jesus answered, If I honour myself, my honour is nothing: it is my Father that honoureth me; of whom ye say, that he is your God: Yet ye have not known him; but I know him: and if I should say, I know him not, I shall be a liar like unto you: but I know him, and keep his saying. Your father Abraham rejoiced to see my day: and he saw it, and was glad. Then said the Jews unto him, Thou art not yet fifty years old, and hast thou seen Abraham? Jesus said unto them, Verily, verily, I say unto you, Before Abraham was, I am. Then took they up stones to cast at him: but Jesus hid himself, and went out of the temple, going through the midst of them, and so passed by.

Chapter VIII

THE PICTURE

Jesus went unto the mount of Olives. And early in the morning he came again into the temple, and all the people came unto him; and he sat down, and taught them. And the scribes and Pharisees brought unto him a woman taken in adultery; and when they had set her in the midst, They say unto him, Master, this woman was taken in adultery, in the very act. Now Moses in the law commanded us, that such should be stoned: but what sayest thou? This they said, tempting him, that they might have to accuse him. But Jesus stooped down, and with his finger wrote on the ground, as though he heard them not.

In this chapter Jesus is dealing with the world and, for the most part with the leaders of the world, that is, the Pharisees.

So when they continued asking him, he lifted up himself, and said unto them, He that is without sin among you, let him first cast a stone at her. And again he stooped down, and wrote on the ground. And they which heard it, being convicted by their own conscience, went out one by one, beginning at the eldest, even unto the last: and Jesus was left alone, and the woman standing in the midst. When Jesus had lifted up himself, and saw none but the woman, he said unto her, Woman, where are those thine accusers? hath no man condemned thee? She said, No man, Lord. And Jesus said unto her, Neither do I condemn thee: go, and sin no more.

The world hates Him, and very obviously it is because He testifies of it that its works are evil.

The first scene runs through eleven verses. Apparently it was not included in the first writing of the Gospel. But whoever added it showed real artistic sense. There is no teaching here but as, a part of the picture that is being drawn, it is a vivid and valuable addition. Here and throughout this chapter Jesus is pitted against the Pharisees and this story is an essential part of the picture.

Jesus is dealing with a woman in great distress. She was about to lose her life. Someone had caught her in the act of adultery, and the Pharisees dragged her, shrinking, terrified, and helpless, to a public exhibition of her disgrace, in order to weaken Jesus' hold on the common people. Coarse, hard brutality could scarcely have found better expression.

Jesus knew that she was guilty, and as far as we are able to tell she had shown no repentance. Nevertheless, He had no sympathy with the demand for her punishment, but rather identified Himself with her. He did not stare at her. He avoided even a look. That would have added to her distress, and Jesus did not add to the distress of the weak and defenseless.

The Pharisees professed great zeal for Moses' law and doubtless also for the good of society, but the real reason why they were willing to bring up the matter in this way, was the gratification it afforded to their cruel and sensual souls. Jesus stood at the opposite pole. He wanted to help this woman.

His delicacy and anxiety to spare her feelings, His gentleness in every word and act, remind us of a surgeon handling an extremely painful broken limb. He was not shocked nor angry with her. He even declined to notice the broken law of Moses. He did not urge her to repent. He carefully refrained from violating the privacy of her sin in the smallest way. He did not want to make her acceptance of His teaching the condition of His help. He did not try to instruct her. She could not have listened intelligently if He had tried.

Jesus wanted to help this woman because she was in trouble, she was suffering. No regard for rules governing society, no fear of possible evil effects of leniency was in His mind at that moment. His sympathies commanded Him in this situation. Is it indeed not by feelings rather than by theological ideas that we enter the Kingdom of God. Pity was Jesus' feeling here. Indeed, why should this sin ever waken in us any feeling except pity?

We gain also a most illuminating view of the Pharisees' fundamental character. No comment is necessary as to the moral texture of the men who would parade an affair of this sort before the crowd, simply to embarrass a wandering preacher. And scarcely less glaring than their coarseness is their heartlessness and cruelty. Their victim was a trembling defenseless woman but they showed no gleam of pity for her. There were regular ways of trying such offenders but the Pharisees wanted to put Jesus at a disadvantage. So, inspite of the unspeakable distress it caused her, the woman was dragged before the crowd to be exhibited for that purpose. Every feeling of delicate femininity was crucified by so doing. She suffered to the very limit of her capacity. They probably did not give her feelings a moment's thought.   ,

And with all the rest there stands out the meanness and cowardice of their souls. The man was taken in the very act too, but he was not brought forward. It is safe to suppose that he was equally guilty, probably more so. He would have served their purpose just as well, but it was easier and safer to sacrifice the woman. She would suffer more because she was completely defenseless.

It has often been regarded as a mistake to put this little story here. The argument of the Gospel is not helped by it. But if we consider the picture of Jesus which the author is trying to give,

Then spake Jesus again unto them, saying, I am the light of the world:
he that followeth me shall not walk in darkness, but shall have the light
of life. The Pharisees therefore said unto him, Thou bearest record of
thyself; thy record is not true.

---

we gain a different impression. The writer is giving us a picture
of Jesus and here particularly of his relationship to the Pharisees.

From that viewpoint this story makes an important contribution. Jesus is pitted against the Pharisees. He sides with a helpless and terrified woman, whose death they are demanding. The
rest of chapter 8 is a continuation of this opening picture. John
evidently felt that his portrait of Jesus would be incomplete
without a detailed portrayal of the black background which the
Pharisees afforded.

In the entire Gospel there is nothing more vivid or instructive
than this little story. The power of silent dignity and divine love
faces the self-satisfied and smug insolence of the Pharisees. We
can almost hear that divine sentence "The blameless one among
you, let him cast the first stone." The devastating impact of that
word from God, in the silence of the great temple created a profoundly dramatic moment.

This chapter continues the story of chapter 7. Jesus is talking
to the same people. Again He heals none who are sick and feeds
none who are hungry. The crowds who listen are divided. Some
accept Him and His message more and more completely, and
others reject what He says with more and more bitterness.

The Pharisees merge into clearer view — a disturbing picture.
Here is a group of outstanding men. They have devoted themselves with unremitting diligence to the study of God's wonderful
revelation. Pride and intolerance have ruined them? Why? At
least partly because political as well as religious power was in
their hands. The union of church and state is always dangerous
because religious earnestness grows into intolerance. In this chapter it grows into murder.

Furthermore, religious law is dangerous anywhere. It is looked
on as the perfect expression of God, and its enforcement, even

Jesus answered and said unto them, Though I bear record of myself, yet my record is true: for I know whence I came, and whither I go; but ye cannot tell whence I come, and whither I go.

---

by intolerably cruel means, is considered Gods will. God is dragged down to the level of a heathen idol.

It is worth nothing, too, the picture John draws of the Roman empire. We see a good deal of Pilate and the Roman soldiers before this Gospel is finished. Heathen as they were, and cruel and wicked, they were not nearly as far from God and His righteousness, as the Sanhedrin. They did not hate Jesus. In the Roman Empire there was a union of church and state, too, but it was loose and ineffective. In the Jewish nation it was close and effective and utterly deadly. By murdering Jesus the Pharisees thought that they were rendering service to God. The Roman centurion knew better. There were political and business leaders then, too, just as there are now. These men did not hate Jesus, did not even oppose Him, and He was not compelled to pit Himself against them.

But He pitted Himself without compromise against the Pharisees. He told them that they were sons of the Devil. Out of Jesus' mouth, that is a very terrifying word. It is only too clear what Jesus had in mind. They were dominated by the pride and sin of the Devil. His desires were their desires, and his works their works. What are "the lusts of the flesh?" Not the indulgences of the flesh, nor the self-satisfied haze of infidelity and doubt. The Devil thirsts for domination and power, for self-aggrandizement by wrecking others. Murder and lies are his characteristic works.

The deterioration of the Pharisees is a dreadful thing to see. No others were called sons of the Devil. They were sunk in sin as far as it is possible for men to get. They stood at the bottom in blasphemy too, for they projected back into their picture of God every sin that they nourished in their own hearts. They supposed that the murder of Jesus was the will and desire of God.

Ye judge after the flesh; I judge no man. And yet if I judge, my judgment is true: for I am not alone, but I and the Father that sent me.

This legalistic system had almost as bad an effect on the
common people. They, too, were shut away from God. The
legalistic God of the Pharisees' imagination was the only God
they knew. It is not surprising that they were perplexed, indifferent and frivolous, neither knowing nor greatly caring when or
how the Messiah was to come. They had no genuine touch with
God and no concern over their lack.

At this feast Jesus is a teacher. Even His patience must have
been tested by some of the reactions which He met. Several times
He started an address to the people. The opening statement of
such a talk is likely to be a particularly beautiful gem, and we
wait with as much anticipation as they waited for its complete
development.

But no complete development was allowed. Hostile and captious questions were constantly thrown back into Jesus' face. He
was used to this. No doubt He expected it. He always replied
with great sincerity and depth. Jesus probably stirred up intentionally the objections which He wanted to discuss. At this
feast all He needed to do was to select from many objections the
few which He wanted to take up.

At the end Jesus had advanced beyond the lessons of the earlier
days. It would seem that on the last day the discussion continued
through the afternoon, with growing intensity. Jesus was telling
these listeners why His Kingdom is better than the world, giving
reasons for transferring themselves from the world to Himself.

And evidently the writer intends that we gain from these feast
experiences a much more complete idea of the Pharisees than we
have had before. The comon people were increasingly friendly
to Jesus. In the course of the days many came to believe on Him.
But not the leaders. Their hostility increased. In the exchanges
of the debate, Jesus gives us a good deal of information about
the Pharisees.

It is also written in your law, that the testimony of two men is true. I am one that bear witness of myself, and the Father that sent me beareth witness of me. Then said they unto him, Where is thy Father? Jesus answered, Ye neither know me, nor my Father: if ye had known me, ye should have known my Father also. These words spake Jesus in the treasury, as he taught in the temple: and no man laid hands on him; for his hour was not yet come. Then said Jesus again unto them, I go my way, and ye shall seek me, and shall die in your sins: whither I go, ye cannot come. Then said the Jews, Will he kill himself? because he saith, Whither I go, ye cannot come.

They were a conspicuous part of the Jewish world, but He reckoned them mostly part of its sin. As Jesus met the world, its sin crystallized to a definite and bitter opposition, hatred, and finally murder. The surprising thing here is that this sin embodied itself in the religious leaders.

The situation was singularly free from political or social factors. What these people needed was God. If they only knew Him, other things would take care of themselves. Jesus was reaching out in complete simplicity to give them that knowledge. He taught the people because teaching was the one thing they needed. Moreover, it has a very special sort of teaching. It was new. Jesus might have stood and cried, "I am the successor of Moses. I am the prophet whom he promised, saying: "A prophet shall the Lord your God raise up for you from among your brethren, like unto me.' " What he did say was, "I am the light of the world."

We must try to get a glimpse of Jesus' mind here. What was He trying to persuade these people to do? Apparently, simply to understand and believe that He came from God. The Heavenly Father had sent Him. Whatever He said and did came from that source. They must believe it and abide in it.

This seems a modest demand on men's capacity to believe, and, as a matter of fact, His listeners did not find believing Him difficult. But it meant a radical break with their previous faith, and, worse, a sharp and definite break with their religious leaders. It was difficult and dangerous to follow Jesus, and break away from the legalistic system which bound them.

And he said unto them, Ye are from beneath; I am from above: ye are of this world; I am not of this world. I said therefore unto you, that ye shall die in your sins: for if ye believe not that I am he, ye shall die in your sins. Then said they unto him, Who art thou? And Jesus saith unto them, Even the same that I said unto you from the beginning. I have many things to say and to judge of you: but he that sent me is true; and I speak to the world those things which I have heard of him. They understood not that he spake to them of the Father.

To what motives did Jesus appeal in this situation? What inducements could He offer, strong enough to make men welcome ostracism and unpopularity and even hunger and death for the sake of following Him? Some of His audience were willing, even anxious to follow Him. The Pharisees were willing to commit murder to prevent anything of that sort. What could Jesus give to this mixed company?

"I am the light of the world." The beauty and power of that sentence were such that Jesus' enemies stopped Him immediately by a hostile and insincere rejoinder. We can almost shed a tear at this discourteous check to what might have developed into a discussion of the greatest beauty and depth. Jesus was not forced to acquiesce in this abrupt stop. He could have prolonged the discusson. Apparently He preferred to leave it just as it was, complete to an extraordinary degree, and in its brevity and brillance quite unforgettable. Years later those who had heard Jesus could recall and quote it.

Jesus was talking to a varied group. In it were the educated and the uneducated, the rich and the poor, the well-fed and the hungry. What class was He trying to reach? Probably He did not expect His teaching to appeal to any special class. Jesus knew that it would remain in men's minds and that they would think about it in the months and years to come.

The discussion died down and Jesus began again. He walked away, probably to where a different crowd could listen. "I am going away," He said, "and you will seek me and will die in your sins. Where I am you cannot come." Hostile questions were thrown up to stop this line of thought, but this time it was

Then said Jesus unto them, When ye have lifted up the Son of man, then shall ye know that I am he, and that I do nothing of myself; but as my Father hath taught me, I speak these things. And he that sent me is with me: the Father hath not left me alone; for I do always those things that please him. As he spake these words, many believed on him. Then said Jesus to those Jews which believed on him, If ye continue in my word, then are ye my disciples indeed; And ye shall know the truth, and the truth shall make you free.

They answered him, We be Abraham's seed, and were never in bondage to any man: how sayest thou, Ye shall be made free?

Jesus' intention to keep on. "You are from beneath. I am from above. Unless you believe that I am from above you will die in your sins."

The hostility of the listeners gave Jesus the opportunity which He wanted. He explained just what it was that they must believe. The Greek text is a little ambiguous here. It reads "Except ye believe that I am. That I am what? "That I am from above" seems the most natural reading.

But Jesus wanted a more definite and deeper faith than that. He spoke not merely as one "from above." "I speak thus as the Father taught me and he that sent me is with me. He has not left me alone for I do always that which is pleasing to him."

We see repeatedly in this chapter Jesus' sense of companionship with His Heavenly Father. It was the dominant note in His teaching. It was this that He wanted men to believe about Him.

He especially wanted these men to recognize His teachings as from God. "As my Father taught me I speak these things." Of all that Jesus came to accomplish the thing most constantly on His mind was the delivery of His Father's message. He came not because He desired to, but because the Father sent Him; not to do His own will but the will of the Father. For this purpose He delivered not His own message, but the message which the Father had given Him. Jesus knew that the validity of His claims and His whole power to save men depended on His loyalty to the Father's will.

Jesus answered them, Verily, verily, I say unto you, Whosoever committeth sin is the servant of sin. And the servant abideth not in the house
for ever: but the Son abideth ever. If the Son therefore shall make you
free, ye shall be free indeed. I know that ye are Abraham's seed; but
ye seek to kill me, because my word hath no place in you. I speak that
which I have seen with my Father: and ye do that which ye have seen
with your father. They answered and said unto him, Abraham is our
father. Jesus saith unto them, If ye were Abraham's children, ye would
do the works of Abraham.

This explanation captured the indifferent crowd. He was
talking of a Heavenly Father who was with Him always, never
leaving Him alone. The beauty of this presentation pierced
through the atmosphere of indifference and hostility. I have
watched the same process in Arabia. There is almost no hostility
which does not yield to a sympathetic presentation of God as our
Heavenly Father.

At this point Jesus dropped His effort to reach the whole crowd
gave His attention to the smaller company which had believed
on Him. Their faith was genuine, but it was only a beginning.
How could Jesus develop it into something deep and strong and
adequate for eternal life? They had accepted His word, and had
caught a genuine vision of God as their Heavenly Father. They
must abide in Jesus word now, and the truth would make them
free.

It was a superb teaching. Given to the Jews of that day,
smarting under the Roman yoke, the very word "freedom" might
have been expected to command immediate attention and approval. The Pharisees especially resented the Roman domination. But this teaching was not accepted at all. However
friendly and earnest the majority of this little group may have
been, their reply came from an enemy. "We have never been
in bondage to any man. How sayest thou, Ye shall be made
free?" But Jesus refused to be deflected.

"Whosoever committeth sin is the slave of sin."

What follows is worthy of special study, for it is the only discussion in this Gospel where Jesus allowed this sort of emotion

But now ye seek to kill me, a man that hath told you the truth, which I have heard of God: this did not Abraham. Ye do the deeds of your father. Then said they to him, We be not born of fornication; we have one Father, even God. Jesus said unto them, If God were your Father, ye would love me: for I proceeded forth and came from God; neither came I of myself, but he sent me. Why do ye not understand my speech? even because ye cannot hear my word. Ye are of your father the devil, and the lusts of your father ye will do: he was a murderer from the beginning, and abode not in the truth, because there is no truth in him. When he speaketh a lie, he speaketh of his own: for he is a liar, and the father of it.

---

to appear. He was sharp and personal, and denunciatory. He usually showed the most perfect emotional detachment when speaking to enemies. In the early part of the discussion He met captious questions with sincere and wholehearted explanations, and His forbearance and patience were rewarded by the belief of a large number. The tone at the end is very different.

It is not easy to understand this attitude on Jesus' part. The Pharisees were enemies. Their one desire was to destroy Jesus' work and nothing would be more natural than for Him to reply in kind. Jesus however was not natural in that sense. He had the ability to meet hostility and denunciation with an unruffled spirit. One reason for this different attitude was probably his concern for the beginners. They were sincere and with a litttle further instruction would enter into the Kingdom of God. The Pharisees wanted to prevent this with all their strength. Everything depended on which leader these men chose, Jesus or the Pharisees. Jesus apparently felt that the grip of the Pharisees on them must be broken. His teaching was as sincere and profound as ever. It was stirred up by hostile questions, as was usually the case, but it was certainly colored by very unusual emotion.

Jesus made no effort to soften His message down so that it might give less offense to the Pharisees. In fact, He seems to utilize this hostile atmosphere as an introduction for His last and most unacceptable statement: "Verily, verily, 'if a man keep my word he shall never see death.'"

And because I tell you the truth, ye believe me not. Which of you convinceth me of sin? And if I say the truth, why do ye not believe me? He that is of God heareth God's words: ye therefore hear them not, because ye are not of God. Then answered the Jews, and said unto him, Say we not well that thou art a Samaritan and hast a devil? Jesus answered, I have not a devil; but I honour my Father, and ye do dishonour me. And I seek not mine own glory: there is one that seeketh and judgeth. Verily, verily, I say unto you, If a man keep my saying, he shall never see death. Then said the Jews unto him, Now we know that thou hast a devil. Abraham is dead, and the prophets; and thou sayest, If a man keep my saying, he shall never taste of death. Art thou greater than our father, Abraham, which is dead? and the prophets are dead: whom makest thou thyself?

The Pharisees probably regarded this as the apex of all Jesus' impossible and insolent claims. Why did Jesus present this teaching here? It induced no additional faith even from His friends. But Jesus wanted to finish and He presents the message which He had received from His Father to the last point. The fact that it was extremely offensive to His listeners had nothing to do with the case.

That, of course, is because Jesus never forgot that His message was a divine thing. It was for the whole world and for all ages. This new word did not really make Jesus' position with His listeners much worse. He had already been completely rejected.

As we noted in chapter 5, the very intensity of their rejection of this word from God gave Jesus' listeners the ability to realize its infinite and eternal content. Probably no one except His fierce enemies understood that Jesus was talking of a life and of a death, which pertained not to the body but to the spirit, not to this world, but to eternity.

Pride of race or religion had no place in Jesus' heart. Patriotism seems to us a very fundamental virtue. Jesus did not think so, at least He knew of no patriotism which puts other nations and races in an inferior place. Jesus loved Jerusalem, and Jerusalem stood for the nation. But Jesus loved other nations just as much.

Jesus answered, If I honour myself, my honour is nothing: it is my Father that honoureth me; of whom ye say, that he is your God: Yet ye have not known him; but I know him: and if I should say, I know him not, I shall be a liar like unto you: but I know him, and keep his saying. Your father Abraham rejoiced to see my day: and he saw it, and was glad. Then said the Jews unto him, Thou art not yet fifty years old, and hast thou seen Abraham? Jesus said unto them, Verily, verily, I say unto you, Before Abraham was, I am. Then took they up stones to cast at him: but Jesus hid himself, and went out of the temple, going through the midst of them, and so passed by.

In the face of social abuses Jesus kept silence. But on occasion He was willing to break His silence and be a drastic iconoclast. If we, too only knew when to keep silence, and when to tear evil things down. Jesus' claim to superiority over Abraham costs His hearers no money, and caused them no physical discomfort. They could hardly have claimed that He was attacking anything essential in religion. Why then did it make them so furious? Why are iconoclasts always hated?

Jesus' Teaching

Then spake Jesus again unto them, saying, I am the light of the world: he that followeth me shall nt walk in darkness, but shall have the light of life.

Passing from the account of the woman taken in adultery, we pick up the argument of the Gospel with verse 12. We are still dealing with "the world." How men can be transferred from the world to the Kingdom, we saw in chapter 7. Here Jesus carries His study far deeper. He is teaching about the world, but particularly its contrast with the Kingdom. He wants men to know what the Kingdom of God has to offer.

The first impression is that in this chapter we have disconnected teachings, each very beautiful, but with little connection. Closer study changes that impression. It could easily be that John, writing fifty years after these things happened, assembled in one chapter teachings given in various circumstances. But the account reads extremely well as a connected story. A rough and tumble debate is inevitable with such a hostile audience. Jesus, in the face of captious insincere opposition is carefully and systematically presenting teaching of the greatest importance. Its unity held it in John's mind and he remembered it well.

Jesus is showing the contrast between the world and the Kingdom of God. He discusses this under three heads: light vs. darkness, freedom vs. bondage, and life vs. death.

"I am the light of the world. He that followeth me shall not walk in darkness but shall have the light of life. This is one of Jesus' unforgettable sentences, like, "I am the bread of life," or, "I am the good shepherd." His light illumines vast areas of darkness and obscurity. The "world is the human world, the whole of mankind. It is in darkness, and, in contrast, the man who follows Jesus has the light of life. This is not entirely new. Jesus is "the light that lightens every man." It is not remarkable that men who follow Him will live in the light.

No one can question the statement that those who do not follow Jesus walk in darkness. There are many kinds of darkness in the world. Hundreds of fiercely dancing devotees accompany the transfer of a Hindu idol from one temple to another. Intense devotion lines their faces. Thousands of men and women make the Mohammedan pilgrimage from Northwest China to Mecca.

Often three years are spent on this pilgrimage and hunger and thirst and disease and neglect leave half of the pilgrims buried along the road. And there are other darknesses like the bleak agnosticism which Dr. Warthin of the University of Michigan left behind as his legacy to that center of thought. Henley put it vividly: "Out of the night that covers me, black as the pit from pole to pole."

Men who follow Jesus are to have light, which the world lacks. Jesus rationalizes our universe and shows us the path of duty in it. He saves us from the outlook which gives it neither meaning nor purpose.

We deal here with a very fundamental demand. We want this view of the truth and sometimes that thirst becomes very intense.

Certainly in these days of war and suffering and hunger and cruelty our universe needs rationalizing.

How much search there is in other countries for a faith which will rationalize the universe, the writer is unable to say. In Arabia there is not much evidence of such an attitude. In America, on the contrary, it is a common and sometimes very intense quest. Among younger people, especially students, this demand for a rationalization of the universe is among the sharpest spiritual thirst.

Now if Christ's statement: "He that followeth me shall not walk in darkness, but shall have the light of life," means that His followers are to have their universe rationalized, it should be possible to point out to a sincere inquirer what those rationalizing truths are. Furthermore, if Christ here means exactly what He says it is not to His teaching that we are to look for this light but to His example. Listening to Christ's teaching is one thing, following it is another. Following means not studying His example but imitating it.

The promise is as wide as humanity. There are no exceptions. The man who tries to imitate Christ, will find his universe rationalized. It is possible, indeed it is certain, that different sincere followers wll have this result accomplished by different elements in Christ's life. Perhaps the best that anyone of us can do is to state as simply as possible the things in Christ's life which have done this for him. We will mention three:

First, Christs conception of God. No discourse, formally outlining the nature of the Deity is on record, but from Christ's example as well as from His words we learn that the Omnipotent God is our Father. That truth about God is the foundation of Christ's whole life. It reconstitutes the universe. Every father coming home from work and seeing his three-year-old boy run out to meet him with a shout of joy knows to some extent what kind of a being God is for at that moment he has a picture of God in his own heart.

Second Christ's standard of values. In these days we hear brilliant men of great sincerity and penetration declaring that the supreme and only real value of life are the experiences of human enjoyment, that pleasurable sensations justify themselves under all circumstances; that the soul expands and develops on self-indulgence and pleasure, especially on the stimulation and gratification of the sex desire; that self-control is only another name for hypocrisy; and that self-restraint and discipline are the obsolete sackcloth and ashes of medievalism. The number of people who have been somewhat dazed by this inversion of our previous standards is perhaps not small.

The man who follows Christ finds the standard he needs. The things that afford enjoyable physical sensations, good things to eat and drink, rest and ease after fatigue, pleasant weather and so on seems not so important in this atmosphere. We read four accounts of Christ's life and search without success for any indication of the climate He lived in, what sort of food He ate, or even whether or not He had comfortable quarters. The pleasures and comforts of the body simply did not exist for Jesus. Even the higher values, such as the discovery of scientific truth, or the love of the beautiful which we call art, while these things existed for Christ and He no doubt recognized their value, He gave no such important place as we do. In this world Jesus saw real values in only one field namely, the experiences and enjoyments connected with human association, and cooperation and friendship.

Third, Christ's unmistakable conviction that the good of others is the supreme and indeed the only worthy object of effort. Talk of our duty to ourselves, of self-expression and self-realization sounds childish in the light of Christ's life. He was not trying to express Himself or to realize Himself any more than He wasted time pitying Himself. He lived for others.

Jesus answered and said unto them, Though I bear record of myself, yet my record is true: for I know whence I came, and whither I go; but ye cannot tell whence I come, and whither I go. Ye judge after the flesh; I judge no man. And yet if I judge, my judgment is true: for I am not alone, but I and the Father that sent me.

Those who try to imitate Jesus come to know that these revelations are more than beautiful. They are true. The Almighty God is our affectionate Father. The one thing worth working for is meeting the needs of others. The real values of life are brotherly association and neighborly cooperation with our fellowmen, and worship and fellowship with God.

In his First Epistle John speaks of God as absolute light. "In Him is no darkness at all." That is philosophy. Absolute power, absolute knowledge, and absolute holiness are in that word. Here the thought seems simpler. Jesus' follower walking freely and easly in the daylight is contrasted with a man stumbling in darkness. But there is an overtone here too. Such a follower has the "light of life." The vegetable world demonstrates what that means. All life comes from the light.

The Pharisees, by means of their discourteous interruption, hoped to break the impact of what Jesus had just said. But He used their objection to introduce the topic which He wanted to take up next. This time however, it was not presented in one sentence, but by means of a stormy debate. Debates do not usualy clarify the truth. They obscure it. But Jesus was able to use this one. It bristles with unanswered questions, but the helm was always firmly in Jesus' hands. A good helmsman uses a contrary wind to drive his boat forward, and that is just what Jesus was doing here.

The teaching so astonishingly well presented in this stormy discussion we have met before, and we will meet it again. That is because it is the foundation on which Jesus' whole life was built. Jesus had been sent by His Heavenly Father. Everything which He said and did was an absolute replica of the Father's will. Jesus loved this term "Father." The Word "God" does not appear in the early discussion at all. It appears once in verse 54 when Jesus tells them plainly that His Father is their God.

I am one that bear witness of myself, and the Father that sent me beareth witness of me. Then said they unto him, Whence is thy Father? Jesus answered, Ye neither know me, nor my Father: if ye had known me, ye should have known my Father also. . . . Then said Jesus again unto them, I go my way, and ye shall seek me, and shall die in your sins: whither I go, ye cannot come. . . . And he said unto them, Ye are from beneath; I am from above: ye are of this world; I am not of this world. I said therefore unto you, that ye shall die in your sins: for if ye believe not that I am he, ye shall die in your sins.

This was difficult to follow for His hearers, for the whole idea of God as a Heavenly Father was utterly new and strange. Jesus had told them about His Heavenly Father before, but something new was added that day, something new and very difficult. Unless these people could believe that Jesus came from His Heavenly Father, from above, they would die in their sins.

For sheer brazen effrontery, the Pharisees probably ranked this as the apex, the most grotesquely absurd of all Jesus' assertions. He repeated it so its significance could not be missed or its meaning misunderstood. Even for us it is difficult.

In the company Jesus was addressing every sort of sin was represented. The sin of the Pharisees was there. The sin of the woman of Samaria was there. The money lenders with their avarice and their calousness were there. Not one of them could escape from their sins except as he came to believe that Jesus was from above.

And the belief that Jesus came from God, and represented God in every word, every deed, in every thought, carries with it the belief that God was like Jesus. This is a step further than recognizing that God is our Father: God, the omnipotent Creator, is like Jesus.

These people were bound by a very terrible legalistic conception of God. It represented a great deterioration of what Moses had given them. But we need not read into this statement an assertion that every man there was hopelessly bound. Those who still retained a connection with God through the faith of the Old Testament would without difficulty recognize the fact that Jesus was from above, and so the door of salvation was open to them.

Where could they get the conception of God they needed? Only from Jesus. Only by seeing God in Jesus. Only by believing that He came from above. It is from His human life that we gain the picture of God. Cherishing in our hearts the legalistic Pharisaic picture of God not only subjects us to sin, but is itself terrible sin.

Then said Jesus unto them, When ye have lifted up the Son of man, then shall ye know that I am he, and that I do nothing of myself; but as my Father hath taught me, I speak these things. And he that sent me is with me: the Father hath not left me alone; for I do always those things that please him.

We see now a new and deeper significance in Jesus' word, "I am the light of the world." His own life, His own, person standing before them was itself the picture of God, the light which emancipates from the overwhelming power of sin.

As the stormy debate continued Jesus was able to paint a picture of the divine relationships that was so transparently beautiful that "many believed on Him." Those were doubtless the common people not the Pharisees.

This is one of the places where we wish that we had Jesus' address in greater detail. How did He present this truth so that it melted their hearts? Even from this meager account we catch a glimpse of the greatness of His accomplishment.

Perhaps the main reason was, that He gave them a new and unbelievably beautiful picture of God. The one Christian teaching that can melt a Bedouin heart in the deserts of Arabia is this one that melted the hearts of Jesus' listeners that afternoon in Jerusalem, namely, that the omnipotent God is our Heavenly Father. Added to that was the almost involuntary revelation of warm and deep affection which flowed as a constant current between Jesus and his Heavenly Father. Simple people the world over can understand that. They understood it that afternoon in Jerusalem. It emancipated them from the hard, legalistic God of the Pharisees.

This discussion is probably best understood as the continuation of Jesus' opening word, "I am the light of the world." This new conception of God was a very great part of the "light of life" which Jesus' followers were to have. It is the development and

completion of that little sentence which was so abruptly termi-
nated by Jesus' hostile listeners.

Jesus gained the ear of the crowd and carried them with Him
till it is recorded that many believed on Him. It was a personal
triumph of the first order. He dropped the role of a debater and
was a teacher again, and so we pass to the consideration of the
next great truth which Jesus wanted to present to His Jerusalem
audience that afternoon.

Then said Jesus to those Jews which believed on him, If ye continue in
my word, then are ye my disciples indeed; And ye shall know the truth,
and the truth shall make you free.

It was a very beautiful word that He had for them: "If ye
abide in my word, then are ye my disciples and ye shall know
the truth and the truth shall make you free." There is a considerable development here beyond what we have seen in the
teaching immediately preceding this. People have been promised
the light of life if they follow Jesus, and that light of life has
been seen to include a recognition of Jesus' heavenly origin and,
most important of all, a view of God as our Heavenly Father.

Here Jesus' demands are greater. He wants something permanent. It is a deeper demand too, for abiding in Jesus' words,
that is, His teachings, means in addition to permanence, a profound meditation on these teachings till we understand them and
accept them. Jesus did not regard these believers as stable members of the new order. They believed that He came from His
Heavenly Father just as He had told them was necessary. He
hastened to tell them now how this beginning could be carried to
completion. The further progress which He was anxious for them
to make also concerned this matter of sin. "Ye shall know the
truth and the truth shall make you free."

"Truth" is a new word and it catches our attention immediately.
What truth? First of all the truth that God is like Jesus, but
Jesus did not follow up this idea. His mind was on something
else. We would like to stop for a time with the word "abide."
Just how can we abide in Jesus' words? But here, too, we are

disappointed. Jesus had His mind on freedom. It was in that direction that His further teaching was to come.

The people whom Jesus was addressing believed on Him. They had made the necessary beginning, but their faith was incomplete. A further word was needed. They had accepted Jesus' teaching as coming from God. They must abide in it. Then they would know the truth. We wish that we had a definition here, but all that we are told is that the truth will make us free.

They answered him, We be Abraham's seed, and were never in bondage to any man: how sayest thou, Ye shall be made free? Jesus answered them, Verily, verily, I say unto you, Whosoever committeth sin is the servant of sin. And the servant abideth not in the house for ever: but the Son abideth ever. If the Son therefore shall make you free, ye shall be free indeed.

It is the picture of a school. "If ye abide in my word then are ye truly my pupils." Jesus is the teacher and we are His pupils. But these pupils are in bondage. They have iron collars around their necks, and their hands are manacled. They are slaves. Now, if we will abide in the word that the teacher gives us we will know the truth, and most remarkable of all, once we know the truth, those iron collars and chains will dissolve and we will be free.

The important thing, then, is to understand just what is meant by abiding. The easiest figure is that of a house that we live in. We have a permanent residence there. We wish that Jesus had developed this particular theme a little. Is the figure equally valid if we think of a mantle which we constantly wear? He gives us no further help at this point.

Jesus put in a word about freedom. The very fragrance of Heaven was on it, but it evoked from His listeners a most astonishing rejoinder. Smarting under the Roman yoke with its harsh and unfeeling brutality, we would have supposed that any discussion of freedom would be water for the thirsty. But human pride is a curious thing, and it flared up here. "We are Abraham's seed, and have never been in bondage to any man." Jesus began this discussion with friends and believers, but He is debating with enemies now. It was a mixed crowd, and both friends and enemies were in it.

Evidently He welcomed this particular objection for its extremely hostile tone, for it moved the discussion into the area where He wanted it, and we hear an exceedingly profound and important word about sin. "The truth shall make you free." Free from what? From slavery. "Whosoever committeth sin is the slave of sin." At this point we would like to have a definition of sin but we will have to do without it. Sin works itself out in many hideous carnal forms, but these do not seem to be in Jesus' mind. So far as we can see it is the self-directed life that He is thinking of, the life that is far away from God. Such a life then is slavery. There is food for thought here, for many aspects of such a life are far from unattractive. Some of these types of slavery are very much loved and the grip they have on men is stronger on that account.

One of the unexpected things in this discussion is Jesus' attitude of pity to sin. A slave is compelled by force to do what he does not want to do and hence he is to be pitied. It is as if we were discussing something shameful, but impossible to shake off, like a small boy who wakes up wet in the morning in spite of all he can do to break the habit.

We have become so accustomed to the ideas of guilt and condemnation and punishment in connection with sin, that Jesus' word here comes as a surprise. In His mind the sinning world is not so much blameworthy as helpless. Jesus evidently intends to leave no possibility of misunderstanding here. "Every one who committeth sin is the bondservant of sin," that is, the slave of sin. A slave is one who is compelled to do what he does not want to do, and every one who commits sin comes in this category.

On the other hand, the man who follows Jesus, who enters the new order, is free. He does what he wants to do. That is not the way we are accustomed to look at it, but like everything that Jesus says, it is profoundly true. A man commits sin because, as James puts it, "he is drawn away by his own lust and enticed." A man can sin in this business. He can fill it with oppression and dishonesty, but business procedure is right in the right place. The relations between men and women can be filled with sin. The most evil things in the world would rise out of them. But those relations are right in the right place. Every lovely thing in our lives is built on this foundation.

Slavery to sin is the first part of this picture. There is a second part. We see a teacher, and these slaves are His pupils. The schools of Arabia are to this day made up of a little group of perhaps fifteen or twenty boys with a single teacher before whom they sit and recite their lessons. In Jesus' school the pupils enter chained in their bondage, and the teacher teaches them a wonderful lesson which dissolves the chains off their necks and the manacles off their hands. However, for this to happen it is necessary to remain in school for a long time, indeed for always.

No one but Jesus could have put so much into a few simple words. He surely must have brought this straight from God. "If ye abide in my words, then are ye truly my pupils, and ye shall know the truth, and the truth shall make you free. It is the truth that makes us free, not a miraculous exercise of divine power. And what truth? The divine truth that the teacher gives to each pupil. That must mean that our slavery to whatever sin it may be, is not a physical necessity. It is a matter of enslaved emotion and mind and will. That, of course, is why the psychiatrist is able to do so much for these men and women. If we can learn this lesson and catch the truth that Jesus is trying to give us, then the truth will make us free. The promise is without qualifications. A real vision of the truth, and that includes acceptance, will free us from every bondage. It is a long and gloriously complete list of emancipations: drink and drugs and sex, resentments and frustrations and fears. "The truth shall make you free."

The writer is giving us a very complete lesson on sin. The path of its development is plain enough. It begins as darkness. We walk in darkness. The hard-faced industrialist, responsible for malnourished babies and the untimely death of their mothers, began by following his New England grandmother's maxims of thrift and hard work. The wrecks that the Bowery Mission tries to reach began by making themselves socially pleasant and gracious for business or even for religious purposes. The social glass with its charm was their first step in a very deep descent.

Bondage in Jesus' mind calls not for blame, but for pity. There is perhaps no address of His on record where He condemns these slaves. "Judge not, He said, "that ye be not judged." His patience and pity for the men and women in bondage had no limits. But sometimes the process of deterioration goes farther. Men can become children of the Devil. Apparently it is the thirst for domination, especially religious domination, that leads to this. In Jesus time as also in our own, slaves have at times been adopted by their masters. They are his children then. Perhaps the most terrifying element in this situation is the fact that it was the orthodox religious leaders who had been so adopted and were children of the Devil.

I know that ye are Abraham's seed; but ye seek to kill me, because my word hath no place in you. I speak that which I have seen with my Father: and ye do that which ye have seen with your father. They answered and said unto him, Abraham is our father. Jesus saith unto them, If ye were Abraham's children, ye would do the works of Abraham. But now ye seek to kill me, a man that hath told you the truth, which I have heard of God: this did not Abraham.

The surprisingly hostile rejoinder on the part of Jesus' hearers to His statement about freedom, did not keep Him from finishing that discussion. They were slaves right then, slaves to sin in spite of their descent from Abraham. Jesus had lost touch by this time with the group who believed on Him so He took up the discussion with His usual skill along the lines His critics suggested. They were Abraham's children, they asserted and from that they deduced very naturally that they were Gods children. In the first place they were descended from Abraham and in the second place because they were following Abrahams sacred law.

Jesus' reply to this is terrible: "Ye are of your father the Devil." The Pharisees were entirely sincere in their belief that they were serving God in their opposition to Jesus. By carrying this service further, they were soon to crucify Him. To us this seems simply impossible, but Jesus was not at all surprised by it. They had so terribly changed and corrupted and debased their conception of God, that now their service to God was really service to the Devil. Every ounce of zeal in "God's service pulled them down deeper into the bottomless pit.

Ye do the deeds of your father. Then said they to him, We be not born of fornication; we have one Father, even God. Jesus said unto them, If God were your Father, ye would love me: for I proceeded forth and came from God; neither came I of myself, but he sent me. Why do ye not understand my speech? even because ye cannot hear my word. Ye are of your father the devil, and the lusts of your father ye will do: he was a murderer from the beginning, and abode not in the truth, because there is no truth in him. When he speaketh a lie, he speaketh of his own: for he is a liar, and the father of it.

"The lusts of your father it is your will to do." The word reaches out in several directions. What had happened? The presentation of God in the Old Testament is not the same as that given us by Jesus, but it is not a picture of the Devil. These men had fashioned their God gradually but none the less certainly after the pattern of their own sins. It was a vicious circle. Their debased conception of God justified and encouraged them in their sins, and this deeper descent into sin in turn resulted in a further debasement of their picture of God. Finally, when this account was written, they thought that they were serving God when they crucified Jesus.

Jesus' analysis of their deteriorated character, and thereby of the character of the Devil is worth noting. Lies and murder were his characteristics. Murder is the direct result of intolerance. It is a characteristic of legalistic religion everywhere. Lies are more difficult to understand. In a general way we might suppose that the Devil tells lies only when it serves his purpose better than telling the truth. But the suggestion here is that he actually prefers lies to the truth. Their conviction that Jesus was an evil menace who should be murdered, was built on nothing else.

The fiery debate went on to unusual intensity this time. Jesus'

listeners were His enemies now. Finally they took up stones
to kill Him right there on the spot.

And I seek not mine own glory: there is one that seeketh and judgeth.
Verily, verily, I say unto you, If a man keep my saying, he shall never
see death. Then said the Jews unto him, Now we know that thou hast a
devil. Abraham is dead, and the prophets; and thou sayest, If a man
keep my saying, he shall never taste of death. Art thou greater than
our father Abraham, which is dead? and the prophets are dead: whom
makest thou thyself?

Jesus brought forward one further point before the discussion
closed. He regarded it as a word of great importance. "Verily,
verily, I say unto you, if any man keep my word he shall never
see death." Jesus must have felt it absolutely necessary to bring
this point forward, and so make the presentation complete. So
far as the account indicates it added nothing to what His listeners
could understand or accept. Instead it so infuriated them that
they took up stones to kill Him. It is not easy to see any reasonable basis for this excessive reaction. There was no blasphemy
in it even from their point of view. A claim of superiority to
Abraham is hardly a capital crime.

It is a great and profound word, the final difference between
the world and the Kingdom. We have to take it on faith, for
physical death, the death that we can see, comes in precisely the
same way to all men whether they belong to the world or the
Kingdom. No doubt Jesus had a different definition of death in
His mind, but what definition? The death, perhaps, that is separated from God. That idea comes from Hebrews rather than
from this Gospel but Jesus apparently had something like this
in mind, for He had just been speaking of His Father and their
rejection of Him. That is just what death is rejection of our
Heavenly Father and the separation from Him which is its
result. These men were dead, spiritually dead, and it was the
most natural thing in the world to bring up at this point the final
and most profound difference between the world and the Kingdom.

This "verily, verily" of Jesus points to another lesson too, the inexpressible importance of Jesus' words. They came from God and had been given to men with the most scrupulous care. The very omnipotence of God is in those words, but what Jesus wanted them to understand here is the fact that His life was in these words. We must keep them.| If we keep them the life of God will flow into our souls in an uninterrupted stream, and we will never see death, never even taste it.

Jesus answered, If I honour myself, my honour is nothing: it is my Father that honoureth me; of whom ye say, that he is your God: Yet ye have not known him; but I know him: and if I should say, I know him not, I shall be a liar like unto you: but I know him, and keep his saying. Your father Abraham rejoiced to see my day: and he saw it, and was glad. Then said the Jews unto him, Thou art not yet fifty years old, and hast thou seen Abraham? Jesus said unto them, Verily, verily, I say unto you, Before Abraham was, I am. Then took they up stones to cast at him: but Jesus hid himself, and went out of the temple, going through the midst of them, and so passed by.

We do not have to understand them, and we do not have to explain them, still less defend them. But we do have to keep them. And if we keep those divine words that Jesus gives us. life is ours, divine life, eternal life, God's own life, and nothing puzzling and perplexing demands from all manner of sources, here is what we are to live by the Words of Jesus.

As Jesus finishes the debate, He asks that His words be kept. He gives different words to different people. The simplest He puts first: "He that followeth me." That is simple imitation. There are many people who seem unable to enter by any other door. "Except ye believe that I am He" is another door.| To us it might not seem adequate but the word is from Jesus Himself. "If ye abide in my word" is perhaps the most complete word of all, and leads the most complete experience. "The truth shall make you free." But they are all doors, doors to the Kingdom, doors to the circle around Jesus. And this final word, the command to "keep" the words of Jesus, is probably the simplest and the deepest of them all.

JOHN 9

And as Jesus passed by, he saw a man which was blind from his birth. And his disciples asked him, saying, Master, who did sin, this man, or his parents, that he was born blind? Jesus answered, Neither hath this man sinned, nor his parents: but that the works of God should be made manifest in him. I must work the works of him that sent me, while it is day: the night cometh, when no man can work. As long as I am in the world, I am the light of the world. When he had thus spoken, he spat on the ground, and made clay of the spittle, and he anointed the eyes of the blind man with the clay, And said unto him, Go, wash in the pool of Siloam, (which is by interpretation, Sent.) He went his way therefore, and washed, and came seeing.

The neighbours therefore, and they which before had seen him that he was blind, said, Is not this he that sat and begged? Some said, This is he: others said, He is like him: but he said, I am he. Therefore said they unto him, How were thine eyes opened? He answered and said, A man that is called Jesus made clay, and anointed mine eyes, and said unto me, Go to the pool of Siloam, and wash: and I went and washed, and I received sight. Then said they unto him, Where is he? He said, I know not.

They brought to the Pharisee him that aforetime was blind. And it was the sabbath day when Jesus made the clay, and opened his eyes. Then again the Pharisees also asked him how he had received his sight. He said unto them, He put clay upon mine eyes, and I washed, and do see. Therefore said some of the Pharisees, This man is not of God, because he keepeth not the sabbath day. Others said, How can a man that is a sinner do such miracles? And there was a division among them. They say unto the blind man again, What sayest thou of him, that he hath opened thine eyes? He said, He is a prophet. But the Jews did not believe concerning him, that he had been blind, and received his sight, until they called the parents of him that had received his sight. And they asked them, saying, Is this your son, who ye say was born blind? how then doth he now see? His parents answered them and said, We know that this is our son, and that he was born blind: But by what means he now seeth, we know not; or who hath opened his eyes, we know not: he is of age; ask him: he shall speak for himself. These words spake his parents, because they feared the Jews: for the Jews had agreed already, that if any man did confess that he was Christ, he should be put out of the synagogue. Therefore said his parents, He is of age; ask him. Then again called they the man that was blind, and said unto him, Give God the praise: we know that this man is a sinner. He answered and said, Whether he be a sinner or no, I know not: one thing I know, that, whereas I was blind, now I see. Then said they to him again, What did he to thee? how opened he thine eyes? He answered them, I have told you already, and ye did not hear: wherefore would ye hear it again? will ye also be his disciples? Then they reviled him, and said, Thou art his disciple; but we are Moses' disciples. We know that God spake unto Moses: as for this fellow, we know not from whence he is. The man answered and said unto them, Why herein is a marvellous thing, that ye know not from whence he is, and yet he hath opened mine eyes. Now we know that God heareth not sinners: but if any man be a worshipper of God, and doeth his will, him he heareth. Since the world began was it not heard that any man opened the eyes of one that was born blind. If this man were not of God, he could do nothing. They answered and said unto him, Thou wast altogether born in sins, and dost thou teach us? And they cast him out. Jesus heard that they had cast him out; and when he had found him, he said unto him, Dost thou believe on the Son of God? He answered and said, Who is he, Lord, that I might believe on him? And

Jesus said unto him, Thou hast both seen him, and it is he that talketh with thee. And he said, Lord, I believe. And he worshipped him.

And Jesus said, For judgment I am come into this world, that they which see not might see; and that they which see might be made blind. And some of the Pharisees which were with him heard these words, and said unto him, Are we blind also? Jesus said unto them, If ye were blind, ye should have no sin: but now ye say, We see; therefore your sin remaineth.

Chapter IX

THE PICTURE

And as Jesus passed by, he saw a man which was blind from his birth. And his disciples asked him, saying, Master, who did sin, this man, or his parents, that he was born blind? Jesus answered, Neither hath this man sinned, nor his parents: but that the works of God should be made manifest in him. I must work the works of him that sent me, while it is day: the night cometh, when no man can work. As long as I am in the world, I am the light of the world.

We see three figures in this picture. First of all, Jesus and second, the man born blind, and third, the Pharisees. In a minor role we see the man's parents. We will try to get a clear picture of the background and surroundings before we study the picture of Jesus Himself.

Years before, a baby had been born blind, and now, as a man, he sat by the road, begging. Jesus with some of His disciples, passed by. The man undoubtedly called attention to himself by asking for a contribution. The disciples most likely gave him a small coin, and their minds passed easily from his pitiful condition to the very natural question why God had visited such affliction on him. They followed the teaching of the times. It is the easy answer. Such affliction is a punishment for sin. This man was punished before he was born, so it must be his parents who had sinned.

Apparently Jesus had not intended to heal this man. He had not been asked. Jesus did not try to relieve all the suffering of the community as if He were a divine health department. Just what suffering did He relieve? Whom did He heal? Usually but not always men who asked for it with faith in His power to perform the miracle.

When he had thus spoken, he spat on the ground, and made clay of the spittle, and he anointed the eyes of the blind man with the clay, And said unto him, Go, wash in the pool of Siloam, (which is by interpretation, Sent.)   He went his way therefore, and washed, and came seeing.

The neighbours therefore, and they which before had seen him that he was blind, said, Is not this he that sat and begged?   Some said, This is he: others said, He is like him: but he said, I am he.   Therefore said they unto him, How were thine eyes opened?   He answered and said, A man that is called Jesus made clay, and anointed mine eyes, and said unto me, Go to the pool of Siloam, and wash: and I went and washed, and I received sight.   Then said they unto him, Where is he?   He said, I know not.

The question of the disciples' broke Jesus' attention away from whatever was preoccupying Him, and brought vividly before Him this man's pathetic need. It brought forward just as vividly the disciple's need for some improvement in their religious thinking. "Master, who sinned, this man or his parents?" showed that the disciples were perhaps in as deep a need as the blind man himself.

Jesus gave them a very profound, and somewhat brusque reply. "Neither did this man sin nor his parents but that the works of God might be manifested in him," and saying this He proceeded to demonstrate such a work of God right on the spot. That took care of the man's need, and the disciple's too, with promptness and adequacy.

But Jesus with His alert perception saw in this situation an opportunity to do something further. Probably He had been waiting for such an opening. Jesus had a certain number of important teachings to present to the world. His skill in presenting them was very great indeed. "I am the bread of life," "I am the good shepherd," are examples. He also had a certain number of destructive iconoclastic tasks to perform. He suddenly realized that here was the opportunity He had been waiting for.

So He spat on the ground and made some mud with the spittle, and putting a little of this mud on the man's eyes, sent him off to wash in a nearby pool. The man returned with his sight completely restored.

They brought to the Pharisees him that aforetime was blind. And it was the sabbath day when Jesus made the clay, and opened his eyes. Then again the Pharisees also asked him how he had received his sight. He said unto them, He put clay upon mine eyes, and I washed, and do see. Therefore said some of the Pharisees, This man is not of God, because he keepeth not the sabbath day. Others said, How can a man that is a sinner do such miracles? And there was a division among them.

We are tempted to pause here and ask several questions. This use of mud is not a good example of cleanliness, to say the least, and what is worse, that filthy mud lacked all therapeutic significance, and its use in this way seems hardly honest. Saliva is collected at the doors of the mosques in Arabia to this day, for use in treating the sick. However, even the Arabs look on this as a bit of superstition.

But evidently Jesus gave all this not a thought, nor does the writer of the Gospel. Bystanders were not at all distressed, indeed they were not even surprised. Jesus had His mind on something else, and the outcome shows what it was. The mud offered him an easy and effective means of breaking the Sabbath. As matters worked out it was also an effective way to repudiate the pretensions to spiritual authority on the part of the Pharisees.

The essence of the opportunity which Jesus saw here was that He could put back of His destructive iconoclasm the tremendous authority of a spectacular, public miracle. A man born blind had been healed. He could see perfectly now. People had known him for years, and his blindness was a matter of common knowledge. Here was an unheard of achievement whose genuineness could not be questioned.

The Sabbath had been broken that is the impossible Sabbath of the Pharisees. It was a definite challenge to them, and they were quick to recognize it. The controversy was bitter right from the beginning. "It was the Sabbath day when Jesus made the clay and opened his eyes." It was the clay that made the trouble. Simple healing on the Sabbath was frowned on by the Pharisees, as can be seen in several accounts in the other Gospels, but healing the man with the withered hand did not stir up a riot, in

They say unto the blind man again, What sayest thou of him, that he hath opened thine eyes? He said, He is a prophet. But the Jews did not believe concerning him, that he had been blind, and receiveth his sight, until they called the parents of him that had received his sight. And they asked them, saying, Is this your son, who ye say was born blind? how then doth he now see? His parents answered them and said, We know that this is our son, and that he was born blind: But by what means he now seeth, we know not; or who hath opened his eyes, we know not: he is of age; ask him: he shall speak for himself.

---

fact, nothing worse than criticism, for the Sabbath had not been broken.

In the account here, no one, or at least no Pharisee takes any notice of the fact that a very beautiful act of mercy had been done, and that the unbelievable blessing of sight had come to a man who had been blind all his life. All they noticed was that a great miracle had been performed, but that the Sabbath had been broken.

This chapter is a study in sin, the sin of the Pharisees. Their fundamental sin was the love of domination. Their control of the people was so dreadful that the first reaction of this man's friends was not to run and bring others who needed similar help. They did not even rejoice with him over his unheard of blessing. They took him to the Pharisees so that competent spiritual monitors could pass judgment on this subversive act of getting healed on the Sabbath. The Pharisees did not know that this complete domination was a sin. They were sure that the people needed it. "This multitude that knoweth not the law is accursed," they said in another place, and here their remark is self-revealing enough. "Thou wast altogether born in sins and dost thou teach us?"

Their self-confidence and pride were simply unlimited, but with it their spiritual blindness was very great. They did not even see the beauty of Jesus' life and teaching. In that life they saw nothing that called for admiration. His miracles were tremendous, but His breaking of the Sabbath dreadful. That He

These words spake his parents, because they feared the Jews: for the
Jews had agreed already, that if any man did confess that he was Christ,
he should be put out of the synagogue.   Therefore said his parents, He
is of age; ask him.   Then again called they the man that was blind, and
said unto him, Give God the praise: we know that this man is a sinner.
He answered and said, Whether he be a sinner or no, I know not: one
thing I know, that, whereas I was blind, now I see.

---

brought men closer to God they would not have understood if it
had been told to them.

So far as the man is concerned, this is a study in courage. He
showed real faith in the first place. Accosted and treated by
Jesus without previous notice and with a bit of mud on each lid,
he had faith enough in this heavenly voice and the gentleness
and authority of Jesus' manner to go to the pool of Siloam and
wash. He knew that it was the Sabbath, and that handling this
mud had put both Jesus and himself outside the law, but beggars
are an independent lot. At least this one was.

The thing that saved this man was his loyalty and gratitude.
We probably do not realize how important these virtues are. His
sight had returned, an incredible blessing, and this he recognized as pure heavenly good. All the religious authority of the
Pharisees could not shake that loyalty and make him think it had.

It takes great courage to do this. All the religious ideas and
all the worship of God this man knew had come from the Phar-
sees. Our vague convictions are hard to keep when ostracism lies
at the end of the road. He did not have any book to quote against
the Pharisees, and no human friend stood by his side. Even his
parents deserted him as soon as a collision with the Pharisees
developed. But he had his eyes to quote against them, and that
was enough.

There was an extraordinary honesty about this man, too. He
defended nothing and asserted nothing except what he had seen
and experienced. The man's impudence saved him, and sent
him to Jesus. That statement is not quite correct. His impudent
and reckless loyalty stirred up the Pharisees so they put him
out. Jesus found him and saved him. The main purpose of this

Then said they to him again, What did he to thee? how opened he thine eyes? He answered them, I have told you already, and ye did not hear: wherefore would ye hear it again? will ye also be his disciples? Then they reviled him, and said, Thou art his disciple; but we are Moses' disciples. We know that God spake unto Moses: as for this fellow, we know not from whence he is. The man answered and said unto them, Why herein is a marvellous thing, that ye know not from whence he is, and yet he hath opened mine eyes. Now we know that God heareth not sinners: but if any man be a worshipper of God, and doeth his will, him he heareth. Since the world began was it not heard that any man opened the eyes of one that was born blind. If this man were not of God, he could do nothing.

---

whole story is to show that we have to break away from the world, if we want to enter the Kingdom of God. Courage is needed for that.

But as far as Jesus is concerned, this is a lesson in iconoclasm. Jesus broke down three idols in this chapter. The first one was a mental idol, or rather, theological one. The closed legalistic system explained all human misfortune as punishment for sin. The Pharisees' sabbath was the second idol to go down, and the domination of the common people by the Pharisees was the third.

Jesus' reply to the disciples when they asked Him, "Who sinned, this man or his parents?" was abrupt and brusque. The question stirred Him unusually. It may not look important to us, but Jesus considered it very important. Jesus gave a great deal of attention to teaching the disciples. Apparently that was very definitely in His mind as He turned aside to heal this blind man.

But with the lesson to the disciples went an effort to do His utmost for the man himself. The man had not asked for healing and he had shown no faith. One wonders what his thoughts were as he, with the mud on his eyes, went to the pool to wash. Why Jesus put the mud there has been a debated question for many earnest disciples, ever since. Jesus did many things that we find difficult to understand. He never defends or even explains Him-

They answered and said unto him, Thou wast altogether born in sins, and dost thou teach us? And they cast him out. Jesus heard that they had cast him out; and when he had found him, he said unto them, Dost thou believe on the Son of God? He answered and said, Who is he, Lord, that I might believe on him? And Jesus said unto him, Thou hast both seen him, and it is he that talketh with thee. And he said, Lord, I believe. And he worshipped him.

And Jesus said, For judgment I am come into this world, that they which see not might see; and that they which see might be made blind. And some of the Pharisees which were with him heard these words, and said unto him, Are we blind also? Jesus said unto them, If we were blind, ye should have no sin: but now ye say, We see; therefore your sin remaineth.

---

self. But here Jesus' purpose is not difficult to make out. He could have healed the man just as well without the mud. It would have been more convenient. But that mud broke the law. It was needed, for Jesus' purpose that morning was to break the Pharisees' Sabbath.

By this gratuitous addition to the healing, Jesus broke a purely human command. The Sabbath played an astonishingly large part in the religion of the Pharisees, and of the people under them. It had become an idol.

But there was another reason and perhaps a deeper one. Jesus wanted to save this man, and the only way he could be saved was to break away from the Pharisees. Jesus killed two birds with one stone here. He repudiated the whole notion of the Pharisees' Sabbath, and He created a situation in which the Pharisees would ostracize and expel this man, so Jesus could look him up and save him.

The most dreadful idol that Jesus threw down that day was the whole authority and position of the Pharisees. This miracle was perhaps one of the most radical of all Jesus' deeds. The man who had been healed on the Sabbath and had joined in Sabbath breaking to do it, came at once into a sharp collision with the Pharisees. He refused to accept their authority when they pitted themselves against the light in his own soul and he defied their ostracism. Jesus looked him up and enrolled him as a follower. He endorsed by implication all that the man had done. The issue is a very deep and important one. Are we to follow the vision of truth, and goodness, and beauty that we have in our own hearts, or are we to bow to religious authority? It was not simply on this particular issue, that is on the character of Jesus, that the Pharisees were wrong. It is wrong to dominate or to attempt to dominate any of our fellow men in matters of worship. We must learn to follow with all loyalty and courage the vision of truth and of God that we have in our own hearts, and this against any opposition whatever.

Jesus' Teaching

And as Jesus passed by, he saw a man which was blind from his birth. And his disciples asked him, saying, Master, who did sin, this man, or his parents, that he was born blind? Jesus answered, Neither hath this man sinned, nor his parents: but that the works of God should be made manifest in him. I must work the works of him that sent me, while it is day: the night cometh, when no man can work.

Chapter 9 seems to have been put in here because of the picture which it affords, first of all of Jesus, but also of the Pharisees, and their domination over the hearts of the common people. But there is very important teaching in it too.

First, the overall teaching that to enter the Kingdom of God we must break away from the world which is a kingdom of evil. Men are not like loose stones simply waiting for some spiritual stone mason to build them into the Kingdom of God. They are set in a wall of concrete, to be blown loose with dynamite. That however, is an imperfect and objectionable figure, for they have to break themselves loose, and there is much difference in the difficulty which they experience in accomplishing this. In this instance the difficulty was very great and the figure of dynamite is not out of place.

But it is worth nothing that simple loyalty is the only weapon which this man used to break himself away from the world.

Evidently it is not possible to serve two masters, the world and God as we see Him in Christ. There are many questions that arise, for the Pharisee's too, were teaching men to serve God, just as Jesus was. They lived for nothing else. Here as in so many other places, everything depends on our conception of God. Jesus defined God for us by His human life. Other pictures of God we have to reject. Our salvation depends on it.

As long as I am in the world, I am the light of the world. When he had thus spoken, he spat on the ground, and made clay of the spittle, and he anointed the eyes of the blind man with the clay, And said unto him, Go, wash in the pool of Siloam, (which is by interpretation, Sent.) He went his way therefore, and washed, and came seeing.

But in the course of giving us this picture, Jesus presented some important lessons, with extraordinary brevity and depth. First a contribution to our understanding of suffering. A man had been born blind. "Who sinned, this man or his parents," that God should punish him so? This assumption has been the easiest answer from the beginning to this day. Suffering is a punishment for sin. In this case, inasmuch as the man punished before he was born, it must have been his parents who were at fault.

Jesus responds to this idea with a brusque, absolute answer that rather takes our breath away. "Neither did this man sin nor his parents." That is the negative part of it. There is an absoluteness here that is beautiful. Punishment for sin literally has nothing to do with suffering, at least the type of suffering which results from the operation of natural causes. No doubt, if a man steals and is tied up and flogged as a punishment, there is some relation between his sin and his suffering, but then it is not God who is punishing him.

The postive part is more important. There is much suffering that comes from the simple operation of natural causes. We have a sure hope that much of this will be eliminated eventually, but such a hope does not help us now. God has permitted it.

Jesus heard that they had cast him out; and when he had found him, he said unto him, Dost thou believe on the Son of God? He answered and said, Who is he, Lord, that I might believe on him? And Jesus said unto him, Thou hast both seen him, and it is he that talketh with thee. And he said, Lord, I believe. And he worshipped him.

And Jesus said, For judgment I am come into this world, that they which see not might see; and that they which see might be made blind. And some of the Pharisees which were with him heard these words, and said unto him, Are we blind also? Jesus said unto them, If ye were blind, ye should have no sin: but now ye say, We see; therefore your sin remaineth.

One has the uncomfortable feeling that Jesus would not have cared for the argument that an omnipotent Heavenly Father might have been expected to devise a universe without suffering and pain, or at least a better one than this.

God has a purpose in the unmerited suffering which arises from the operation of natural causes. He has permitted it so that He can manifest His works in such men. God's Spirit then can do things in such men that are impossible without these experiences. Such a man has an opportunity to demonstrate in a special way the power and the love and the salvation of God. Jesus does not say anything about the part that the man himself must play in this. From our experience we may suppose that this co-operation from the human side is very important indeed, for some of these victims of circumstance are warped and twisted and rendered terribly unfit for God's Kingdom.

The question of rectification on the other side of the grave arises here too. There surely must be a large place in God's plan for this if Jesus' conception of Our Heavenly Father is to stand at all.

Jesus added a word on one other subject which evidently had a prominent place in His mind. "While I am in the world, I am the light of the world." He was the light to that man's eyes that morning, and hinted that His stay might be short. But He is in the world forever in another sense, and He will be its light always.

He was light that morning, too, to the disciples as He guided their minds from darkness and ignorance to light and wisdom, and a better understanding of God. And He was light to the man himself eventually, in a most absolute sense.

JOHN 10

Verily, verily, I say unto you, He that entereth not by the door into the sheepfold, but climbeth up some other way, the same is a thief and a robber. But he that entereth in by the door is the shepherd of the sheep. To him the porter openeth; and the sheep hear his voice: and he calleth his own sheep by name, and leadeth them out. And when he putteth forth his own sheep, he goeth before them, and the sheep follow him: for they know his voice. And a stranger will they not follow, but will flee from him; for they know not the voice of strangers. This parable spake Jesus unto them; but they understood not what things they were which he spake unto them. Then said Jesus unto them again, Verily, verily, I say unto you, I am the door of the sheep. All that ever came before me are thieves and robbers: but the sheep did not hear them. I am the door: by me if any man enter in, he shall be saved, and shall go in and out, and find pasture. The thief cometh not, but for to steal, and to kill, and to destroy: I am come that they might have life, and that they might have it more abundantly. I am the good shepherd: the good shepherd giveth his life for the sheep. But he that is a hireling, and not the shepherd, whose own the sheep are not, seeth the wolf coming, and leaveth the sheep, and fleeth: and the wolf catcheth them, and scattereth the sheep. The hireling fleeth, because he is a hireling, and careth not for the sheep. I am the good shepherd, and know my sheep, and am known of mine. As the Father knoweth me, even so know I the Father: and I lay down my life for the sheep. And other sheep I have, which are not of this fold: them also I must bring, and they shall hear my voice; and there shall be one fold, and one shepherd. Therefore doth my Father love me, because I lay down my life, that I might take it again. No man taketh it from me, but I lay it down of myself. I have power to lay it down, and I have power to take it again. This commandment have I received of my Father.

There was a division therefore again among the Jews for these sayings. And many of them said, He hath a devil, and is mad; why hear ye him? Others said, These are not the words of him that hath a devil. Can a devil open the eyes of the blind?

And it was at Jerusalem the feast of the dedication, and it was winter. And Jesus walked in the temple in Solomon's porch. Then came the Jews round about him, and said unto him, How long dost thou make us to doubt? If thou be the Christ, tell us plainly. Jesus answered them, I told you, and ye believed not: the works that I do in my Father's name, they bear witness of me. But ye believe not, because ye are not of my sheep, as I said unto you. My sheep hear my voice, and I know them, and they follow me: And I give unto them eternal life; and they shall never perish, neither shall any man pluck them out of my hand. My Father, which gave me them, is greater than all; and no man is able to pluck them out of my Father's hand. I and my Father are one. Then the Jews took up stones again to stone him. Jesus answered them, Many good works have I shewed you from my Father; for which of those works do ye stone me? The Jews answered him, saying, For a good work we stone thee not; but for blasphemy; and because that thou, being a man, makest thyself God. Jesus answered them, Is it not written in your law, I said, Ye are gods? If he called them gods, unto whom the word of God came, and the Scripture cannot be broken; Say ye of him, whom the Father hath sanctified, and sent into the world, Thou blasphemest; because I said, I am the Son of God? If I do not the works of my Father, believe me not. But if I do, though ye believe not me, believe the works; that ye may know, and believe, that the Father is in me, and I in him. Therefore they sought again to take him; but he escaped out of their hand, And went away again beyond Jordan into the place where John at first baptized; and there he abode. And many resorted unto him, and said, John did no miracle: but all things that John spake of this man were true. And many believed on him there.

Chapter X

THE PICTURE

Verily, verily, I say unto you, He that entereth not by the door into the sheepfold, but climbeth up some other way, the same is a thief and a robber. But he that entereth in by the door is the shepherd of the sheep. To him the porter openeth; and the sheep hear his voice: and he calleth his own sheep by name, and leadeth them out. And when he putteth forth his own sheep, he goeth before them, and the sheep follow him: for they know his voice. And a stranger will they not follow, but will flee from him; for they know not the voice of strangers.

In this chapter Jesus is facing a crowd dominated by very hostile Pharisees. As far as numbers are concerned it was made up of hundreds of common people. They were indifferent to spiritual things and far away from God. This seems to be a continuation of chapter 9, and if that is so, the miracle of restoring sight to a man born blind, was fresh in their minds.

Jesus had used that miracle with great skill to break down three very evil things. First the idea that physical suffering and deformity are punishments for sin. "Neither did this man sin nor his parents." Second, the slavish, observance of the Sabbath, which was the keystone of the whole structure of Pharisaism; third the autocratic and pitiless domination by the Pharisees of the worship of the common people. All these things were repudiated, and publicly discredited. Jesus succeeded in putting behind His iconoclastic teaching the force of a very great and absolutely indisputable miracle. The hostile attitude of the Pharisees under such circumstances does not surprise us at all.

But Jesus has finished, for the moment, His destructive task. Now He has constructive work to do. He turns away from the fiercely controversial subjects of only a few hours before. It may have been even less than that. We would not be able to

This parable spake Jesus unto them; but they understood not what things they were which he spake unto them. Then said Jesus unto them again, Verily, verily, I say unto you, I am the door of the sheep. All that ever came before me are thieves and robbers: but the sheep did not hear them. I am the door: by me if any man enter in, he shall be saved, and shall go in and out, and find pasture. The thief cometh not, but for to steal, and to kill, and to destroy: I am come that they might have life, and that they might have it more abundantly.

---

get our minds away so quickly from a struggle with evil. Jesus could. There is no trace of conflict in His beautiful parable.

Even we with our imperfect vision can realize that Jesus faced a difficult task that afternoon. His audience was composed of two extremely dissimilar elements, the highly trained and educated Pharisees, and the indifferent, careless common people. However, they had much in common. Jesus may not have looked on them as dissimilar at all. Both leaders and those led were all bound by the same chains. The same legalistic conception of God filled their minds. The same iron religious system dictated their worship.

Probably the disciples waited with a good deal of apprehension to see how Jesus was going to put his words into the listeners' minds. They had seen Him accomplish the impossible along these lines many times. We can imagine them whispering to each other, "What will He say to this impossible crowd?"

How much of what Jesus said and taught was planned by Him beforehand, we can not tell, but we know that He came to earth with a very definite understanding of the message that the Father wanted Him to present. His skill in putting these indispensable truths into unforgettable words was marvelous. "Ye must be born again," was an example, and, "I am the bread of life."

The dramatic and somewhat overwhelming developments described in chapter 9 may or may not have been anticipated by Jesus when He intentionally broke the Sabbath by using a bit of fresh mud in healing the blind man's eyes. But whether He

I am the good shepherd: the good shepherd giveth his life for the sheep. But he that is a hireling, and not the shepherd, whose own the sheep are not, seeth the wolf coming, and leaveth the sheep, and fleeth; and the wolf catcheth them, and scattereth the sheep. The hireling fleeth, because he is a hireling, and careth not for the sheep. I am the good shepherd, and know my sheep, and am known of mine. As the Father knoweth me, even so know I the Father: and I lay down my life for the sheep.

---

anticipated this result or not, it put into His hands an opportunity He had been waiting for. One of His most important messages had not as yet been given. It had to do with the extremely important matter of leadership in spiritual things.

Jesus came to redeem us from the guilt and the power and the punishment of sin. He came to redeem us from the law. But that idea comes from Paul. Jesus in this address presents a different facet of salvation. He came to redeem us from the curse of wrong human leadership. Until He came, such leadership had been unavoidable. A law must be administered by human leadership. Until He came, such leadership had been unavoidable. A law must be administered by human leaders. This inevitably deteriorates into a very evil thing, as Jesus was seeing every day. The most evil men whom He met were the Pharisees. They hated Him. And the people whom they led were victims of sin, perplexed and helpless wanderers.

Jesus realized, as He faced that mixed crowd, that now was the time to speak the emancipating word. It is perhaps the most marvelous of all the miraculous little seeds that Jesus planted in men's hearts: "I am the good shepherd."

This time it is more surprising than ever that He did not fall back on the Old Testament. What a wonderful introduction to what He had to say, could have been gotten from the Twenty-third Psalm: "The Lord is my shepherd." Jesus did not use that, and He did not use any other of the religious ideas or teachings of the Pharisees.

And other sheep I have, which are not of this fold: them also I must
bring, and they shall hear my voice; and there shall be one fold, and
one shepherd. Therefore doth my Father love me, because I lay down
my life, that I might take it again. No man taketh it from me, but I
lay it down of myself. I have power to lay it down, and I have power
to take it again. This commandment have I received of my Father.

There was a division therefore again among the Jews for these sayings. And many of them said, He hath a devil, and is mad; why hear
ye him? Others said, These are not the words of him that hath a
devil. Can a devil open the eyes of the blind?
And it was at Jerusalem the feast of the dedication, and it was winter.
And Jesus walked in the temple in Solomon's porch. Then came the
Jews round about him, and said unto him, How long dost thou make us
to doubt? If thou be the Christ, tell us plainly. Jesus answered them,
I told you, and ye believed not: the works that I do in my Father's name,
they bear witness of me.

He chose a new pattern. He had never before compared Himself with any type of man. His comparisons had been of a different sort. "I am the true vine." "I am the bread of life." "I
am the way." It is interesting to observe this new pattern. In it
is no element of human training or education. He could have
said, "I am the good teacher." There was no human religious
element either. He could have said, I am the good priest." Fifty
years later, the writer of the Epistle to the Hebrews did say
just that.

But for this picture of the mercy and love and beauty of
God, Jesus resorted to the realm of pure, untwisted, unpolished
human nature. "I am the good shepherd." The word was presented simply. There was no effort to argue or prove or even
explain.

It is not surprising that this figure came easily to Jesus' mind.
As a boy He had probably led out the sheep and the goats of
the village to graze on the hills around, and, staying with them
all day, brought them home at night. A lamb might be born out
on those hills and he would carry the tiny baby home in his
arms, with the mother following trustfully behind.

Jesus probably sat on the hillside many times with His dis-

But ye believe not, because ye are not of my sheep, as I said unto you. My sheep hear my voice, and I know them, and they follow me: And I give unto them eternal life; and they shall never perish, neither shall any man pluck them out of my hand. My Father, which gave them me, is greater than all; and no man is able to pluck them out of my Father's hand. I and my Father are one. Then the Jews took up stones again to stone him.

---

ciples watching the flocks led by their shepherds over the hills, from one pasture to another, and home at night to protection and peace in their owner's house. He must have realized many times that He was a shepherd too. No doubt He told the disciples just that. There are good shepherds and there are bad ones. There are thieves and robbers too, who come at night to steal a sheep and to kill it, if it makes any noise. Jesus loved that picture of the good shepherd with a weak little lamb in his arms.

On this simple pattern Jesus painted what by common consent is our most perfect picture of God and His love and salvation. The nature of faith and discipleship is there. The nature of eternal life, and the beauty of God's will are there. As we read it there is not one lesson or one emphasis that we would like to add or to take away; not one thing that we would want to change. That afternoon Jesus faced the great Pharisaic system with its domination and slavery, with all the incredible power of its evil conception of God, and its great iron chains binding the souls of men. It stood there like a huge impregnable Roman fortress. Jesus pitted against it a shepherd with a happy little lamb in his arms.

This picture penetrated their indifference and overcame their hostility. It divided the crowd into two fractions, the one following on to hear and believe more, their hostility gone, and their souls open; and the other more hostile than ever, now planning definitely to murder this dangerous teacher just as soon as they could possibly compass it.

Jesus answered them, Many good works have I shewed you from my Father; for which of those works do ye stone me? The Jews answered him, saying, For a good work we stone thee not; but for blasphemy; and because that thou, being a man, makest thyself God.   Jesus answered them, Is it not written in your law, I said, Ye are gods?   If he called them gods, unto whom the word of God came, and the Scripture cannot be broken; Say ye of him, whom the Father hath sanctified, and sent into the world, Thou blasphemest; because I said, I am the Son of God?

Jesus made His lesson complete, even though by so doing He made it more difficult for them to accept. "Other sheep have I which are not of this fold." To those intense nationalists, this was probably the most unacceptable thing that He said that day. It would seem to us that the parable was a heavy enough load of hostility without adding this to it, but the message that God had given Him to deliver would not have been complete without this final paragraph.

The discussion which followed brought a new question: "If thou be the Christ, tell us plainly."   From the Pharisees' point of view, nothing could be more reasonable than this request. At first we are surprised that Jesus did not welcome the opportunity to clarify His position. But the situation was not as simple as that. The questioners had such a defective and wrong conception of the Messiah that it would have been farther from the truth for Jesus to say, Yes, than to say No. They wanted a military leader who would conquer the earth, and set up a kingdom like the Romans. Jesus did not want these nationalistic and warlike patriots to look at Him as the Messiah. He, pacifistic sufferer that He was, could not possibly have fitted into their Messianic pattern. They would have reckoned that as a sort of blasphemy, for blasphemy in their minds included reviling and insults to the king as well as the reviling of God.

Blasphemy at that moment was regarded as a capital crime. Just why might have been difficult for those patriots to say, except that it came down from the past in the Old Testament. It is one of the world's most dangerous delusions, this assurance

If I do not the works of my Father, believe me not. But if I do, though ye believe not me, believe the works; that ye may know, and believe, that the Father is in me, and I in him. Therefore they sought again to take him; but he escaped out of their hand, And went away again beyond Jordan into the place where John at first baptized; and there he abode. And many resorted unto him, and said, John did no miracle: but all things that John spake of this man were true. And many believed on him there.

---

that we have been made legal and official custodians of the dignity and honour of God.

Jesus' defense is a very great surprise. He found a verse in the Eighty-second Psalm which they must have been acquainted with. It rather takes our breath away even now. One wonders just what content Jesus wanted them to put into His phrase, "the Son of God."

But we must not miss the fact that Jesus accepted these questioners as sincere inquirers. They received from Him a very sincere reply. Whether or not He was the Christ they could learn by observing His works, and this is a more profound and complete reply than appears on the surface. Men whose ideas of the Messiah were even approximately right, would find in those works all the proof they could ask or want. Those who were looking for the wrong sort of Messiah would find in them nothing at all.

Only faith based on Jesus' works can possibly be valid faith. It was only by observing His works, and His words were part of them, that the disciples could see the real Jesus. That was true of the Pharisees, and it is true of us. There are two elements in this faith. In the first place |Jesus' works must delight us. We approve of them and admire them, and plan to imitate them. We must see that they are good. But that is only the first part of belief, at least it is only the first part of belief in Jesus. Jesus' works are not only good as opposed to bad. They are a part of God's goodness and wisdom as opposed to man's. They represent God, our Heavenly Father. Here we see again Jesus' own definition of saving faith. We must believe that He is in the Father, and the Father in Him.

JESUS' TEACHING

Verily, verily, I say unto you, He that entereth not by the door into the sheepfold, but climbeth up some other way, the same is a thief and a robber. But he that entereth in by the door is the shepherd of the sheep. To him the porter openeth; and the sheep hear his voice: and he calleth his own sheep by name, and leadeth them out. And when he putteth forth his own sheep, he goeth before them, and the sheep follow him: for they know his voice.

This chapter, together with chapter 9, can very easily be considered as one account. From the space it occupies, if from nothing else, we would know that John, regarded the subject discussed as very important. The topic under discussion is the same in both chapters.

Leadership in the things of the spirit is an extremely fundamental and important matter. Perhaps the only genuinely iconoclastic chapter in this Gospel is chapter 9 where Jesus repudiates conclusively the leadership of the Pharisees. He musters all the weight of a very remarkable miracle to reinforce His teaching.

But obviously such a lesson is incomplete. Here we have the positive, the immensely important part. Nothing could be more incredible than, the claims that Jesus makes for Himself here. The whole leadership of the Pharisees is brushed away. Jesus takes their place. He is to be our leader.

Jesus surprises us by presenting this very profound and difficult truth, not to earnestly sympathetic disciples, but to an extremely hostile crowd, dominated by the Pharisees. Looking at it from any ordinary viewpoint, such an effort was simply foolish, and impossible.

And a stranger will they not follow, but will flee from him; for they know not the voice of strangers. This parable spake Jesus unto them; but they understood not what things they were which he spake unto them.

But from the standpoint of presenting truth to difficult crowds, Jesus could do anything. The discussion begins with a parable which is beautiful in its transparent simplicity and realism. It is taken from the commonest happenings of the daily life of the people. "I am the good shepherd." From this simple story we gain perhaps our most vivid and useful picture of the fundamental nature of the new order.

We gain first of all a definition of discipleship. "The sheep hear his voice," and "they follow him." They want to follow. It is not a matter of compulsion. Furthermore it is not a picture of intellectual belief, but of personal loyalty. We become Christians then, when we choose the leadership and companionship of Christ. And how long is this leadership to last? "I go to prepare a place for you, that where I am there ye may be also.' (John 14:3-4). His leadership and companionship are to last through all eternity. The essence of the Christian's choice is that he has chosen Christ as his good shepherd for time and eternity.

For a little while we must walk by faith, which means that we walk in a foggy atmosphere, for we grasp very imperfectly Jesus' teachings, and example, and will. The fog will not last long, and after it we are to enter an eternity of unclouded companionship.

Sometimes we envy the men and women who lived in Jesus' time. Faith must have been simple for the disciples, no theological creeds, no developed rituals, personal loyalty only. We feel that for us now faith has become a staggering matter involving insoluble problems of both philosophy and history. In the light of this parable we see that our difficulties are of our own making. Faith is still simple, personal loyalty to Christ. None of these hard questions has essentially anything to do with it, and eventually they will all be forgotten.

Then said Jesus unto them again, Verily, verily, I say unto you, I am the door of the sheep. All that ever came before me are thieves and robbers: but the sheep did not hear them. I am the door: by me if any man enter in, he shall be saved, and shall go in and out, and find pasture. The thief cometh not, but for to steal, and to kill, and to destroy: I am come that they might have life, and that they might have it more abundantly.

In the second place we have here a picture of Jesus' leadership. The parable itself seems to picture Him as the good shepherd. His explanation shows that He thought of Himself also as the door. Two different parables may be amalgamated here into one. For people outside the fold, He is the door. For those within, He is the good shepherd.

But just what did Jesus have in mind when He said, "I am the good shepherd"? What is the picture He is trying to give us? The picture is beautifully clear to the Arab mind. In the morning the shepherd leads his sheep out from the fold where they have spent the night. All day long he leads them, finds them places where the grass is fresh and green and other places where they can drink sweet water. As the day wears on toward noon, and the sun gets hotter and hotter, he leads the sheep to some overhanging rock where they will be sheltered from the burning sun. Sometimes he leads them up a steep hill. That may be for exercise of it may be because better pasture lies in that direction. In the afternoon they will be led to further pastures, and at sundown he brings them home to the sheepfold. Throughout the entire day they have met no single experience that the shepherd did not choose for them. The food they ate and the water they drank, he selected. He chose their hill to climb, and their shelter from the hot sun at noon. It was he who brought them home tired at night, by an easy and pleasant path.

I am the good shepherd: the good shepherd giveth his life for the sheep. But he that is a hireling, and not the shepherd, whose own the sheep are not, seeth the wolf coming, and leaveth the sheep, and fleeth: and the wolf catcheth them, and scattereth the sheep. The hireling fleeth, because he is a hireling, and careth not for the sheep.

That is the picture. Jesus is our shepherd, and if we constitute a more difficult flock than the sheep of the parable, with more needs than the needs of those sheep, the difference is not nearly as great as the difference between our shepherd and theirs. Our shepherd, too, "calleth his own sheep by name and leadeth them out." He too, "goeth before them." Our day consists of one experience after another, one contact after another, one temptation, one humiliation, one success after another. Like the sheep in the parable, throughout the whole day we meet with not the smallest experience that He has not chosen for us, granted only that we follow, not perfectly, to be sure, but at least sincerely.

Most of our thorns we encounter when we fail to follow. Other leaders attract us for a little while, and tears and repentance bring us back. Sometimes the good shepherd leads us in thorny paths because He sees that we need the discipline, or perhaps some weaker Christian is to be helped by our suffering. But whether we meet such responsibility that we tremble before it, or such neglect of our abilities that our pride is dreadfully wounded, whether we find ease and comfort, or tears and blood, Christ is walking before us, and not one of these experiences comes except by His selection, a selection that has in view our growth into His likeness, and the good of the whole flock, the great Kingdom of God.

I am the good shepherd, and know my sheep, and am known of mine. As the Father knoweth me, even so know I the Father: and I lay down my life for the sheep. And other sheep I have, which are not of this fold: them also I must bring, and they shall hear my voice; and there shall be one fold, and one shepherd.

From this picture we learn something further as to how we are to follow. Christ leads us sometimes, into responsibilities, perplexities, and temptations. The way may seem confused and the path impossible. We still have no reason for strain and worry. The Good Shepherd led us into this situation, and the responsibility for the outcome is His. What does He want us to do? Perhaps to work out of the trying situation, perhaps to render service in it. Whatever the situation, only two things need concern us — that our reaction to this problem be what Christ wants it to be, and that we learn from it what He wants us to learn.

These are human experiences, concerned with our affairs and those of our fellow men. There are more important things. Our life of faith, our attitude toward God, is more important than our attitude toward men. Our conception of God, the picture of Him we carry in our hearts, is the most precious and important possession of all. Surely, if our Good Shepherd guides us any-where we can trust Him to guide us here. There are no problems of devotion, or worship, or of listening to God, that He has not faced. He solved them all. For many of us this is the most im-portant lesson of this great chapter. We are to let Him guide us into that faith, and that certainty, that love, and above all, that conception of God, that He wants us to have. Under His guidance our faith will grow, and our picture of God will be-come more and more beautiful, as He leads our spirits step by step from one splendid vision to another.

Therefore doth my Father love me, because I lay down my life, that I might take it again. No man taketh it from me, but I lay it down of myself. I have power to lay it down, and I have power to take it again This commandment have I received of my Father.

That is why our religious outlook, our faith, our understand-ing of God and His Word, is not the same this year as it was ten years ago, and it will be something still different ten years hence. Jesus knows that it will be so. He wants us to make prog-ress and change. Every growing thing changes. This is the reason for the differences between earnest followers of Christ in what they can see and hold with great conviction. Jesus has led them different distances, and along different paths. If our stock of clear and definite convictions seems less than that of some of our friends, that need not worry us. When Jesus wants us to hold their convictions and see their visions. He will guide us to those experiences. The fact that we do not see them now, simply indicates that it is not His present will that we should have these treasures. And if some of our friends seem to have less than we, our mind will be equally undisturbed. When Jesus wants them to see these visions with us, our Good Shepherd and theirs will lead them along that path, and show them that vision.

Finally we have here the contrast between this leadership and that of the world. This parable is known as the parable of the Good Shepherd, but it is not that only. It is a parable of the good shepherd contrasted with something else. The parable opens with this contrast, and both in the parable and in its explantation a large space is given to this "thief and robber." Just whom did Jesus mean when He spoke of the thief and the robber? His own statement seems clear. The thief does not enter by the door into the sheepfold, but climbs up some other way. There is only one door leading into the little enclosure, and the thief must climb over the wall. The thief is trying to take away the sheep so they will follow him and be his. The distinguishing mark of the thief is how he gets in.

Jesus was speaking of leadership in spiritual things. The Pharisees and the leadership they offered was being contrasted to Jesus. How had the Pharisees entered to lead the sheep, and how did Jesus come in?

The Pharisees had what looks like a very strong case. They had come in through the Old Testament, the law and the prophets. They had immersed themselves in that law since childhood, and their whole life's aim was to carry out its most minute command. They led the people, the sheep, along the same road. Surely, they had come in by the door into the fold of the sheep.

But Hebrews tells us, No. The new priesthood which Jesus brought is not after the law of a carnal commandment, but after the power of an endless life. The shepherd, Jesus, comes in to the fold through the new door.

The whole parable is a contrast between these two leader-ships, the shepherd on, the one hand, and the thief on the other. And the Pharisees were the most deeply sunk in sin and evil of any whom Jesus met in His entire life. Jesus adds a further word about the thief and the robber: "All that came before me are thieves and robbers." The word can indicate precedence in point of time, or of place, or of rank. The last is the meaning that Jesus seems to have had in mind here. All who place them-selves before Christ in spiritual leadership, are thieves and robbers. He goes on to say that the thief cometh not but to steal and kill and destroy.

Spiritual leadership, Jesus unhesitatingly divides into two classes, His own on the one hand, and on the other human leadership in the affairs of the spirit. It is Christ vs. human spiritual leaders.

It is not difficult to see this once our attention is called to it. The Wahabees of central Arabia, twenty years ago, slaughtered timid women with the babes in their arms, feeble old men and innocent children, because someone in the caravan smoked to-bacco. They did this not because they lacked affection for children, or regard for the aged. They are unusually endowed with both of these virtues. But their religious leaders taught them to do it, taught them that God's will demanded this atro-city. Religious zeal which is humanly guided is not something beneficial. It is perhaps the worst and most destructive evil in the world.

Christ's will for us takes on a new aspect in the light of this parable. The one thing we are to do is to follow Christ. The one thing we are to avoid is following any religious leader, however popular and good. Our friends, earnestly sincere men and women, can help us to see in Christ's teaching and ex-ample, things we have missed before. They have no further function. And in what they show us, the point of supreme im-portance is that we see these things with our own eyes. Creeds,

venerated because of their history, theological systems devised
by fallible men in our own day, dictatorial and emotional evangelists with their exhortations, are all interesting and instructive, but they possess no authority over our spirits. From them,
as from every source, we welcome the finger which points to
something in Christ we had not seen before. When they attempt
to speak to us with authority, the authority of the church, or
of the creed, the authority of scholarship or of science, then
they are to be cast away, for then it is the voice of Satan himself
which we hear in them.

Christ wants us to gain our light and guidance from Him,
light as to conduct, light as to belief, light as to motive, light
as to our life's objective. All our light is to come from Him,
and from Him directly. This means that we will listen to a ser-
mon with critical ears and read a book with critical eyes. We
must discriminate between truth from Christ which is our greatest need, and human contributions which we do not want.

That is what it means negatively. Positively it means something
still more important. It means that we shall give Christ the opportunity to show us the things He wants us to see. We must
sit down with His teachings and His example and study them
carefully, and ponder them patiently. We must take time for
contact with Christ. We must give Him an opportunity, every
day, to illumine our minds and guide our steps. Indeed, is not
this Christ's own word? "If ye abide in my word, then are ye
my disciples indeed, and ye shall know the truth, and the truth
shall make you free."

Jesus leads us out and goes before us. No matter where the
sheep of the parable found themselves, the shepherd was leading them. He was there with them, and ahead of them, and this
is one of the things that we are to appropriate for ourselves. In
days of physical danger He is there. But there are deeper things
than that. In days of desperate grief, of unmerited suffering,
He goes before us, and when the blackness of complete doubt
submerges us He is there. Perhaps the most important thing of

all is to remember that in days of great and deserved success He is with us. Usually we do not realize it, but often we find the most dangerous and slippery places in those lovely periods when we are successful and popular.

This is one of Jesus' simplest parables. It is of the earth, and earthly experiences. But after Jesus finished that lesson, and completed it with great care He went on and carried the teaching right up to the throne of God.

He brought a further lesson and a very important one. "The good shepherd giveth his life for the sheep." In Arabia and the Near East it would not happen often, but it does occur. Doubtless in Jesus' day it was a more frequent thing. It happens usually when the shepherd is a little boy, for a full grown wolf can kill such a shepherd. An adult man, especially an outdoor man like a shepherd, is more than a match for a wolf. But even he is not safe when robbers come. The love and loyalty of those shepherds, particularly of the small shepherds of ten years or thereabouts, would be sufficient for this. They would not run away.

The hireling runs away and lets the wolf kill a sheep. Probably he will kill only one or two. To save the sheep it is necessary to kill the wolf and that is dangerous. The hireling can easily say that the life of a sheep is not worth the life of a man.

That last argument behind the cowardice of the hireling has real weight and we must give it some thought. It was Jesus Himself who said, "How much then is a man of more value than a sheep." Here the Pharisees could have presented a real argument against the soundness of Jesus' teaching. Unquestionably the life of the shepherd is worth infinitely more than the life of the sheep which he tries to save.

Our everyday life gives us some good examples of this. A very moving illustration came recently from the underprivileged mountain districts where a colored man had a very loyal dog. He was a common, everyday dog but there was nothing common about his loyalty. When his master went to work in the forest the dog was left guarding the dinner pail. A sudden forest fire swept over them all, and with some difficulty the men escaped with their lives. The dog could have escaped too. He knew what the fire meant, and he knew the way out, but they found his charred body still guarding the blackened dinner pail.

We see without difficulty why Jesus chose this figure. Here is a parable where Jesus teaches the atonement, for Jesus died in just this way, an infinitely more valuable life sacrificed to save valuable ones.

The boy or the man who takes care of the sheep and loses his life doing it, loves those sheep very deeply. He loves every one of them. When they are sick or hurt, he carries them home on his shoulder. That is pure love at work. They are usually not his own property, but belong to other people. The shepherd leads them out for the day, to bring them back at night. They are committed to him, and he is responsible for their welfare and safety. That is reckoned as a sacred responsibility. The small boy's father, when he finds the mangled body, looks with shining eyes on that scene of loyalty and heroism. The love that sacrifices itself for the sheep is a beautiful divine thing, the most vivid picture of the atonement that Jesus could find.

The shepherd does not love the wolf. He drives the wolf away and kills it if he can. Moreover, the shepherd does not save the sheep's life by lying down and letting the wolf eat him instead of the sheep. The wolf's appetite might be satisfied in that way . . . and then no sheep would be killed, but the parable points in no such direction.

To our limited minds it would seem impossible to add either depth or height to this, but Jesus had a further lesson. Apparently in His mind it was the deepest and highest lesson of all. Jesus' sacrifice of Himself for us results in His knowing us and we Him. Probably we will never know why that result comes from this cause. Most certainly we cannot see such a profound thing now. No doubt it is the depth of His love that brings this about. We do not understand it at all, but we take off our shoes and bow our heads and worship.

The degree of this knowledge surprises us most of all. The love and knowledge between us and Jesus, our shepherd, is cut to a divine pattern — "As the Father knows me and I know the Father." We are moving in sacred territory here, standing before our Heavenly Father's throne. Jesus' death saves us, and we have given much time and thought to meditation on what that death saves us *from*. Evidently we need to meditate also on the things which that death saves us *to*. It saves us to a fellowship with Jesus that is of the same sort as His fellowship with the Father.

And as He looks at the cross, Jesus finds it easy to catch a glimpse of His universal mission. "Other sheep I have which are not of this fold." To the Pharisees that was a very unacceptable teaching, but the love reaching out from the Cross could not be other than universal.

There is a beautiful final touch. "For this reason the Father loves me, that I lay down my life, that I may take it again." No doubt Jesus' love, as incredible as it was, simply reflected the love of the Heavenly Father. Even the Heavenly Father can let His love flow out completely only toward a Son who manifested His divine love by dying for us. And if we want to know Jesus and be known by Him, our path is plain. We must love as He loved. "My sheep hear my voice and they follow me." Probably the most important thing that we have to do is to follow Him in His love.

Then came the Jews round about him, and said unto him, How long dost thou make us to doubt? If thou be the Christ, tell us plainly. Jesus answered them, I told you, and ye believed not: the works that I do in my Father's name, they bear witness of me. But ye believe not, because ye are not of my sheep, as I said unto you. My sheep hear my voice, and I know them, and they follow me: And I give unto them eternal life; and they shall never perish, neither shall any man pluck them out of my hand. My Father, which gave them me, is greater than all; and no man is able to pluck them out of my Father's hand. I and my Father are one.

The writer has recorded for us Jesus' further development of the parable of the Good Shepherd. Questioners gathered around Him. Some of them were hostile and some were greatly impressed with the beauty and power of His teachings. It was a time of national expectation. Men longed for the appearing of the Messiah. It was inevitable that a teacher of such extraordinary power and holiness should be asked if he was the expected one.

This question was in the minds of the people, but it was phrased here by an enemy, or at least by a hostile critic. "If you are the Christ, tell us plainly." We should have reckoned this a great opportunity to present His claims. The audience at least was ready to listen. But Jesus refused to discuss it. He never discussed such things with unbelievers, or, shall we say, outsiders. Indeed. He never discussed it in this way even with His disciples, though it is evident that He was very anxious that they should come to this conclusion about Him.

Jesus knew the Old Testament, and that His coming had been predicted by the prophets. He was indeed the King. Unfortunately, His type of kingship was not at all what the nation expected or wanted. Spiritual renewal was not in their remotest thought. This was true of both the Pharisees and of the people they led.

Then the Jews took up stones again to stone him. Jesus answered them, Many good works have I shewed you from my Father; for which of those works do ye stone me? The Jews answered him, saying, For a good work we stone thee not; but for blasphemy; and because that thou, being a man, makest thyself God. Jesus answered them, Is it not written in your law, I said, Ye are gods? If he called them gods, unto whom the word of God came, and the Scripture cannot be broken; Say ye of him, whom the Father hath sanctified, and sent into teh world, Thou blasphemest; because I said, I am the Son of God? If I do not the works of my Father, believe me not. But if I do, though ye believe not me, believe the works; that ye may know, and believe, that the Father is in me, and I in him. Therefore they sought again to take him; but he escaped out of their hand,

For Jesus to have said, Yes to this question would have been further from the truth than to say No. He was not the Messiah they were waiting for. On the other hand, there are indications in the Old Testament that the Messiah was to bring spiritual renewal, and even to be an atonement for Israel's sins. Some had noted these things and we understand why Jesus insisted that men come to a realization of His Messiahship by considering His works.

Jesus' works were outstanding. They showed divine power, and they had in them the potency for spiritual renewal, but only those who had caught some glimpse of the Messiah as an atonement would eventually recognize His Messiahship.

But the man who was looking for an earthly military Messiah, a great king who would conquer the Romans and rule the world could only conclude from Jesus' works that this man could not possibly be the expected one. No doubt that was exactly the conclusion Jesus wanted such a man to reach. A man whose heart was filled with such wrong conception would only cause more trouble if he supposed that Jesus was the Messiah. Perhaps Judas had a divided heart on this point, and that was one of the reasons for his downfall.

Now a certain *man* was sick, named Lazarus, of Bethany, the town of Mary and her sister Martha. (It was *that* Mary which anointed the Lord with ointment, and wiped his feet with her hair, whose brother Lazarus was sick.) Therefore his sisters sent unto him, saying, Lord, behold, he whom thou lovest is sick. When Jesus heard *that,* he said, This sickness is not unto death, but for the glory of God, that the Son of God might be glorified thereby. Now Jesus loved Martha, and her sister, and Lazarus. When he had heard therefore that he was sick, he abode two days still in the same place where he was. Then after that saith he to *his* disciples, Let us go into Judea again. *His* disciples say unto him, Master, the Jews of late sought to stone thee; and goest thou thither again? Jesus answered, Are there not twelve hours in the day? If any man walk in the day, he stumbleth not, because he seeth the light of his world. But if a man walk in the night, he stumbleth, because there is no light in him. These things said he: and after that he saith unto them, Our friend Lazarus sleepeth; but I go, that I may awake him out of sleep. Then said his disciples, Lord, if he sleep, he shall do well. Howbeit Jesus spake of his death: but they thought that he had spoken of taking of rest in sleep. Then said Jesus unto them plainly, Lazarus is dead. And I am glad for your sakes that I was not there, to the intent ye may believe; nevertheless let us go unto him. Then said Thomas, which is called Didymus, unto his fellow disciples, Let us also go, that we may die with him. Then when Jesus came, he found that he had *lain* in the grace four days already. Now Bethany was nigh unto Jerusalem, about fifteen furlongs off: And many of the Jews came to Martha and Mary, to comfort them concerning their brother. Then Martha, as soon as she heard that Jesus was coming, went and met him: but Mary sat *still* in the house. Then said Martha unto Jesus, Lord, if thou hadst been here, my brother had not died. But I know, that even now, whatsoever thou wilt ask of God, God will give it thee. Jesus saith unto her, Thy brother shall rise again. Martha saith unto him, I know that he shall rise again in the resurrection at the last day. Jesus saith unto her, I am the resurrection, and the life: he that believeth in me, though he were dead, yet shall he live: and whosoever liveth and believeth in me shall never die. Believest thou this? She saith unto him, Yea, Lord: I believe that thou art the Christ, the Son of God, which should come into the world. And when she had so said, she went her way, and called Mary her sister secretly, saying, The Master is come, and calleth for thee. As soon as she heard that, she arose quickly, and came unto him. Now Jesus was not yet come into the town, but was in that place where Martha met him. The Jews then which were with her in the house, and comforted her, when they saw Mary, that she rose up hastily and went out, followed her, saying, She goeth unto the grave to weep there. Then when Mary was come where Jesus was, and saw him, she fell down at his feet, saying unto him, Lord, if thou hadst been here, my brother had not died. When Jesus therefore saw her weeping, and the Jews also weeping which came with her, he groaned in the spirit, and was troubled. And said, Where have ye laid him? They say unto him, Lord, come and see. Jesus wept. Then said the Jews, Behold how he loved him And some of them said, Could not this man, which opened the eyes of the blind, have caused that even this should not have died? Jesus therefore again groaning in himself cometh to the grave. It was a cave, and a stone lay upon it. Jesus said, Take ye away the stone. Martha, the sister of him that was dead, saith unto him, Lord, by this time he stinketh: for he hath been dead four days. Jesus saith unto her, Said I not unto thee, that, if thou wouldest believe, thou shouldest see the glory of God? Then they took away the stone from the place where the dead was laid. And Jesus lifted up his eyes, and said, Father, I thank thee that thou hast heard me. And I knew that thou hearest me always: but because of the people which stand by I said it, that they may believe that thou hast sent me. And when he thus cried with a loud voice, Lazarus, come forth. And he that was dead came forth, bound hand and foot with graveclothes; and his face was bound about with a napkin. Jesus saith unto them, Loose him, and let him go. Then many of the Jews which came to Mary, and had seen the things which Jesus did, believed on him. But some of them went their ways to the Pharisees, and told them what things Jesus had done.

Then gathered the chief priests and the Pharisees a council, and said, What do we? for this man doeth many miracles. If we let him thus alone, all men will believe on him and the Romans shall come and take away both our place and nation. And one of them, named Caiaphas, being the high priest that same year, said unto them, Ye know nothing at all, Nor consider that it is expedient for us, that one man should die for the people, and that the whole nation perish not. And this spake he not of himself: but being high priest that year, he prophesied that Jesus should die for that nation; and not for that nation only, but that also he should gather together in one the children of God that were scattered abroad. Then from that day forth they took counsel together for to put him to death. Jesus therefore walked no more openly among the Jews; but went thence unto a country near to the wilderness, into a city called Ephraim, and there continued with his disciples.

And the Jews' passover was nigh at hand; and many went out of the country up to Jerusalem before the passover, to purify themselves. Then sought they for Jesus, and spake among themselves, as they stood in the temple, What think ye, that he will not come to the feast? Now both the chief priests and the Pharisees had given a commandment, that, if any man knew where he were, he should shew it, that they might take him.

Chapter XI

THE PICTURE

It is easy to see the literary outline here. This chapter is a series of pictures, and the different pictures are parts of a single story. One of the most remarkable of Jesus' miracles serves as its climax.

But even the miracle is not what the writer has principally in mind. The story, miracle and all, is a means to an end. It may be questioned whether the picture itself, arresting and beautiful as it is, adds anything really significant to what we have seen of Jesus before.

But as a pedestal from which Jesus could say, "I am the resurrection and the life," its value, and, indeed, its necessity is obvious. Moreover, it is obvious that the unity of this account is no writer's achievement. The suitability of these different events as an introduction to Jesus' teaching cannot be questioned, but

Now a certain man was sick, named Lazarus, of Bethany, the town of Mary and her sister Martha. (It was that Mary which anointed the Lord with ointment, and wiped his feet with her hair, whose brother Lazarus was sick.) Therefore his sisters sent unto him, saying, Lord, he whom thou lovest is sick.

When Jesus heard that, he said, This sickness is not unto death, but for the glory of God, that the Son of God might be glorified thereby. Now Jesus loved Martha, and her sister, and Lazarus. When he had heard therefore that he was sick, he abode two days still in the same place where he was. Then after that saith he to his disciples, Let us go into Judea again. His disciples say usto him, Master, the Jews of late sought to stone thee; and goest thou thither again?

---

what the writer did was to put down, simply and naturally, different things as they happened. Jesus planned the events. Apparently even from the start He foresaw what the later developments would be.

Scene 1
Jesus and the Bethany Family

There are four figures in this scene, — three in the Bethany family, and Jesus.

Lazarus is the first to be mentioned. He was the official head of the house. The father and mother were probably dead. And Lazarus was sick. This family was bound together by very unusual affection. They had come to love Jesus very deeply. What had led to this we do not know, but all three loved Jesus and He loved them. There seems to have been no other such family. As far as we are told, relatively little such affection persisted between Jesus and His own family. His brethren repudiated Him and even between Jesus and His mother there seems to have been no such warm confidence and familiarity as we see here.

Lazarus was the man of the house. The whole atmosphere of the account leads to the conclusion that this was a family of some prominence in Jerusalem, and Lazarus a man of some position, young and popular.

We know very little about Lazarus, except that at this time he fell sick. The nature of his illness we cannot even guess, but it

Jesus answered, Are there not twelve hours in the day? If any man walk in the day, he stumbleth not because he seeth the light of this world. But if a man walk in the night, he stumbleth, because there is no light in him. These things said he: and after that he saith unto them, Our friend Lazarus sleepeth; but I go, that I may awake him out of sleep. Then said his disciples, Lord, if he sleep, he shall do well.

---

was a serious thing, for it caused his death in a few days. It struck hard and suddenly, and the sisters recognized that his life was in danger. In their need they sent for Jesus. He was the one friend who could deal with such a serious situation. They felt sure that Jesus' love for them and Lazarus would bring Him immediately to their help. Their message was simplicity itself. "Lord, he whom thou lovest is sick." Jesus never refused to heal anyone who asked for it. Faith was necessary, no doubt, but the faith involved in asking was evidently adequate. Jesus never refused such a request, how much more here, where a very deep personal affection was felt.

Scene 2

Jesus and the Disciples

The message reached Jesus. In those days a horse was the fastest method of travel. Most people walked. A message like this would take two or three days to reach its destination, even if it was hurried.

But Jesus, after receiving this call for help, remained where He was. He stayed on for two days. No doubt the disciples who were with Jesus asked the messenger about his message, and they interpreted Jesus' action, or rather His lack of action, as simple caution. They had just come from very stormy scenes in Jerusalem, and Jesus had barely escaped with His life.

They were therefore much surprised when at the end of two days Jesus announced that the group would now go back to Judea. This looked reckless. Thomas, the somber realist, said, "Let us also go that we may die with Him."

Howbeit Jesus spake of his death: but they thought that he had spoken
of taking of rest in sleep.   Then said Jesus unto them plainly, Lazarus
is dead.   And I am glad for your sakes that I was not there, to the intent
ye may believe; nevertheless let us go unto him.   Then said Thomas,
which is called Didymus, unto his fellow disciples, Let us also go, that we
may die with him.

Jesus waited so that Lazarus might die.   Then He could go and
raise him to life again.   It is safe to say that the disciples did not
grasp this at the moment, even though Jesus explained it and
they eventually did understand.

The first thing that Jesus wished to accomplish by the tremendous miracle which He had in mind was to glorify God.   This is
one of the things which, with a little attention, we can partially
understand.   We have already learned that in Jesus' mind one of
the important features of His redemption of men on the cross
is the fact that it was a voluntary sacrifice.   No man took Jesus'
life away from Him.   He laid it down of Himself.   We can penetrate very little into the mysteries of the atonement, but here
we can see something.   If Jesus' execution was a human thing,
if His death was forced upon Him by men, however great and
strong, nearly all of its divine redemptive element is taken away.

At first sight it is exceedingly difficult to see how Jesus could
demonstrate to us humans with our weak minds the voluntary
nature of this sacrifice.   Looked at from the earthly aspect it was
a human thing, the triumph of pure sin over pure righteousness.
Jesus' assertion that this sacrifice on His part is a voluntary thing
remains an empty word, even though that sacrifice was sublimely
beautiful even from the earthly standpoint.

Jesus wants us to see that it is more than that.   As we meditate on the tremendous miracle of this chapter, the fog lifts a
little.   It is here that the miracle ministers to the glory of God.
In the raising of Lazarus Jesus did not give us a preview of the
resurrection.   After everything was over, Lazarus had the same
body as before and it was subject to the same limitations.   His

evidently had the same mind and no doubt he died again when his time came.

But here Jesus did show Himself to be in complete command of both life and death, and, having seen this miracle, no one can imagine that His own death on the cross was other than completely voluntary. His body was surrendered to the laws and forces of death only by His consent.

When Jesus said that this death was "for the glory of God, that the Son of God may be glorified," He was speaking of the glory that ordinary people, the community as a whole, would give God as a result of it. We may be sure that God's essential glory will neither be increased nor diminished by anything humans can do. And no doubt the community as a whole did give glory to God as they saw this miracle and its results. The Pharisees were made more hostile by it, but many of the people believed on Jesus.

Jesus mentioned, as a second result, the fact that the disciples would believe on Him. Jesus gave a great deal of attention to building up the faith of the disciples. Many of His miracles had this as their purpose. It is impossible to doubt that this demonstration of His power would have such an effect.

It is not mentioned, but we can be sure that Jesus knew that the family and especially the sisters would be strengthened by the experience. They suffered very deeply and it seems hardly fair to subject them to such a trial, even for the sake of others, unless it helped them too.

Scene 3

Jesus and Martha

On arrival Jesus found that Lazarus had been dead four days. This was what He had planned on. The attention of Jerusalem was still on this death. Dozens and scores of consolers were there to comfort the sisters and mourn their dead brother. In

Then when Jesus came, he found that he had lain in the grave four days already. Now Bethany was nigh unto Jerusalem, about fifteen furlongs off: And many of the Jews came to Martha and Mary, to comfort them concerning their brother. Then Martha, as soon as she heard that Jesus was coming, went and met him: but Mary sat still in the house. Then said Martha unto Jesus, Lord, if thou hadst been here, my brother had not died. But I know, that even now, whatsoever thou wilt ask of God, God will give it thee. Jesus saith unto her, Thy brother shall rise again.

Martha said unto him, I know that he shall rise again in the resurrection at the last day. Jesus said unto her, I am the resurrection, and the life: he that believeth in me, though he were dead, yet shall he live: And whosoever liveth and believeth in me shall never die. Believest thou this? She saith unto him, Yea, Lord: I believe that thou art the Christ, the Son of God, which should come into the world. And when she had so said, she went her way, and called Mary her sister secretly, saying, The Master is come, and calleth for thee.

---

that part of the world, even to this day, men and women come to weep with those who have been bereaved. Tears come to the surface easily but there is deep sincerity in them, and they soothe the dreadful ache as nothing else can.

Jesus had an extraordinary ability to surround His critically important miracles with such clouds of witnesses that no one could question what happened, no matter how tensely he might disapprove. Here were witnesses in dozens, the most prominent figures in the city who had watched Lazarus when he was desperately sick. They had seen him breathe his last. They had wrapped the long white grave clothes around his stiff, cold body after it was washed, and they themselves had carried the corpse to the cave and rolled against the door the gigantic stone which closed it. Later, in the fierce, bitter hostility which broke out against Jesus, and which put even Lazarus' own life in danger, no one thought of questioning what had happened.

Jesus did not refer to this by so much as a syllable. Its effect was better by being left alone. Jesus knew when not to stress a point.

It was Martha who met Him. She had everything under control, herself included. There were no tears in this interview.

Her disappointment at Jesus' delay was great and she felt free
to tell Him so, which shows a very beautiful degree of confidence
and intimacy. Martha's faith, however, went far beyond that.
She still had hopes that Jesus could take care of the situation.
Moreover, hers was the type of faith that Jesus particularly
prized, faith that He was in the Father and the Father in Him.
Jesus practically told her that this unusual faith was to be honored.

But Jesus did not give her the simple and unequivocal answer
that she wanted. He saw an opportunity here to give to the world
one of His supremely important words. She would not understand it then. Indeed, where is the man who now, after centuries
of Christian experience, can fathom that great word even with
his boldest imagination? But she would never forget it. It was
one of those teachings which Jesus succeeded in expressing in a
short, unforgettable sentence — "I am the resurrection and the
life." All that we know about the next world, all that we need to
know, and all that we can know, is in that word.

Martha evidently caught some real assurance from Jesus, and
went away comforted and reassured. She probably could not
have told just what she had expected. She knew that Mary would
want to see Jesus, too. She did not feel sure enough of herself
to pass on to Mary her new confidence. Perhaps she would not
have called it more than a new hope.

Scene 4

Jesus and Mary

Martha told Mary that Jesus had come, and Mary went out to
meet Him. Here is an emotional scene. Tears were always close
to the surface with Mary, and, as we would have expected, there
were many of them here. Jesus showed no displeasure. At such
a time people weep, and it is well that they do. The sympathizing
friends from Jerusalem were weeping. They felt the loss of their
old friend.

As soon as she heard that, she arose quickly, and came unto him. Now Jesus was not yet come into the town, but was in that place where Martha met him. The Jews then which were with her in the house, and comforted her, when they saw Mary, that she rose up hastily and went out, followed her, saying, She goeth unto the grave to weep there. Then when Mary was come where Jesus was, and saw him, she fell down at his feet, saying unto him, Lord, if thou hadst been here, my brother had not died.

When Jesus therefore saw her weeping, and the Jews also weeping which came with her, he groaned in the spirit, and was troubled. And said, Where have ye laid him? They say unto him, come and see. Jesus wept. Then said the Jews, Behold how he loved him! And some of them said, Could not this man, which opened the eyes of the blind, have caused that even this man should not have died?

Mary was completely devastated. Her faith had not begun to take hold of the situation yet, and even in Jesus she saw no ray of hope. She fell at His feet weeping, and those with her were weeping, too.

Jesus' sympathies were very vivid and quick. He was a man of intense emotions, and the keen grief around Him entered into His soul. It is easy to imagine that this was not what He preferred or planned, for He alone of that great company knew that this grief within a few minutes was to be turned into very great joy. Jesus wept with them, an involuntary evidence of His keen sympathy.

All Jesus could do was to ask, "Where have ye lain Him?" and follow the invitation, "Come and see." Jesus entered into their grief and wept with them, but it would seem that He was better pleased with Martha's faith. So far as we can see He was not able to do anything with this intense grief of Mary. The grief did not displease Him, or, if it did, He did not show it. And indeed we can be sure that it did not displease Him for He shared in it. Repression was not Jesus' way, and it is not the best way, but such abandonement to the instinctive reaction of the moment has its disadvantages for it leaves no place for faith, and Mary was not able to give her faith in Jesus any opportunity at all while grief had such complete sway over her.

Jesus therefore again groaning in himself cometh to the grave. It was a cave, and a stone lay upon it. Jesus said, Take ye away the stone. Martha, the sister of him that was dead, saith unto him, Lord, by this time he stinketh: for he hath been dead four days. Jesus saith unto her, Said I not unto thee, that, if thou wouldest believe, thou shouldest see the glory of God?

Grief as intense as this for the time being excludes faith. If we are looking into the eyes of our Heavenly Father our surrender to grief cannot be complete. This time it was Martha and not Mary who sat at Jesus' feet and heard His words.

Scene 5

Jesus at the Tomb

Jesus was greatly moved as He approached the tomb. Was He praying? Not exactly, perhaps; more likely He was simply feeling. Feeling for what? For the assurance that He was still within His Father's will.

The people standing around needed the lesson. This miracle was a manifestation of His Father's will. That was the one thing that Jesus hoped the bystanders would realize. "That they may believe that thou hast sent me." Jesus hoped they would learn that.

Martha shrank from having the stone taken away. Her faith quailed at the prospect of realizing that her beloved brother had become a stinking and dreadful corruption. Her faith, vague and unformed at best, was not equal to this. Perhaps she wanted Jesus to raise him before the stone was taken away.

But Jesus knew that it was better the other way, so they took away the stone, and Jesus, with a word of prayer to throw the whole effort back into the hands of His Heavenly Father, "cried with a loud voice, Lazarus, come forth." There is something superbly simple in this. No explanations and no preliminaries.

Then they took away the stone from the place where the dead was laid. And Jesus lifted his eyes, and said, Father, I thank thee that thou hast heard me. And I knew that thou hearest me always; but because of the people which stand by I said it that they may believe that thou hast sent me.

A simple command, and simple obedience. Lazarus came forth. Jesus paid no attention to the details of unwrapping him. He did not seek for any further contact with the miracle. He did not exult over it. He did not exploit it. He made no comment on it.

We may well give a moment's thought to the miracle itself. Just what happened? Lazarus had been dead for four days. The actual material which composed his body was more or less in place, but the cells were all dead and disintegrated, and that whole mass of matter was under the laws of death. We know a good deal about the laws of death. The complicated chemical compounds formed under the influence of life break down, one after another, till not a great deal is left except water and carbon dioxide and ammonia. The intermediate products are very offensive to the eye and even more so to the nose. In Lazarus' case these disintegrative processes were well started, though their completion would take several months.

The laws of life we understand much less. Under the influence of life the energy of the sun, indirectly and directly, is able to build up complicated chemical compounds of symmetry and utility. They are integrated with each other in arrangements that are supremely beautiful and balanced, but these compounds do not become more and more complicated. Rather, a plateau is reached, and then this complex and bautiful and adjusted level is steadily maintained.

Along with this complex chemistry there is maintained a separate activity which in humans we call thought and which we can see in its beginnings in animals. We do not know the rela-

And when he thus had spoken, he cried with a loud voice, Lazarus, come forth. And he that was dead came forth, bound hand and foot with graveclothes; and his face was bound about with a napkin. Jesus saith unto them, Loose him, and let him go.

---

tionship between this and the complex chemistry of life but when life departs mental activity disappears with it.

There is another aspect of this miracle that we must notice. Jesus stood before the grave of Lazarus with the pose and manner of a king. His unostentatious authority is very impressive. When He spoke men obeyed, and when He spoke again death obeyed, or, perhaps we should say that it was life which obeyed and returned to that disintegrated corpse. We would like to know whether death is an entity of itself, as the ancients supposed, or whether it is simply the absence of life as we tend to think. But whichever it was that Jesus was commanding, He was able to take by His simple fiat that hundred and fifty pounds of putrefaction, and place it again under the laws of life. It was a complete work, as Jesus' signs always were. Lazarus came back, as his old self, a normal man as we learn in the following chapter.

We are going to see more of this consciousness of kingship. So far as the account gives us to know, this was a new thing. In a curious way we see Him here fulfilling the predictions of the Old Testament prophets, and the hopes of His short-sighted disciples. It is interesting and thrilling to let the imagination marshall before us the kingdom that Jesus ruled. The kingdom of death and the kingdom of life, also the Kingdom of truth, as He told Pilate. But the kingdom of men's hearts, did He rule over that? He ruled over some of them, but the kingdoms of pride and sin and selfishness, He did not as yet rule over them. They were soon to rule over Him, at least to rule over His body. His crucifixion was only a few days away as He stood before Lazarus' grave, King of this world and the next.

Then many of the Jews which came to Mary, and had seen the things which Jesus did, believed on him.   But some of them went their ways to the Pharisees, and told them what things Jesus had done.

Then gathered the chief priests and the Pharisees a council, and said, What do we? for this man doeth many miracles.   If we let him thus alone, all men will believe on him; and the Romans shall come and take away both out place and nation.   And one of them, named Caiaphas, being the high priest that same year, said unto them, Ye know nothing at all, nor consider that it is expedient for us, that one man should die for people, and that the whole nation perish not.   And this spake he not of himself: but being high priest that year, he prophesied that Jesus should die for the nation;

Scene 6

The Pharisees

Jesus may not have made any comment on the miracle but the Pharisees did. However there was one comment they did not make. They did not question what had happened. They were stunned by it, but it was not possible to discredit a single detail.

They manifested not the slighest joy over the sisters' relief. Sorrow had been turned into joy, but the Pharisees were not concerned with that.

The miracle that had brought such joy to the sisters and to Lazarus, to their friends and to the disciples, and indeed to Jesus, brought something else to the Pharisees. What? It brought fear to them. It is a little difficult for us in our day to understand just what it was that those men feared. "The Romans will come and take away both our place and our nation." Just what the connection was between this miracle and their fear, is perhaps beyond us. But they reacted as men do when fear dominates their hearts. They planned to murder Jesus just as soon as they could possibly compass it. Where had their conscience gone? Where does conscience always go when fear rules?

Jesus was not at all surprised by this. We will not say that this was one of His objects when He planned the miracle, but

And not for that nation only, but that also he should gather together in one the children of God that were scattered abroad. Then from that day forth they took counsel together for to put him to death. Jesus therefore walked no more openly among the Jews; but went thence unto a country near to the wilderness, into a city called Ephraim, and there continued with his disciples.

And the Jews passover was nigh at hand: and many went out of the country up to Jerusalem before the passover, to purify themselves. Then sought they for Jesus, and spake among themselves, as they stood in the temple, What think ye, that he will not come to the feast? Now both the chief priests and the Pharisees had given a commandment, that, if any man knew where he were, he should shew it, that they might take him.

Then said Martha unto Jesus, Lord, if thou hadst been here, my brother had not died. But I know that even now, whatsoever thou wilt ask of God, God will give it thee. Jesus saith unto her, Thy brother shall rise again. Martha saith unto him, I know that he shall rise again in the resurrection at the last day. Jesus said unto her, I am the resurrection, and the life: he that believeth in me, though he were dead, yet shall he live: And whosoever liveth and believeth in me shall never die. Believest thou this?

He knew it would happen. There had been many times when His listeners, led by the Pharisees, had wanted to kill Him. Now it was a definite and dreadful policy which was soon to be successful. But Jesus, we can be sure, was satisfied. It had been a great day's work. The last of His tremendous signs He had successfully executed, and with a certainty that was unshakable. The last of His great words He had successfully planted in the human mind where it was to grow through the centuries. He was almost ready now for the cross.

Jesus' Teaching

The teaching which the writer presents in this chapter is certainly a short lesson. It seems at first that such a small contribution can hardly be a matter of very great importance. But the build-up that John gives this little word is one of the most elaborate in the entire Gospel. Evidently he thought it important. But Jesus Himself arranged this tremendous introduction. He put the force of a great miracle behind a number of His great teachings. "I am the bread of life" and "I am the good shepherd" both had such introductions. Raising Lazarus from the dead was a tremendous miracle.

This is one of Jesus' greatest words. Here He deals with our life and death. Paul realized its importance. Said he, "If we have hoped in Christ only in this life, we are of all men most miserable." A faith which does not reach beyond the grave is no faith at all. This world and its experiences give no picture of God which satisfies the most elementary demands of the human spirit.

The imagination of the dullest Christian is captivated by this wonderful sentence. The resurrection is to bring us into a new type of life, infinitely different from and more beautiful than the old one. Lazarus was raised from the dead, and this most wonderfully demonstrated that Jesus is life. But Lazarus did not taste the resurrection. He came back to the same life he had lived before.

"I am the resurrection." Even as we begin to meditate on that little sentence we see visions and dream dreams. Jesus will be our guide at first — ". . . And are sons of God, being sons of the resurrection." We are sons of God now but not very good ones. It is only by His infinite grace that we could even think of using such a term. In the days of the resurrection it will be a true description, for Paul says, "We shall be changed, for this corruptible shall put on incorruption and this mortal must put on immortality."

And the most beautiful element in the resurrection life is its partnership with Jesus. We have been united with Christ in the likeness of His death, but the future glows with the glory of God. We are to be "united with Him in the likeness of His resurrection." We are to bear the image of the Man of Heaven. Our body is to be raised in glory.

This body of ours is a beautiful thing. God has put His divine artistry into it. His truth is there, and real life too. The anatomist and the physiologist and the psychologist all stand in awc of what their investigations show of the glory and the beauty and the precision and symmetry of the laws of God.

After the resurrection it will have God's glory in it. It is sown in dishonour for when the laws of death take hold of it, nothing is left except putrefaction and disintegration. But it is is to be raised in, the likeness of Jesus' resurrection body. It will be emancipated from the laws of death, "death no more has dominion over it." "For this mortal must put on immortality, this corruptible must put on incorruption."

The emancipation brought by the resurrection goes beyond this. The material limitations under which our bodies place us are to disappear and our spirits be free. "On the evening of that day, the doors being shut, Jesus came and stood among them." Perhaps this is why Jesus never showed much interest in human devices for overcoming our material environment. He knew that just around the corner was the world where such limitations are gone.

But Jesus was careful to indicate, even in this single sentence, that the life which we have in Him continues. Indeed the resurrection is not a new life at all but the complete development and flowering of the life which He has already given us. Any florist will illustrate it for us. We will let him show us some hyacinth plants. They are young and show real life. There is beauty in that life, and if we put under the microscope the stem or the leaves of that plant, real beauty and truth to be seen, and symmetry and balance, real beautiful life.

But quite surely the florist will also have a hyacinth in full bloom. The beauty and the fragrance of that great spike of God's loveliest flowers is almost overpowering. It is same life, but now we are looking at its consummation. And the ultimate purpose of that plant is only seen when we see it in its resurrection dress.

Months and years afterward, when Martha's mind went over and over again that wonderful dialogue, she came to realize that what Jesus wanted her to catch was simply that as she looked at Him she was looking at the resurrection. When Jesus said, "I am the resurrection." He did not have in mind, except in a very minor way, the changes that would take place in His body. The essence of the resurrection is that we are to be like Jesus, not on the outside, but on the inside. With the resentments and the fears and the frustrations all gone, our souls will be like the hyacinth spike with its fragrance and beauty. Our spirits will roam as untrammeled as our redeemed bodies, roam through the great beautiful thoughts of God, thoughts of truth and beauty and love, great wonderful fragrant thoughts that we cannot even imagine now. It is one of Jesus' greatest words — "I am the resurrection and the life."

Then Jesus six days before the passover came to Bethany, where Lazarus was which had been dead, whom he raised from the dead. There they made him a supper; and Martha served: but Lazarus was one of them that sat at the table with him. Then took Mary a pound of ointment of spikenard, very costly, and anointed the feet of Jesus, and wiped his feet with her hair: and the house was filled with the odour of the ointment. Then saith one of his disciples, Judas Iscariot, Simon's son, which should betray him, why was not this ointment sold for three hundred pence, and given to the poor? This he said, not that he cared for the poor; but because he was a thief, and had the bag, and bare what was put therein. Then said Jesus, Let her alone: against the day of my burying hath she kept this. For the poor always ye have with you; but me ye have not always. Much people of the Jews therefore knew that he was there: and they came not for Jesus' sake only, but that they might see Lazarus also, whom he had raised from the dead.

But the chief priests consulted that they might put Lazarus also to death; Because that by reason of him many of the Jews went away, and believed on Jesus.

On the next day much people that were come to the feast, when they heard that Jesus was coming to Jerusalem, took branches of palm trees, and went forth to meet him, and cried, Hosanna: Blessed is the King of Israel that cometh in the name of the Lord. And Jesus, when he had found a young ass, sat thereon; as it is written, Fear not, daughter of Sion: behold, thy King cometh, sitting on an ass's colt. These things understood not his disciples at the first but when Jesus was glorified, then remembered they that these things were written of him, and that they had done these things unto him. The people therefore that was with him when he called Lazarus out of his grave, and raised him from the dead, bare record.

For this cause the people also met him, for that they heard that he had done this miracle. The Pharisees therefore said among themselves, Perceive ye how ye prevail nothing? behold, the world is gone after him.

And there were certain Greeks among them that came up to worship at the feast: The same came therefore to Philip, which was of Bethsaida of Galilee, and desired him, saying, Sir, we would see Jesus. Philip cometh and telleth Andrew: and again Andrew and Philip tell Jesus.

And Jesus answered them, saying, The hour is come, that the Son of man should be glorified. Verily, verily, I say unto you, Except a corn of wheat fall into the ground and die, it abideth alone: but if it die, it bringeth forth much fruit. He that loveth his life shall lose it; and he that hateth his life in this world shall keep it unto life eternal. If any man serve me, let him follow me; and where I am, there shall also my servant be: if any man serve me, him will my Father honour. Now is my soul troubled; and what shall I say? Father, save me from this hour: but for this cause came I unto this hour. Father, glorify thy name. Then came there a voice from heaven, saying, I have both glorified it, and will glorify it again. The people therefore that stood by, and heard it, said that it thundered: others said, An angel spake to him. Jesus answered and said, This voice came not because of me, but for your sakes. Now is the judgment of this world: now shall the prince of this world be cast out. And I, if I be lifted up from the earth, will draw all men unto me. This he said, signifying what death he should die. The people answered him, We have heard out of the law that Christ abideth for ever: and how sayest thou, The Son of man must be lifted up? who is this Son of man? Then Jesus said unto them, Yet a little while is the light with you. Walk while ye have the light, lest darkness come upon you: for he that walketh in darkness knoweth not whither he goeth.

While ye have light, believe in the light, that ye may be the children of light. These things spake Jesus, and departed, and did hide himself from them.

But though he had done so many miracles before them, yet they believed not on him: That the saying of Esaias the prophet might be fulfilled, which he spake, Lord, who hath believed our report? and to whom hath the arm of the Lord been revealed? Therefore they could not believe, because that Easias said again. He hath blinded their eyes, and hardened their heart; that they should not see with their eyes, nor understand with their heart, and be converted, and I should heal them. These things said Esaias, when he saw his glory, and spake of him.

Nevertheless among the chief rulers also many believed on him; but because of the Pharisees they did not confess him, lest they should be put out of the synagogue: For they loved the praise of men more than the praise of God.

Jesus cried and said, He that believeth on me, believeth not on me, but on him that sent me. And he that seeth me seeth him that sent me. I am come a light into the world, that whosoever believeth on me should not abide in darkness. And if any man hear my words, and believe not, I judge him not: for I came not to judge the world, but to save the world. He that rejecteth me, and receiveth not my words hath one that judgeth him: the word that I have spoken, the same shall judge him in the last day. For I have not spoken of myself; but the Father which sent me, he gave me a commandment, what I should say, and what I should speak. And I know that his commandment is life everlasting: whatsoever I speak therefore, even as the Father said unto me, so I speak.

Chapter XII

THE PICTURE

Episode I

The Bethany Feast

Then Jesus six days before the passover came to Bethany, where Lazarus was which had been dead, whom he raised from the dead. There they made him a supper; and Martha served: but Lazarus was one of them that sat at the table with him. Then took Mary a pound of ointment of spikenard, very costly, and anointed the feet of Jesus, and wiped his feet with her hair: and the house was filled with the odour of the ointment.

As we look on this scene we are reminded of the marriage feast at Cana. Here as there we see how keenly Jesus enjoyed friendly association with ordinary people, and these were not merely people, but the one family group where He found complete relaxation and love and understanding. In some ways this is the most beautiful view of Jesus we are given. The

Then saith one of his disciples, Judas Iscariot, Simon's son, which should betray him, Why was not this ointment sold for three hundred pence, and given to the poor? This he said, not that he cared for the poor; but because he was a thief, and had the bag, and bare what was put therein. Then said Jesus, Let her alone: against the day of my burying hath she kept this. For the poor always ye have with you; but me ye have not always.

---

simplicity and perfection of the picture make it hard to analyze and discuss. It is a picture of perfect love and harmony of joy and peace. The writer is a dramatist and he does not fail to draw in the contrasting background. But Judas is not part of the picture. He is its background.

Jesus' enjoyment of this atmosphere of happiness, comradeship and quiet devotion was undisturbed by His knowledge of the terrible experiences which lay just ahead. It was a time of disintegration and disorder in Israel, and outside was a distressed, hungry and cruelty-ridden world. But this little group took the environment that God had given them and the world they found themselves living in, and utilized the opportunity to enjoy each others' and Jesus' fellowship with a peace and poise and completeness that shows us a little of Heaven on earth.

As we meditate on this picture we realize that here at last we catch a glimpse of the end for which God is striving as He guides us and trains us. Here is the object for which we have been created. Most of the things we see are means to an end. What end? What is the chief end of man? "To glorify God and enjoy Him forever" and with Him to enjoy each other.

The significance of this beautiful picture goes even further. Jesus in King now. We realized that at Lazarus' tomb and we feel it here. Jesus is King and this is His Kingdom.

Four figures move in and out of this picture — Jesus and three others, all remarkable individuals. But it is more than four individuals. This is a group. Its binding force was loyalty to Jesus, a complete and overwhelming loyalty. But the Kingdom of God is not a group of individual human atoms characterized by great loyalty to Jesus. That would be a small and poor Kingdom. This group was a unit, knit not to Jesus only but to each other, and the fragrance of Heaven was in it.

Jesus was happy in this atmosphere. His enjoyment of the evening was just as undisturbed and beautiful as the others' was. Living as they were in the joy over Lazarus' raising they probably did not feel the cold and bitter storm outside at all.

Every one brought the best gifts re possessed. Jesus gave without restraint or limitation Himself, His perfect, flawless comradeship.   Martha served Jesus and all the others too.   She found here loveliest self-expression in that service. Lazarus was a gracious comrade to everyone there, just back from the grave, unchanged, poised and happy.

Even Mary's gift was brought to Jesus not when He was off by Himself, but in the group where all the company could share its beauty and fragrance. Utter self-giving and love were behind it. Mary wanted it to be a public affair so that all the group could share in the giving of it. The pure love of that gift has come down to us so that we can share in it too.

Episode 2

The Triumphal Entry

Much people of the Jews therefore knew that he was there: and they came not for Jesus' sake only, but that they might see Lazarus also, whom he had raised from the dead.

But the chief priests consulted that they might put Lazarus also to death; Because that by reason of him many of the Jews went away, and believed on Jesus.

A crowd collected to see Lazarus. Raising him from the dead had been a tremendous miracle. This would seem to offer a good opportunity for preaching, but Jesus did not think so. If anyone had asked for spiritual help, doubtless He would have responded quickly and gladly, but no one did. If there had been opposition and hostile questions, He would have replied earnestly and sincerely to the interest and need that even such an attitude showed

On the next day much people that were come to the feast, when they
heard that Jesus was coming to Jerusalem, Took branches of palm trees,
and went forth to meet him, and cried, Hosana: Blessed is the King
of Israel that cometh in the name of the Lord. And Jesus, when he had
found a young ass, sat thereon; as it is written, Fear not, daughter of
Sion: Behold, thy King cometh, sitting on an ass's colt.

---

but the desire to see a miracle did not open any door whatever
in Jesus' mind.

We see here the apex of Jesus' popularity. These people
were attracted by the raising of Lazarus and underneath was a
fierce patriotism, a vivid hope for the social and political liber-
ation of their country by this great prophet. They wanted to expel the Romans and gain independence and national self-respect.
they would gladly endure any suffering and make any sacrifice
Here at last was a man who could lead them to victory.

Jesus took no interest in all this. He was absolutely sincere,
and it is impossible to suppose that He merely regarded their
ambitions as impossible for the moment, and therefore agitation
for them inexpedient. The gulf between His mind and theirs
was far deeper than that. Jesus worked for the personal regen-
eration of individuals. He wanted to give them eternal life.
Social and political rearrangements He seemed to regard as utterly valueless. The enthusiastic crowd offered Him no opportunity for His work and He did not even try to win their permanent allegiance so He could teach them later.

This attitude in Jesus comes as a good deal of a shock. Those
patriots longed to sacrifice themselves for ends which we reckon
as part of the fundamental righteousness of the universe. They
were trying to abolish wrongs which are among the fundamental
evils. For generations they had suffered the bitterly oppressive
rule of heathen overlords. It would seem that at least a word of
sympathy was due them.

Jesus here cuts so squarely across the whole mind pattern of
the West that it is very difficult for us to understand and more
difficult still to loyally follow Him. Stamped from the day of

These things understood not his disciples at the first: but when Jesus was glorified, then remembered they that these things were written of him, and that they had done these things unto him. The people therefore that was with him when he called Lazarus out of his grave, and raised him from the dead, bare record. For this cause the people also met him, for that they heard that he had done this miracle. The Pharisees therefore said among themselves, Perceive ye how ye prevail nothing? behold, the world is gone after him.

---

our birth in the modern nationalistic mold, we find it hard to throw overboard the whole conception of patriotism as we know it. Nor is it quite certain that Jesus' thought went as far as that. This is one of the questions that merge from any deep study of the Gospel of John. Unfortunately the answer does not emerge with it.

For this is a picture of Jesus the King. He Himself arranged for the donkey and the official entrance and so fulfilled the old prophecies, but He was not the sort of a king they wanted or expected. He was offering to the people of Jerusalem a Kingdom which they were at liberty to accept or reject as they wished. Kings do not usually rule in that way. The kingdoms of this world are filled with coercion.

We may gain a little insight into this question by reviewing the previous episode. Jesus stood before Lazarus' grave as a King. The whole scene radiates regal authority. The Bethany group which we admired so deeply is an example of Jesus ruling as King. This is a new sort of Kingdom. There is no coercion and no class superiority. Yet no Caesar ever ruled his subjects as Jesus rules His

No doubt, when that group is expanded to include millions, some organization will be necessary, but the essence of the Kingdom of Jesus is the harmonious interplay of human spirits united in their devotion to Jesus, and in their devotion to each other. The large group is just as possible as the small one, granted there is complete devotion to Jesus and to each other. Harmony and love and joy are the marks of the Kingdom of Heaven.

Episode 3

Jesus' Universal Vision

And there were certain Greeks among them that came up to worship at the feast: The same came therefore to Philip, which was of Bethsaida of Galilee, and desired him, saying, Sir, we would see Jesus. Philip cometh and telleth Andrew: and again Andrew and Philip tell Jesus.

And Jesus answered them, saying, The hour is come, that the Son of man should be glorified. Verily, verily, I say unto you, Except a corn of wheat fall into the ground and die, it abideth alone: but if it die, it bringeth forth much fruit. He that loveth his life shall lose it; and he that hateth his life in this world shall keep it unto life eternal. If any man serve me, let him follow me; and where I am, there shall also my servant be: if any man serve me, him will my Father honour.

We come to the final scene of this chapter, and so far as the world is concerned, this is the final scene of the book. Jesus is about to ascend His throne. When Jesus met His Greek visitors and was transfigured by His great vision, the cross was only a few hours away.

There are two startling things here. First, we are looking at the world, not the Jewish nation. "If I be lifted up I will draw all men unto me." "Now is the judgment of this world." "Now shall the prince of this world be cast out." No doubt Jesus' vision often took in the world. But the disciples did not capture that part of His thought and it does not appear in the records.

But there is a greater lesson than that. "The hour is come that the Son of man should be glorified." Jesus is about to ascend His throne. It was for this that He marched into Jerusalem as a King. It was for this that He allowed Mary to wipe His feet with her hair. Such devotion is for kings. Jesus did not give up His throne to accept the cross instead. The Cross is His throne. The Kingdom of Death and the Kingdom of Life, the Kingdom of Truth, the Kingdom of Suffering, the Kingdom of Redemption, the Kingdom of God. This King did not sit on His throne. He hung on it that Friday afternoon, the throne of divine reality Jesus Christ the ruler of the Kings of the earth.

Now is my soul troubled; and what shall I say? Father, save me from this hour: but for this cause came I unto this hour. Father, glorify thy name. Then came there a voice from heaven, saying, I have both glorified it, and will glorify it again. The people therefore that stood by, and heard it, said that it thundered: others said, An angel spake to him. Jesus answered and said, This voice came not because of me, but for our sakes. Now is the judgment of this world: now shall the prince of this world be cast out. And I, if I be lifted up from the earth, will draw all men unto me. This he said, signifying what death he should die.

And there was a terrible word added: "If any man would serve me, let him follow me. If any man serve me, him will the Father honor."

Jesus regarded the cross as the climax of His life's work. It saves us as we look at it. "As Moses lifted up the serpent in the wilderness even so must the Son of man be lifted up." All men did was look at that serpent, and that is all we can do with Jesus on the cross. What we see there changes us, but what do we see? We see, in the first place, how it is that God can forgive our sins instead of punishing us. That is an important thing to see. We see another thing, God loves us. Without the cross we could never be sure of that. Nature does not tell us that.

It was by the cross that God's love made the example and the sufferings and the teachings of Christ adequate for the salvation of all men. We owe to the Apostle Paul the clarity of our understanding that God's forgiveness of our sins depends upon Christ's sacrifice. The Christian experience of the West has been built largely on that foundation. But while Paul seems largely concerned with our guilty past, John seems concerned with God's provision for our eternal future. Eternal life is his word.

Here Christ gives eternal life to His followers and without question it was at the cross that Christ's separation from the Father was consummated, and with it His dedication to broken, defeated and helpless men. We will never penetrate to the depths of this accomplishment but even with our limitations we can see that Christ saves by "falling into the earth and dying," i. e. by complete self sacrifice.

The people answered him, We have heard out of the law that Christ abideth for ever: and how sayest thou, The Son of man must be lifted up? who is this Son of man? Then Jesus said unto them, Yet a little while is the light with you. Walk while ye have the light, lest darkness come upon you: for he that walketh in darkness knoweth not whither he goeth. While ye have light, believe in the light, that ye may be the children of light. These things spake Jesus, and departed, and did hide himself from them.

JESUS' TEACHING

Then Jesus six days before the passover came to Bethany, where Lazarus was which had been dead, whom he raised from the dead. There they made him a supper; and Martha served: but Lazarus was one of them that sat at the table with him. Then took Mary a pound of ointment of spikenard, very costly, and anointed the feet of Jesus, and wiped his feet with her hair: and the house was filled with the odour of the ointment. Then saith one of his disciples, Judas Iscariot, Simon's son, which should betray him, Why was not this ointment sold for three hundred pence, and given to the poor? This he said, not that he cared for the poor; but because he was a thief, and had the bag, and bare what was put therein. Then said Jesus, Let her alone: against the day of my burying hath she kept this. For the poor always ye have with you; but me ye have not always.

There are three sections in this chapter, and three lessons. The Bethany feast is the first. It is our most beautiful picture of Jesus. We see Jesus accepting the devotion and the gifts of three people. Each gift was accepted. Martha served and it was generous hospitality that she brought. Lazarus sat with Jesus in comradeship and love, and we can be sure that Jesus enjoyed that gift very much indeed. Mary's gift was one of the most beautiful acts of love that the entire Bible records.

These all show personal devotion to Jesus and each one of them cost money. Judas raised a question. It is a question of importance. We are inclined to answer it as John did on the basis of Judas' bad record, personally. However it is worth a moment's real thought. We face that same question very often. Judas wanted to take Mary's exquisite gift and sell it and donate the proceeds to the poor. It would have fed a good many people. Martha's gift of a large amount of expensive food might have been diverted to the poor, too. It would not have fed so

many, but it would have done something. Judas did not bring
that up. No doubt he was enjoying Martha's gift himself.

Jesus puts the stamp of priority on personal devotion to Himself. Jesus was one of the poor and His comradeship has lifted
them up ever since. Their personal relations to Jesus would
make every one of those at the feast real helpers of the poor from
that day forward, and that help would be personal comradeship
and love. Charity is a poor way to help anyone. We must give
ourselves.

And there were certain Greeks among them that came up to worship
at the feast: The same came therefore to Philip, which was of Bethsaida
of Galilee, and desired him, saying, Sir, we would see Jesus. Philip
cometh and telleth Andrew: and again Andrew and Philip tell Jesus.
And Jesus answered them, saying, The hour is come, that the Son of
man should be glorified. Verily, verily, I say unto you, Except a corn
of wheat fall into the ground and die, it abideth alone: but if it die, it
bringeth forth much fruit.

But the real lesson of this paragraph is not to be looked for
in Judas' question. Jesus sits here a King. Gifts of loyal subjects in His Kingdom were brought to Him that day. Gifts like
Mary's are not properly brought to any one except a king.

The second scene in this chapter also shows Jesus as King.
He is riding into Jerusalem on a donkey with a great crowd of
enthusiastic followers who hailed Him as their ruler. No one
can miss the feeling of kingship here. He was a monarch with
an impressive retinue. The Old Testament prophecies were fulfilled in that triumphal entry.

But here is one of the most puzzling episodes of Jesus' life.
His mind and that of His shouting followers were as far apart
as the poles. We have seen before that the conception of the
Messiah in the minds of the Pharisees was so far from Jesus'
mind that He refused to make use of the idea. He declined to
even discuss His Messiahship with them. We see the same situation here. What these men wanted their King to do and what
Jesus intended to do were diametrically opposed. They wanted
a military leader who would lead them to political independence,

and eventually to political domination of the world. A notion more abhorrent to Jesus would have been impossible to find.

Jesus was a different kind of king. He loved every Jew, but He loved every Roman too. What about patriotism? Was Jesus a patriot? The people who took Him into Jerusalem were full of fierce patriotism.

He that loveth his life shall lose it; and he that hateth his life in this world shall keep it unto life eternal. If any man serve me, let him follow me; and where I am, there shall also my servant me: if any man serve me, him will my Father honour. Now is my soul troubled; and what shall I say? Father, save me from this hour: but for this cause came I unto this hour.

Jesus took no interest in all this. Why? We regard patriotism as a capital virtue. Jesus seemed to feel that any man who has eternal life in his soul, whose motive comes from a vision of God's will and whose life objective is giving to others the blessing that God has given to him, can be injured by no external maladjustment whatever, and conversely that no possible material blessings can help in any significant way the man who is materialistic and self-centered.

This is perhaps a correct statement of Jesus' mind and of the truth with regard to mature men, but we would still think that the developing child can be bent in the right or the wrong direction by outside influences. A free and helpful environment must be important for them.

There is another thing that Jesus saw more clearly than we do. Is it possible that social and political institutions, however oppressive and evil, are really a reflection of the mind and desire of the people among whom they are found? If in a community where slavery exists the only desire of the slaves is to become slave drivers, the abolition of the institution of slavery will accomplish nothing. Where the working class is downtrodden and oppressed and hopes for nothing so much as for the time when it can rule society as a dominant minority, no possible reconstruction offers hope for real progress. Who knows?

This much we do know. Jesus saw no hope except in a change of people's hearts. He came to give men eternal life, and that is nothing less than changing them completely by means of the new birth. They would be new men and women then. The question is obvious. What of the long interim period when some of the citizens will be changed men and women with God's life in them, and some selfish and predatory?

Father, glorify thy name. Then came there a voice from heaven, saying, I have both glorified it, and will glorify it again. The people therefore that stood by, and heard it, said that it thundered: others said, An angel spake to him. Jesus answered and said, This voice came not because of me, but for your sakes. Now is the judgment of this world: now shall the prince of this world be cast out. And I, if I be lifted up from the earth, will draw al lmen unto me. This he said, signifying what death he should die.

It is here that we begin to understand Jesus as He teaches that the good things we dream of must grow. The new birth is a sudden thing, but after that the individual must grow in grace. And when we think of the Kingdom of God as a whole then it is evident that the principle of growth is still more important. "The Kingdom of Heaven is like leaven which a woman took and hid in three measures of meal." The Kingdom of God will eventually grow until it includes whole societies and whole states. That will take a long time.

Jesus longed to tell that shouting enthusiastic company some of these things. He wept over Jerusalem. Eventually He will rule communities and states. It is to be a universal Kingdom and an eternal one. How close to the thoughts of those shouting patriots Jesus thoughts were, and how very far away!

The great pageant moved forward and Jesus entered Jerusalem. "The hour is come," He said. For what? "For the Son of man to be glorified," that is, for the King to ascend His throne. "The hour." What hour? The hour when, after centuries and millenniums of preparation, God could send Jesus to hang on the cross, "God having spoken to the fathers in the prophets in divers manners and in divers portions hath at the end of these days spoken to us in His Son." It is a breath-taking picture, God coming down through the ages laying the necessary foundations, and clearing away the obstructions so His program can culminate in the cross.

The people answered him, We have heard out of the law that Christ abideth for ever: and how sayest thou, The Son of man must be lifted up? who is this Son of man? Then Jesus said unto them, Yet a little while is the light with you. Walk while ye have the light, lest darkness come upon you: for he that walketh in darkness knoweth not whither he goeth. While ye have light, believe in the light, that ye may be the children of light. These things spake Jesus, and departed, and did hide himself from them.

Where was this preparation? In the Hebrew nation, no doubt. But what about the magnificent ethics of the Greeks and the Romans? Plutarch's parallel gives us a wonderful picture of God working in those minds. But perhaps the preparation that God found necessary did not consist mostly of things that we can see and understand. There are more subtle things that grow slowly out of simple human association. Perhaps it took thousands of years to teach men to value each other as they should.

Jesus understood the world as we cannot understand it. In the midst of all the triumphant wickedness surrounding Him, amid all the little failing currents of good, in the midst of an apostasy in Israel that seems complete, Jesus stood, and as He looked over that shocking landscape of the human spirit and of human history, and said, "The hour is come, that the Son of man should be glorified."

If our first question is about the word "hour" our second takes up the word "glory." What glory? The glory of the cross. We would have supposed that being one with the Father must be Jesus' glory. Jesus felt otherwise. His glory He found in the cross, the glory of saving mankind by His suffering. The glory is in the suffering as well as in man's salvation, for if Jesus could have saved us without suffering there would have been no glory of that sort in it. There was public disgrace in the cross and much physical suffering. There was the spiritual suffering of having our sins wrapped around His exquisitely sensitive soul, but apparently it was His death that saved us. Its somber glory has illuminated the world from that day to this.

This teaching is difficult, so Jesus gives us a parable. "Except a grain of wheat fall into the earth and die, it abideth by itself alone, but if it die, it bringeth forth much fruit." Jesus Himself was such a grain of wheat. He was about to die. His followers, too, are in this category. In His case and in ours, fruit bearing depends absolutely on dying.

Only those organic things that partake of the nature of seeds bring forth fruit if they die. We will add a word to the parable and say that all those in whom the life of God dwells, as it did in Jesus, are, in this sense, seeds. This is a word to His followers. Jesus is not here outlining the path that leads into the Kingdom of God but for us who have God in our hearts, the word comes with great force, for the rule is absolute. Every one of these seeds that die brings forth fruit, and, lacking that death, there is no possibility of fruit for anyone.

We know more about the processes of death than people did in Jesus' time. We know that in the most literal way, barring the few cells that constitute the germ of that wheat grain, it is death in its most ordinary form of decay and disintegration that must set in before the germ can grow and become a plant and produce perhaps a hundred kernels. Protected from these processes of death the seed remains alone and useless, shut away from all real life and development.

This is an important and profound parable. Just how does it apply to us? We are like that seed. We have a spark of Jesus' own life in us. But that germ of life is surrounded by selfish ambitions and hopes and desires. They are all centered on our own happiness and development and reputation. The divine life grows by the absorption of all those aptitudes and capacities, but they die first. That is, we have to die to our selfish ambitions and point them toward God and our fellow men.

The terrifying thing about this is the absoluteness of it. Once this death occurs, and our abilities die and decay from our selfish point of view, once they are pointed toward God, fruit is as inevitable as the very will and laws of God. Without that breakdown and surrender of our ambitions, fruit is impossible. What we need is not efficient methods and adequate equipment. What we need is to die.

Jesus must have felt that when the necessary death has taken place, the possibilities of fruit bearing are immeasurable. He looked out over the earth with a faith that fairly staggers us. "Now (that I am about to die on the cross) is the judgment of this world." The Jewish nation was a small part in that vision. "Now is the prince of this world cast out." How we wish that we could see the world with Jesus' eyes, at least occasionally. On the day following the cross, or even the resurrection, the world did not seem any different. Evil was as triumphant as ever. The Pharisees were still in control.

But as God saw things everything was different. The Prince of this world had been cast out. It is difficult for us to grasp just what Jesus means here. We have been accustomed to think of Jesus' death on the cross as a propitiation, and there is no contradiction to that thought here, but the cross has many aspects and accomplishes many different things. Certainly the cross, God's supreme work and His supreme glory, reaches out to accomplish things that are beyond the utmost reach of our imagination. It accomplished the dethronement and casting out of this world's prince. Who that prince is, and just what his relation to us is, we would like to know.

Our curiosity is not gratified. God tells us nothing of these things. It is probably not important for us to know them. Jesus goes on to tell us what the cross will accomplish. "I, if I be lifted up, will draw all men unto me." After all, the other things are simply means to this end. We have already been told what Gods purpose in the cross is. It is the salvation of men. And the

cross was no feeble failure. Jesus, when He is lifted up on the
cross, will draw all men to Himself.

"I if I be lifted up will draw all men unto me." The glory
of that vision comes down to reinforce feeble faith in our day.
Jesus knew that disciples then, could gain such a resplendent
vision from no one but Him. Neither can we. To us as to them
He says, "Believe on the light, that ye may become sons of
light."

But though he had done so many miracles before them, yet they believed not on him: That the saying of Esaias the prophet might be fulfilled, which he spake, Lord, who hath believed our report? and to whom
hath the arm of the Lord been revealed? Therefore they could not believe, because that Esaias said again, He hath blinded their eyes, and
hardened their heart; that they should not see with their eyes, nor understand with their heart, and be converted, and I should heal them.
These things said Esaias, when he saw his glory, and spake of him.

Nevertheless among the chief rulers also many believed on him; but
because of the Pharisees they did not confess him, lest they should be
put out of the synagogue: For they loved the praise of men more than
the praise of God.

The author has come to the end of one section of his Gospel.
The account of Jesus' ministry to the public is finished. John
still has important things to tell us. A third of the Gospel is
taken up with them. He must tell us what Jesus taught the disciples on that last memorable evening just before He went to the
cross. The whole somber and glorious picture of the cross is
still to come, and above all, the account of the resurrection.

But the major message has been delivered. "These are written
that ye may believe that Jesus is the Christ the Son of God, and
that believing ye may have life in his name." These signs and
these teachings had been poured into the hearts of men and
women whom Jesus chose carefully. John has faithfully recorded them all.

It was not a record of success. The world had not believed at
all that Jesus is the Christ, the Son of God and they had not
made even a beginning in gaining life in Jesus' name. But this
result did not disturb Jesus and here we can see that it did not

disturb the writer of the Gospel. Evidently that is the way the program of God is carried out. The seed is planted, and to this planting Jesus gave careful attention. Then its eventual growth into faith and eternal life is only a matter of time, for the omnipotence of God is in those words that Jesus planted.

Jesus cried and said, He that believeth on me, believeth not on me, but on him that sent me. And he that seeth me seeth him that sent me. I am come a light into the world, that whosoever believeth on me should not abide in darkness. And if any man hear my words, and believe not, I judge him not: for I came not to judge the world, but to save the world. He that rejecteth me, and receiveth not my words, hath one that judgeth him: the word that I have spoken, the same shall judge him in the last day. For I have not spoken of myself; but the Father which sent me, he gave me a commandment, what I should say, and what I should speak. And I know that his commandment is life everlasting: whatsoever I speak therefore, even as the Father said unto me, so I speak.

This is a review of what Jesus had said, just as the preceding paragraph was a summary of what He had done. But the writer summarizes Jesus' teaching by quotations from Jesus' own mouth, and we see again how very important a part of Jesus' consciousness is this conviction that He came from the Father and represented Him in all that He did.

And the essence of His mission was to bring to us certain "words" from the Father. Those words were beautiful divine things. The power of God was in them. To follow Jesus' own thought here, the light of God was in them.

And the world that Jesus had come to save, had been given those "words." When the day of accounting comes, it is by those words that we all will be judged.

And so the writer of this Gospel closes one section of his Gospel, and prepares us for the next. He is anxious for us to follow the argument as he lays it down. Only so will the full impact of the message be felt, and belief and salvation follow.

JOHN 13

Now before the feast of the passover, when Jesus knew that his hour was come that he should depart of this world unto the Father, having loved his own which were in the world, he loved them unto the end. And Supper being ended, the devil having now put into the heart of Judas Iscariot, Simon's son, to betray him; Jesus knowing that the Father had given all things into his hands, and that he was come from God, and went to God; He riseth from supper, and laid aside his garments; and took a towel, and girded himself. After that he poureth water into a basin, and began to wash the disciples' feet, and wipe them with the towel wherewith he was girded. Then cometh he to Simon Peter: and Pete saith unto him, Lord, dost thou wash my feet? Jesus answered and said unto him, What I do thou knowest not now; but thou shalt know hereafter. Peter saith unto him, Thou shalt never wash my feet. Jesus answered him, If I wash thee not, thou hast no part with me. Simon Peter saith unto him, Lord, not my feet only, but also my hands and my head. Jesus saith to him, He that is washed needeth not save to wash his feet, but is clean every whit: and ye are clean, but not all. For he knew who should betray him; therefore said he, Ye are not all clean. So after he had washed their feet, and had taken his garments, and was set down again, he said unto them, Know ye what I have done to you? Ye call me Master and Lord: and ye say well; for so I am. If I then, your Lord and Master, have washed your feet; ye also ought to wash one another's feet. For I have given you an example, that ye should do as I have done to you. Verily, verily, I say unto you, The servant is not greater than his lord; neither he that is sent greater than he that sent him. If ye know these things, happy are ye if ye do them.

I speak not of you all: I know whom I have chosen: but that the Scripture may be fulfilled, He that eateth bread with me hath lifted up his heel against me. Now I tell you before it come, that, when it is come to pass, ye may believe that I am he. Verily, verily, I say unto you, He that receiveth whomsoever I send receiveth me; and he that receiveth me receiveth him that sent me. When Jesus had thus said, he was troubled in spirit, and testified, and said, Verily, verily, I say unto you, that one of you shall betray me. Then the disciples looked one on another, doubting of whom he spake. Now there was leaning on Jesus' bosom one of his disciples, whom Jesus loved. Simon Peter therefore beckoned to him, that he should ask who it should be of whom he spake. He then lying on Jesus' breast saith unto him, Lord, who is it? Jesus answered, He it is, to whom I shall give a sop, when I have dipped it. And when he had dipped the sop, he gave it to Judas Iscariot, the son of Simon. And after the sop Satan entered into him. Then said Jesus unto him, That thou doest, do quickly. Now no man at the table knew what intent he spake this unto him. For some of them thought, because Judas had the bag, that Jesus had said unto him, Buy those things that we have need of against the feast; or, that he should give something to the poor. He then, having received the sop, went immediately out; and it was night.

Therefore, when he was gone out, Jesus said, Now is the Son of man glorified, and God is glorified in him. If God be glorified in him, God shall also glorify him in himself, and shall straightway glorify him. Little children, yet a little while I am with you. Ye shall seek me; and as I said unto the Jews, Whither I go, ye cannot come; so now I say to you. A new commandment I give unto you, That ye love one another; as I have loved you, that ye also love one another. By this shall all men know that ye are my disciples, if ye have love one to another.

Simon Peter said unto him, Lord, Whither goest thou? Jesus answered him, Whither I go, thou canst not follow me now; but thou shalt follow me afterwards. Peter said unto him, Lord, why cannot I follow thee now? I will lay down my life for thy sake. Jesus answered him, Wilt thou lay down thy life for my sake? Verily, verily, I say unto thee, The cock shall not crow, till thou hast denied me thrice.

Chapter XIII

THE PICTURE

Now before the feast of the passover, when Jesus knew that his hour was come that he should depart out of this world unto the Father, having loved his own which were in the world, he loved them unto the end. And supper being ended, the devil having now put into the heart of Judas Iscariot, Simon's son, to betray him; Jesus knowing that the Father had given all things into his hands, and that he was come from God, and went to God; He riseth from supper, and laid aside his garments; and took a towel, and girded himself. After that he poureth water into a basin, and began to wash the disciples' feet, and to wipe them with the towel wherewith he was girded.

With chapter 13 we enter a new section of the Gospel. Jesus is talking to the disciples. It is the evening before the crucifixion. Jesus knew that His hour had come. In a little more than twelve hours, He would be hanging on the cross. He was departing out of this world unto the Father.

There were many things that we might suppose would be on Jesus' mind under such circumstances. Apprehension, a strained determination to carry through the enormously difficult and trying tasks just ahead and joy at the approaching reunion with his Father. That would be on a divine scale. Now, at long last, He would be free from the unutterable weariness of His uncomprehending disciples. Most of all, escape from the bitter and murderous hostility of the Pharisees. It comes as a revelation from the throne of God with the fragrance and beauty of Heaven in it to see that Jesus here is not thinking of any of these things. His mind is filled with grief at the approaching separation from His beloved disciples. They had not been very good disciples, and they had been slow to learn, but they loved Jesus sincerely, and what is vastly more important, He loved them.

Then cometh he to Simon Peter: and Peter saith unto him, Lord, dost thou wash my feet?   Jesus answered and said unto him, What I do thou knowest not now; but thou shalt know hereafter.   Peter saith unto him, Thou shalt never wash my feet.   Jesus answered him, If I wash thee not, thou hast no part with me.   Simon Peter saith unto him, Lord, not my feet only, but also my hands and my head.   Jesus saith to him, He that is washed needeth not save to wash his feet, but is clean every whit: and ye are clean, but not all.   For he knew who should betray him; therefore said he, Ye are not all clean.   So after he had washed their feet, and had taken his garments, and was set down again, he said unto them, Know ye what I have done to you?   Ye call me Master and Lord: and ye say well; for so I am.

We will not grasp the lesson of this chapter until we have realized something of the depth and intensity of Jesus' love for the disciples. "As my Father hath loved me, even so have I loved you." The love of a mother or a father for their children is what we must have in mind here. Jesus' love was even far greater than that.

Jesus loved them. Inside He was full of tears, for He was going away and He was going to leave them alone. His soul yearned for some avenue of expression for that love. He found it. The supper was half over, and it occurred to Him that their feet had not been washed. Washing a visitor's feet after he came in from outside was something done for rich men. They had slaves to do it. In a company such as this, the lowest man in the company might be expected to do it, but if there was no one who wanted to be considered the lowest, then it would not be done, and probably its omission would not be noted or commented upon. Jesus saw an opportunity to show His love for them, so He rose from supper and laid aside His outer garment, poured some water into a basin and went from one to another of the reclining disciples, knelt down at each pair of feet and washed them with His hands. He dried them with the long towel which was tied around Him.

I remember a personal experience like that. When I was at home from the University on a vacation, my father brought up a

If I then, your Lord and Master, have washed your feet; ye also ought to wash one another's feet. For I have given you an example, that ye should do as I have done to you. Verily, verily, I say unto you, The servant is not greater than his lord; neither he that is sent greater than he that sent him. If ye know these things, happy are ye if ye do them.

I speak not of you all: I know whom I have chosen: but that the Scripture may be fulfilled, He that eateth bread with me hath lifted up his heel against me. Now I tell you before it come, that, when it is come to pass, we may believe that I am he. Verily, verily, I say unto you, He that receiveth whomsoever I send receiveth me; and he that receiveth me receiveth him that sent me.

---

glass of water and put it on the little stand next to my bed, just as I was going to sleep. I do not drink water through the night even now, and did not then. It was an almost involuntary act of pure love. He did it just because he loved me and the impression it made is vivid to this day. Jesus, when He washed the disciples' feet, showed His love for them in much the same way. And it had the same effect. *Seventy* years later when John wrote out the events of that memorable night, his first and most vivid recollection was Jesus washing their feet.

We realize here as we have so many times, what a vivid teller of stories the writer of this Gospel is. The dramatic and vivid details are all here. Jesus knew that the Father had given all things into His hands, and that He came from God and was going to God. To John that was part of the dramatic scene, and surely it is so to us.

And because it was a dramatic scene, all the details remained in his mind. He could not forget one of them, how Jesus rose from supper, laid aside His outer garment, girded Himself with a towel, poured water into a basin and washed the feet of the reclining disciples.

Questions spring up, profound questions and difficult ones. Judas was in that company. Did Jesus love him as He did the others? Probably more, as had been the case with wayward children so many times. Peter too, was tremendously impressed by the sight of Jesus' washing those feet, and the lesson was never

When Jesus had thus said, he was troubled in spirit, and testified, and said, Verily, verily, I say unto you, that one of you shall betray me. Then the disciples looked one on another, doubting of whom he spake. Now there was leaning on Jesus' bosom one of his disciples, whom Jesus loved. Simon Peter therefore beckoned to him, that he should ask who it should be of whom he spake. He then lying on Jesus' breast saith unto him, Lord, who is it? Jesus answered, He it is, to whom I shall give a sop, when I have dipped it. And when he had dipped the sop, he gave it to Judas Iscariot, the son of Simon. And after the sop Satan entered unto him. Then said Jesus unto him, That thou doest, do quickly.

---

forgotten. "Gird yourselves with humility," he wrote decades afterward as he remembered it all.

Jesus usually let His example have its effect, without any moralizing afterward. That example had been transforming the disciples for months and years. But this time He did not leave them to work the lesson out for themselves. He explained it in terms that could not be misunderstood. If I have washed your feet, you ought to wash one another's feet." This is the lesson Dr. Sheldon put into the book, *IN HIS STEPS*, and Dr. Clark into, *WHAT WOULD JESUS DO?* No doubt there are times when, "What would Jesus have me do?" is a better question. But it leaves a big loophole where we can crawl out of difficult requirements. There is no loophole here. "Ye ought to wash one another's feet."

It is worth noting that Jesus had Judas in mind very specifically when He said this to them. He knew that Judas was disloyal, and the question arises, "Why was Judas not put out of the disciples' circle long ago?" Jesus was still trying to win him no doubt, and it was good discipline for the others to have him among them. That was really a difficult lesson, telling the disciples to wash Judas' feet.

John is a dramatist, and so here, right next to the loveliest scene of the evening, he puts the most dreadful and pathetic portrait of the entire New Testament gallery. Something had happened to Judas. We do not know what. Jesus loved him and washed his feet, and longed to reach him. But Judas was lost.

He had separated himself from the company in his heart, apparently some time before, and now he was waiting for an opportunity to betray his Master into the hands of His murderers. Doubtless he was sincere and earnest when Jesus admitted him to the circle of the disciples. It is a very terrifying thing to see Judas taken away, out of Jesus' arms almost, by the insidious sublety of sin.

What happened to Judas? What started him on the downward road? We are not told, but there is a hint that it was the common sin of avarice. It seems simply incredible that avarice could defeat the very grace of God as embodied in Jesus, and wreck Judas before Jesus' own eyes. Jesus might have dismissed him long since, but He did not. He loved Judas, but all His efforts were unavailing. Judas was gone.

But he was there in physical presence. Jesus washed his feet and handed him a morsel of bread dipped in gravy, a graceful gesture of regard and affection in Arabia to this day. "Mangoola," says the Arab host to his favored guest as he hands the morsel to him which means, "Presented." "Makboola," that is "Accepted," says the guest. And having accepted this last evidence of affection, Judas went out to arrange the betrayal of the Master who loved him so much. And, reaching depths of sin unrecorded anywhere else, he betrayed Him with a kiss.

We will never understand Judas, but recent events in India have made him a little less incredible. The impression is that in Judas we are looking at a fierce nationalist, burning for his country, and demanding for its political independence. He looked for the kingdom of God and at first supposed that Jesus had come to usher it in. Now Jesus *had* come to bring in the Kingdom of God.

And so Judas passed day after day and week after week, becoming more and more devoted to the fierce Jewish nationalism of the day, and at the same time seeing more and more clearly the beauty of Jesus' vision of the Kingdom. There is a curious

Now no man at the table knew for what intent he spake this unto him. For some of them thought, because Judas had the bag, that Jesus had said unto him, Buy those things that we have need of against the feast; or, that he should give something to the poor. He then having received the sop went immediately out: and it was night.

Therefore, when he was gone out, Jesus said, Now is the Son of man glorified, and God is glorified in him. If God be glorified in him, God shall also glorify him in himself, and shall straightway glorify him. Little children, yet a little while I am with you. Ye shall seek me; and as I said unto the Jews, Whither I go, ye cannot come; so now I say to you.

---

phrase here — "After the morsel, Satan entered into him." By this time Judas must have been a sort of spiritual Dr. Jekyll and Mr. Hyde. Sitting under the charm of Jesus at the table, and drawn by His love, we can suppose that for that moment Judas was a follower again.

But when Jesus gave him the morsel, something snapped inside of him and his whole soul revolted against this pallid idea of goodness, this stultifying surrender to their enemies. He went out to pit his whole self against Jesus. He saw now that the different visions which he had served at different moments of his life were utterly antithetical. He did not simply dissociate himself from Jesus, He betrayed Him in cold blood to His murderers, and, depth of all infamies, did it with a kiss!

For those of us acquainted with the Middle East such an outcome is not so unbelievable as it once was, for something similar happened to Ghandi. He was murdered by one of his own fellow Hindus, a man previously a great admirer of him. But the gentle and essentially Christian vision of a non-resisting India held by Ghandi, was flatly opposed to the bitter, intolerant, murderous India of his man's dreams, and so Ghandi was murdered by one of the colleagues of his own house, just as Jesus was.

We come away from a study of Judas with a feeling of terror in our hearts. Who is safe in his present faith and position and grace? No one. Let us therefore keep our souls with diligence, close to Jesus and His thoughts, lest avarice or some other sin becomes our undoing.

A new commandment I give unto you, That ye love one another; as I
have loved you, that ye also love one another. By this shall all men
know that ye are my disciples, if ye have love one to another. Simon
Peter said unto him, Lord, whither goest thou? Jesus answered him,
Whither I go, thou canst not follow me now; but thou shalt follow me
afterwards. Peter said unto him, Lord, why cannot I follow thee now?
I will lay down my life for thy sake. Jesus answered him, Wilt thou lay
down my life for my sake? Verily, verily, I say unto thee, The cock
shall not crow, till thou hast denied me thrice.

Through the evening Jesus sat with them, explaining to them
the new things He wanted them to understand. Questions interrupted Him repeatedly, but this did not disturb Him. Jesus liked
to teach that way. Even when He faced hostile crowds that was
His method. His grief over leaving them and His love for them
are like a heavenly fragrance in the account, even now.

He opened to them the truth about the Holy Spirit, the Comforter, the Spirit of truth. They understood very little of it at the
moment, but they remembered it, and that was all that was
necessary. The Church has been meditating on those things ever
since, and they have been our constitution. Fierce and earnest
souls have added to this divine constitution and led great sections
of the Church astray. Blood and tears and suffering accompany
the purification which God in His power always brings to pass
afterwards. Cold and sceptical souls have subtracted from that
divine code, and have led many astray. God always sees to it
that the vacant places are filled up again.

The perils of the Church come from its "friends" much more
than from its enemies. Because God in His omnipotence is in
the church, the gates of Hell will never prevail against it. But
from within deterioration can set in and its faith become weak
and its love cold. The disintegration begins as our love for the
brethren becomes cold or even changes to hatred. The worst
trouble comes from the fierce, determined spirits that add to this
constitution, and make discipleship depend on things unmentioned
by Jesus. They "teach as their doctrines the precepts of men."
From all such Good Lord deliver us.

Jesus Teaching a New Commandment

A new commandment I give unto you, That ye love one another; as I have loved you, that ye also love one another.

These chapters finish John's presentation of Jesus' teaching. They record a long talk with the disciples just before He left them. His previous teachings had been for the general public. In them He described the New Order, the Kingdom of God, and in this way drew men into it. It was the message of His Heavenly Father for the world.

This talk had a different purpose. It was given to men already members of the Kingdom, to guide and strengthen them in it. This is the charter of the Church. It is more than that, it is the constitution of His Church. Jesus had His mind on the centuries to come, and the constitution which He gave us has never been supplemented or changed. It is valid to this day. No doubt, for the world as a whole the most important things that Jesus said are in the first lessons, those we have studied from chapter 2 through chapter 12. But for us who are members of His Church, these chapters are equally important, indeed more so.

Like many of Jesus' discourses this talk was interrupted and its thought dislocated again and again by questions from the puzzled listeners. Jesus' approaching departure cast its shadow over the group, and the unexpressed grief of strong men appears and reappears throughout the account, like a recurring phrase in a symphony.

This was Jesus' farewell to the disciples. He had a good many things He wanted to say to them. The first was an immediate derivative of the object lesson He had just given. He had washed their feet, and the humility and live which found expression in that surprising service was to remain vividly in mind to their dying day.

Therefore, when he was gone out, Jesus said, Now is the Son of man glorified, and God is glorified in him. If God be glorified in him, God shall also glorify him in himself, and shall straightway glorify him.

John mentions a second introductory teaching. Its connection with the main lesson of the evening is not so evident, but it was put in so we may be sure that he thought it important. Perhaps Jesus hoped that by placing this teaching in the very shadow of the cross, as we might say, its importance would be emphasized.

"Now," said He, "is the Son of man glorified, and God is glorified in him, and he will glorify him at once." When Jesus said this with the supper over, and the evening wearing away, not more than six hours distant He saw the cross in all its somber, dreadful glory. Jesus was to suffer on that cross. By His death there, men were to be redeemed. Where is the glory in such a forbidding spectacle? In the suffering? In the death? In the redemption? That is not for us to say, inasmuch as Jesus did not explain that, but the lesson of the paragraph is that the cross is Jesus' glory, and it is God's.

But the disciples did not see anything glorious in the cross. It was the sign and the means of the approaching separation from their beloved Master. Jesus did not try to divert their attention, nor to change their feeling of loneliness and grief. The lesson He had in mind stemmed directly from that loneliness. He wanted them to give very careful and intense attention to their relations to one another.

If ye love me, keep my commandments. . . . He that hath my commandments, and keepeth them, he it is that loveth me: and he that loveth me shall be loved of my Father, and I will love him, and will manifest myself to him. . . . Jesus answered and said unto him, If a man love me, he will keep my words: and my Father will love him, and we will come unto him, and make our abode with him.

Everything in their lives would be changed after His departure, their relations to God, their relations to the world, everything. But He was not thinking of those things just now. It was their relations to each other which were of supreme importance. Why He left all mention of this till the last moment is not easy to see. And at first it is not easy for us to see why Jesus considered this new commandment so very important. It was a new teaching, but to a large extent it had been implied in what He had taught them before. But in Jesus' mind literally everything depended on it. He reveals here an unexplored realm of Christian obligation and experience, the existence of which the disciples had scarcely suspected before. No doubt they understood that they were not to hate each other, but love of the sort that Jesus wanted them to show was a thing that probably seemed to them to show was a thing that probably seemed to them completely out of reach. We in our day are not very different.

It is easy to imagine that the disciples, when they first heard this new commandment from Jesus' lips, were puzzled and a little annoyed to have their grief and loneliness dislocated and jarred by such a commandment.

As the Father hath loved me, so have I loved you: continue ye in my love. If ye keep my commandments, ye shall abide in my love; even as I have kept my Father's commandments, and abide in his love. . . . This is my commandment, That ye love one another, as I have loved you.

Our first realization of the depth and almost impossible intensity of the love Jesus was asking for, comes when we realize that He wanted them to love each other with a love like His own. He had lived for the disciples and He was about to die for them. He looked forward to the coming separation with grief. Jesus' love for the disciples was a deep and infinite thing.

Love is the one characteristic of Jesus' Kingdom. God Himself is love, the writer of this Gospel said later. His Kingdom is love. Upon that love the universe is built. The new life which had grown up in their hearts is simply love growing stronger and stronger.

The disciples probably understood that much then, as we do today. But there was one thing which they did not understand, and to this day we scarcely do.

Jesus puts all His authority behind this new commandment. There is no assumption here. There is no advice. It is a command. Nothing Jesus ever told the disciples received as much emphasis as He puts into this. All the disciples' love for Him He marshals in its support. "The man who loves me, keeps my commandment," says Jesus. "This is my commandment, that ye love one another."

And Jesus' love for each disciple is to be measured by that disciple's love for the brethren, unattractive and unlovely as they may be. To the disciples at this time probably nothing appeared as important as abiding in Jesus' love. They made no mistake there, and the path before them was plain. They were to gain this love and measure its depth and intensity for themselves by their love for one another. "By this," said Jesus, "shall all men know that ye are my disciples." Those who love one another were henceforth, through all the days of separation and reunion as well, His friends, entering into His own counsel and purpose. As friends they are sent out into the great cooperative task of saving the world.

As has been said, it is hard to see why all mention of so important a matter was left until the very last moment. For its importance is very great indeed. We have here the third great characteristic of the new order. We have seen how men are to find their life's motive in doing the Father's will. We have seen that their life objective is devotion to men and their salvation. Here is the third great lesson. Our quickened emotional love is to be directed toward the brethren, shoulder to shoulder, with whom we work and struggle and suffer.

Nowhere is self-deception easier than here. How much did Jesus love the brethren? As different as they were from Him psychologically, as untrained and childish as they were in mind, and as hard and unteachable in spirit, Jesus loved them, loved them so much that He rejoiced to associate with them. He looked forward with a breaking heart to separation from them, and correspondingly with joy to the day when they would be reunited for all eternity.

This is the last great territory of duty and privilege that Jesus opens to members of the new order. It is the most difficult of them all. Men who have surrendered to God are not nearly so numerous as they should be, but they are not rare. They can be found in some numbers the world over. It is the easiest of the three great surrenders. Believers who can add to that a complete devotion to their fellow men are a far smaller company. Scattered over the earth they are seen as lights in the world.

The rarest of all are those unusual saints who have added to these two loyalties a love for the brethren such as Jesus wants us to show. Nothing is going to make this an easy matter, but it is a help to see it through Jesus' eyes, and gain some faint notion of its importance. It is the indication of our love for Jesus and the measure of His love for us. It is the condition of success of His work, and the one road to His friendship. We are to see in chapter 17 that the world's redemption depends on it.

Greater love hath no man than this, that a man lay down his life for his friends. Ye are my friends, if ye do whatsoever I command you. Henceforth I call you not servants; for the servant knoweth not what his lord doeth: but I have called you friends; for all things that I have heard of my Father I have made known unto you. Ye have not chosen me, but I have chosen you, and ordained you, that ye should go and bring forth fruit, and that your fruit should remain; that whatsoever ye shall ask of the Father in my name, he may give it you. These things I command you, that ye love one another.

There were three or four other lessons which Jesus wanted to give the disciples, but first and most important is this one about love, the love to each other of the sort that Jesus Himself had shown to them. This love was more important than appears at first sight. As the discussion developed it was natural that they should think of their love for Jesus. He had led them for three years, and they loved Him very deeply. At the moment it seemed to them that nothing in this world or the next was as important as keeping up this love, preserving it through the days to come.

Jesus goes still further before He is through. "As my father hath loved me, even so have I loved you. Abide ye in my love." Nothing on earth or in heaven seemed as important to the disciples then as abiding in Jesus' love. God loved the world, and Jesus loved the world so much that He gave His life for it. No

matter what we do or do not do, we will never get away from
that love. But the love that Jesus is speaking about here is a
very different thing. It is the love that He is anxious to direct
toward the disciples if only their attitude and love and obedience
make such a thing possible.

Here again we meet the same surprising teaching: "If ye keep
my commandments, ye shall abide in my love, as I have kept
my Father's commandments and abide in his love." But we learn
something further. This is the end of the discussion. All of
it has been based on that first statement. Here we meet it again,
summing up the entire argument. "This is my commandment
that ye love one another."

A few minutes spent in considering this little verse is like
opening a window which reveals a new and beautiful and forbidding landscape of duty and privilege, of fellowship with
God, and of relations with our brethren. Literally everything
hangs on this. On what? On our love for one another. This is
the commandment that Jesus has in mind when He says, "He that
hath my commandments and keepeth them, he it is that loveth
me." The love that we can show toward our brethren is the
precise measure of our love for Christ. No matter what our self-
deceit may assert, and how we may exult in a supposed direct
love for Jesus, this is the measure of that love, and there is
no other.

And if this is not disturbing enough, here is something worse.
Our love for the brethren is the precise measure of the love that
Jesus can feel toward us. How much does Jesus love us? There
is no mystery about the answer to that question. How much do
we love our brethren? In Bahrain there used to be a great well
to which everybody might come to get water. It was free for all.
I have seen men come with a tiny cup, and got the cup full of
water, and I have seen men come with a great barrel hauled on
wheels by a strong donkey. They received a barrel full. We bring
our own measure to Jesus. He fills it up with His love. But the
man who cannot love the brethren goes away empty, and how

many, how many can only love their brethren, a little. It is dreadful to know that so much, no more and no less, is Jesus' love for them.

Jesus turns from His discussion of the new commandment to a careful explanation of the disciples' relationship to Him in the future.

JOHN 14

Let not your heart be troubled: ye believe in God, believe also in me. In my Father's house are many mansions: if it were not so, I would have told you. I go to prepare a place for you. And if I go and prepare a place for you, I will come again, and receive you unto myself; that where I am, there ye may also be. And whither I go ye know, and the way ye know. Thomas saith unto him, Lord, we know not whither thou goest; and how can we know the way? Jesus saith unto him, I am the the truth, and the life: no man cometh unto the Father, but by me. If ye had known me, ye should have known my Father also: and from henceforth ye know him, and have seen him. Philip saith unto him, Lord, shew us the Father, and it sufficeth us. Jesus saith unto him, Have I been so long time with you, and yet hast thou not known me, Philip? he that hath seen me hath seen the Father; and how sayest thou then, Shew us the Father? Believest thou not that I am in the Father and the Father in me? the words that I speak unto you I speak not of myself: but the Father that dwelleth in me, he doeth the work. Believe me that I am in the Father, and the Father in me: or else believe me for the very works' sake. Verily, verily, I say unto you, He that believeth on me, the works that I do shall he do also; and greater works than these shall he do; because I go unto my Father. And whatsoever ye shall ask in my name, that will I do, that the Father may be glorified in the Son. If ye shall ask any thing in my name, I will do it.

If ye love me, keep my commandments. And I will pray the Father, and he shall give you another Comforter, that he may abide with you for ever; Even the Spirit of truth; whom the world cannot receive, because it seeth him not, neither knoweth him: but ye know him; for he dwelleth with you, and shall be in you. I will not leave you comfortless: I will come to you. Yet a little while, and the world seeth me no more; but ye see me; because I live, ye shall live also. At that day ye shall know that I am in my Father, and ye in me, and I in you. He that hath my commandments, and keepth them, he it is that loveth me shall be loved of my Father, and I will love him, and will manifest myself to him. Judas saith unto him, not Iscariot, Lord, how is it that thou wilt manifest thyself unto us, and not unto the world? Jesus answered and said unto him, If a man love me, he will keep my words; and my Father will love him, and we will come unto him, and make our abode with him. He that loveth me not keepeth not my sayings: and the word which ye hear is not mine, but the Father's which sent me. These things have I spoken unto you, being yet present with you. But the Comforter, which is the Holy Ghost whom the Father will send in my name, he shall teach ye all things, and bring all things to your rememberance, whatsoever I have said unto you. Peace I leave with you, my peace I give unto you: not as the world giveth, give I unto you. Let not your heart be troubled, neither let it be afraid. Ye have heard how I said unto you, I go away, and come again unto you. If ye loved me, ye would rejoice, because I said, I go unto the Father: for my Father is greater than I. And now I have told you before it come to pass, that, when it is come to pass, ye might believe. Hereafter I will not talk much with you: for the prince of this world cometh, and hath nothing in me. But that the world may know that I love the Father; and as the Father gave me commandment, even so I do. Arise, let us go hence.

Chapter XIV

THE LESSON ON FAITH

Let not your heart be troubled: ye believe in God, believe also in me. In my Father's house are many mansions: if it were not so, I would have told you. I go to prepare a place for you.

Peter was puzzled by this talk of Jesus' going away. He wanted to go, too. His heart was filled with love for Jesus. He was willing to lay his life down if necessary. There is a tinge of sternness and more than a tinge of grief in Jesus' reply. "The cock shall not crow till thou has denied me three times." And Jesus did not stop to try to fortify Peter for his coming test. Perhaps it was better that Peter learn the lessons of humility the hard way.

For Jesus still had much ground to cover with the disciples and the time was short. The cross was not *twelve* hours away. He had given them His first and most tremendous lesson on love. Now He must say something about faith. Jesus had taught the disciples a good deal about faith in God as He led them along the paths and through the villages of the Holy Land. But now He was going away and they were to be left alone. It was important that their love for the Master should continue through the days and the centuries to come. Scarcely less important was the matter of their faith. Not simply their faith in God. That, Jesus, wanted them to maintain. He mentions it first. "Believe in God." But a new need was emerging. It was a matter of great importance that in addition to their faith in God they have a firm faith in Jesus Himself.

This poses a very difficult problem, indeed a whole series of problems. "Believe in God, believe also in me." We understand immediately that Jesus is talking of two similar types of faith. Our faith in Jesus is to be like our faith in God.

Jesus goes on to tell the disciples just what He wanted the content of this faith to be. For some, that first item must have been difficult. They were to believe that Jesus' leadership took

And if I go and prepare a place for you, I will come again, and receive you unto myself; that where I am, there ye may be also. And whither I go ye know, and the way ye know.

---

them now and led them straight out into eternity, beyond the other side of the grave. They were His followers now. His de-parture did not change this. They were still to be His followers. He is to be with them forever. The path of duty had been simple and plain up to this time. It was not easy. They had found it hard. But it was not a perplexing thing. For them God's will was nothing more nor less than following Jesus. They had left everything so they could follow, and Jesus had become their leader and teacher, their master and friend. For a few months and years they had based their whole lives upon loyalty to Him and in that loyalty they had found eternal life. But this new and wonderful world in which they moved, depended upon their daily association with Jesus. What would they do when He was gone, what sort of lives would they live then? How could they maintain their touch with God?

Jesus' reply was simple. He told them that they had made no mistake. The essence of the new life which they had found was association with Him. They were thinking of their associa-tion as temporary, and the separation as permanent. The exact opposite was true. Their association with Him was permanent. It would continue through eternity. The separation was a temp-orary thing made necessary by matters which He did not stop to explain. He was going away to prepare a place where they could be together forever. Once the significance of this becomes clear we are thankful for Peter's disturbing question. We in our day gain from this message just what Jesus intended the dis-ciples to gain from it. A little later Jesus told them of the provision for the time of separation, but here He did not con-fuse them with these things. He comforted their hearts and doubt-less His own as well with the assurance that the separation was to be short. An eternal reunion lay on the other side of a few years of loneliness and perplexity and struggle.

This has been water for the thirsty through the years that have followed. However dark the future may have looked to the disciples with Jesus gone, they could not foresee more than the smallest fraction of the troubles which were to come. Their own difficulties and perplexities were to be serious enough. Confusion and conflict over creed and ritual and organization arose almost at once. But what of the man who first learned of Jesus a thousand years later, when in the place of eye witnesses nothing was left except a few meager records, and in the place of personal memories, vague and impossible traditions? The centuries have built up such a structure of church organization and theological creed as would have petrified the disciples with dismay, if they could have seen it then.

Voices have never been lacking to assure us that these developments are necessary and desirable, that Jesus' message can be preserved in no other way, but there is a stubborn instinct which insists that they are pathological, signs of disease. Jesus delivered a message that was simple and easy to understand. Most people refused to follow Him, but perplexity kept no one away. Moreover, that simplicity seemed to be what He wanted. He gave no indication that He wished the erection of an elaborate ecclesiastical structure such as we see today. He did not seek the formulation of exact creeds. He outlined no methods of efficient church organization. How can we get back to the simplicity of Jesus? The door opens to us here. This gem was given to the disciples so that they might know that the beautiful simplicity of their faith was not to end with Jesus' departure. After the days of separation, the old relations were to be resumed forever.

If the disciples needed that message to comfort their breaking hearts, we need it even more. Men of Jesus' time were not unique in being able to enter the Kingdom of God by means of simple loyalty to Jesus. We enter just as they did. Like them we have chosen association with Jesus as our destiny, and for us, too, the days of perplexed following through the fog are only a few.

Philip saith unto him, Lord, shew us the Father, and it sufficeth us. Jesus saith unto him, Have I been so long time with you, and yet hast thou not known me, Philip? he that hath seen me hath seen the Father; and how sayest thou then, Shew us the Father?

The assurance that steadied and comforted the disciples can do the same for us. We are to follow Jesus the best we can, through the fogs and difficulties of our increasingly difficult environment. Some will have more pentrating vision than others, but all will one day come out into intimate, unclouded, personal association to live in the sunlight of Jesus' immediate presence forever.

This vision of Jesus, the shepherd of His disciples forever, is the second of the things Jesus wanted them to believe. It was new. About all that Jesus had taught them regarding the next world was that God the Heavenly Father was there. That is all He tells them here except that He Himself is to be there too, and they with Him as His disciples forever.

In the discussion that followed, Jesus took the questions as they came. No doubt many irrevelant ones are omitted from the account that John has given us. Some of the irrelevancies he had forgotten, and if he remembered them, he left them out.

The discussion that John does put in next, is one of the most important of all. Pure bliss in Heaven at Jesus' feet was doubtless in prospect, but in the meantime there were many years ahead of hard struggles in this very imperfect world. Just what was to be the content of the disciples' faith in that difficult period? Jesus' statement is a model of brevity and completeness. We are to believe that Jesus is "the way and the truth and the life." It is essential. "No man cometh unto the Father but by me."

I Am the Way

Thomas saith unto him, Lord, we know not whither thou goest; and how can we know the way? Jesus saith unto him, I am the way, the truth, and the life: no man cometh unto the Father, but by me.

This is one of Jesus' profound and final statements, an important part of what He wanted the disciples to believe. Palestine was full of paths and roads, big and little. They were all "ways" for people to walk in as they went from one place to another.

Jesus and His disciples were on the road often. A number of His teachings are mentioned as given to the disciples "in the way." But these "ways" were simply roads used by travellers. Jesus did not take any interest in them for their own sakes as Stanley Jones does in "The Christ of the Indian road."

A way is a road from somewhere to somewhere, but in Jesus' mind it was simply a road to somewhere, in this case to the Father. The Father is some distance away.

To reach the Father a road is needed, and this for every man. Jesus Himself is the road — the only one.

Jesus met men of different types. They are separated from the Father by different sins. Most dreadful of all were the sins of the Pharisees — their murderous hatred, and smug, self-satisfied pride. They were very far from God. Any road to Jerusalem ran between mountains which, without the road, would have been impenetrable. Think of these mountains as representing the sins which Pharisees must escape if they are to get to the Father.

There were marshes in Palestine, then as now, and perhaps it is not fanciful to think of those as representing the putrescent instinctive sins. Such sin has many victims. Here, too, Jesus the way is the one thing needed.

The case of the ordinary man and woman was different. Only by the greatest effort could he keep body and soul together. His hunger was vividly with him always, but the simplest thought of God perhaps once a week. The disciples to whom Jesus was talking came from just such people. To them Jesus gives a picture of a road made necessary by simple distance. God was far away. They must come to their Heavenly Father not through mountains or marshes, but over long stretches of desert sand of indifference and carelessness, for such people too, are far from God.

Every man needs to come to the Father, no matter what sin separates him from God. Jesus is the way for each of them.

A lifetime of meditation will not exhaust this word of Jesus. Hebrews will help us get started. The "way" is made for us by Jesus' blood. "I am the way" points to the cross. "Therefore, brethren, we have confidence to enter the tabernacle by the blood of Jesus, by the way which He dedicated for us, a new and living way" (Hebrews 10:9). Our sins have separated us from God. Jesus' sacrifice, His blood, makes a way for us to walk in, back to God and His forgiveness.

I Am the Truth

When Jesus said to the disciples "I am the truth" they may have gasped at the incredible character of such a statement, but He went on to make it even more specific and overwhelming. The Spirit whom He promised was to guide the disciples into all the truth. How? By bringing to their remembrance all that Jesus had said and done. What did He mean?

First, without question, Jesus is the truth about God. There is no other truth, no other reality, except God and His thoughts. With utter honesty Jesus said, "I and the Father are one" and He said this to His enemies, who took up stones to kill Him. He added, "The Father is in me, and I in the Father" (Jno. 10:30-31) Here is the one thing for us to study. It is supremely important, for "Except ye believe that I am He, ye shall die in your sins" (Jno. 8:24).

The Pharisees who hated Jesus and finally crucified Him, worshipped God according to all the rules, but inside their shell of ritual and worship and service, which indeed God had given them, their picture of God changed and deteriorated until they thought that by murdering Jesus, they were "rendering service to God." "I am the truth" first of all the truth about God.

There is a further truth, and it is important too. What about man? What sort of life ought we to live? Here again all we need to do is to look at Jesus. "I am the truth" means this kind of truth too. We are to imitate Him just as Peter says. "Leaving us an example that we should follow his steps" (1 Peter 2:21).

There is a third great mountain peak of truth which Jesus shows to us. In one sense it is part of His word: "I am the way." How can Jesus be a wide open way back to God for men who are evil, whose hands are stained with the blood of little children and trusting women, and who grind the faces of the poor? We do not know the truth till we see Jesus suffering on the cross as our Redeemer.

AND THE LIFE

This is another of Jesus' important words, perhaps the most profound of them all. The Gospel of John was written to make it possible for men to gain this life which is in Jesus.

The interview with Nicodemus gives us the first lesson. Life, eternal life, begins as a new birth.

This life is a gift from the very depths of God's own being, as Jesus told a fierce mob which was trying to murder Him. It makes us "partakers of the divine nature." It is maintained by a constant appropriation of Jesus. "I am the bread of life" is one of His loveliest words. Eating Him is a daily affair, and He made it understandable by telling us that it is His words that we are to eat.

And Jesus is our Good Shepherd. That is so we can have more abundant life. He goes before us, and we follow Him. Indeed, we follow Him into the next world. We will be like Him then.

Jesus evidently decided to elaborate "the truth" a little further. "Show us the Father," Philip said. Moses long ago had asked for the same thing. Jesus' reply here is startling and is a bit of a reprimand. Philip should have understood this much before. Jesus had tried to teach him. So the lesson is repeated, specifically and emphatically. We are thankful for this, for we

Believest thou not that I am in the Father, and the Father in me? the words that I speak unto you I speak not of myself: but the Father that dwelleth in me, he doeth the works. Believe me that I am in the Father, and the Father in me: or else believe me for the very works' sake. Verily, verily, I say unto you, He that believeth on me, the works that I do shall he do also; and greater works than these shall he do; because I go unto my Father. And whatsoever ye shall ask in my name, that will I do, that the Father may be glorified in the Son. If ye shall ask any thing in my name, I will do it.

---

had not understood this immensely important matter either. "Have I been so long a time with you and yet you do not know me, Philip?" That is the preface, so that the lesson cannot be misunderstood. "He that hath seen me, hath seen the Father." Jesus is a picture of God, complete and final. That conception of God underlies everything.

So far as faith is concerned this is what we must believe. Based on any other understanding of God, religious faith can pull us down.

This point in the disciples' faith was so important to Jesus that He gave evidence to prove it, or at least to make faith of this kind possible for rational men, and not only possible, but inevitable, if we will give open-minded attention to it. The question is, is the Father in Jesus and Jesus in the Father, each a replica of the other, and each always infusing the other? Where is the evidence for such a statement? Jesus' words and His works. In the nature of the case no other evidence is possible. "Believe me," says Jesus, "or else believe me for the sake of the works that I do." In the case of the disciples, Jesus' own personality would probably carry conviction even on a point as weighty as this, without any further evidence. That may happen even now to a rare soul who sees Jesus with great clearness, but not to many. The works are more important for us than they were for the disciples.

That, however, is perhaps not a disadvantage, for even the disciples knew and understood Jesus by means of His works. And John, who wrote this Gospel, has put them down for us, so that

Peace I leave with you, my peace I give unto you: not as the world giveth, give I unto you. Let not your heart be troubled, neither let it be afraid. Ye have heard how I said unto you, I go away, and come again unto you. If ye loved me, ye would rejoice, because I said, I go unto the Father: for my Father is greater than I. And now I have told you before it come to pass, that, when it is come to pass, ye might believe.

---

we can believe, too. "But these are written that ye may believe that Jesus is the Christ, the Son of God, and that believing, ye may have life in his name."

Jesus adds a further word for us of this sceptical age. The works of Jesus which are recorded to make our faith possible are only a few, and they all happened long ago. But more have happened since, better ones and more of them. Jesus says so, and He adds the "verily verily" which He uses occasionally for emphasis: "The works that I do, shall ye do also, and greater works than these shall ye do." This is made possible by His going to the Father."

It is a very surprising statement, and Jesus put great emphasis behind it for He realized its importance. Perhaps he had in mind the difficulties which centuries to come would have in visualizing His works vividly enough to gain conviction from them.

For this means that in addition to the works and the words that Jesus left us, our own lives can help. Here is a word for the days when doubt overshadows the soul of the disciple. There are days like that when, even a sincere believer wakes up to look out on a universe with no God in it. I have seen missionaries travel for years in that shadow. It seemed impossible to get from the record that has come down to us any vividness and lift at all. Faith does not disappear at a time like that, God knows. But it hides itself and the road is very rough.

To such a man Jesus says, "Look inside." The works that you have done, have in them the footsteps of God, of God in Jesus. They can be seen when no other evidence is to be made out.

THE COMFORTER

And I will pray the Father, and he shall give you another Comforter, that he may abide with you for ever; Even the Spirit of truth; whom the world cannot receive, because it seeth him not, neither knoweth him: but ye know him; for he dwelleth with you, and shall be in you. I will not leave you comfortless: I will come to you.

The third lesson which Jesus had for the disciples concerned the "Comforter." It is impossible to say just what the Greek word means. Paraclete, "Counsellor" is preferred by some. Neither of these words does justice to the lesson that Jesus unfolded to the disciples that evening. The topic was introduced early in the evening's discussion and Jesus returned to it a number of times.

The first lesson about the Holy Spirit was one to comfort the breaking hearts of the disciples. Jesus was leaving them. That much they had finally come to understand. The time they had spent with Him was not so very long, not much more than three years, so far as we can tell. But their whole lives were bound up more and more completely in Jesus, and in His teaching and heavenly personality. The prospect of living without Jesus terrified them.

Jesus had been their guide, their counsellor, their comforter. Now that He was going away, He promises to send them another Comforter. Their minds were full of grief over the temporary character of earthly friendships. The first wonderful thing about this new Comforter was that He would be with them forever.

Jesus made great promises regarding this new Comforter. His association was to be nothing vague and shadowy. He would remove their sense of desolation. The world could not know Him nor see Him, but the disciples would find His abiding friendship and guidance so vivid and compelling that Jesus spoke of it as "beholding" Him.

Jesus discussed this coming Comforter in some detail, but in spite of that, the impression left on the minds of the disciples was very vague.

Yet a little while, and the world seeth me no more; but ye see me: because I live, ye shall live also. At that day ye shall know that I am in my Father, and ye in me, and I in you.

This announcement that the Father was to send "another Comforter" was a piece of good news, something to rejoice over. "It is to your advantage that I go away, for if I go not away the Comforter will not come to you, but if I go I will send him." For some reason, which we cannot see, it was not possible for the Holy Spirit to come and abide in men's hearts while Jesus was still here. Many questions arise, but they deal with divine things, beyond the reach of our limited minds.

However, Jesus tells us regarding the Spirit of truth, the Comforter, that He is to be within us. That was to mean a great deal. Jesus although He was divine, was limited here on earth. He touched one man after another, just as we do, and of this limited number, He only won a small per cent.

But when God the Holy Spirit dwells within His disciples, then the situation is completely changed. The first change comes in the disciple, who is changed to a vastly greater degree when God's Spirit dwells within than when he simply associates with Jesus. There is also a tremendously increased impact on those whom the disciples meet. Jesus made this teaching concrete in a very striking and beautiful parable, the parable of the vine and the branches. Like so many of His words, its depth and suitability are almost limitless.

I am the true vine, and my Father is the husbandman. Every branch in me that beareth not fruit he taketh away: and every branch that beareth fruit, he purgeth it, that it may bring forth more fruit. Now ye are clean through the word which I have spoken unto you Abide in me, and I in you. As the branch cannot bear fruit of itself, except it abide in the vine; no more can ye, except ye abide in me. I am the vine, ye are the branches. He that abideth in me, and I in him, the same bringeth forth much fruit; for without me ye can do nothing. If a man abide not in me, he is cast forth as a branch, and is withered; and men gather them, and cast them into the fire, and they are burned. If ye abide in me, and my words abide in you, ye shall ask what ye will, and it shall be done unto you. Herein is my Father glorified, that ye bear much fruit; so shall ye be my disciples. As the Father hath loved me, so have I loved you: continue ye in my love. If ye keep my commandments, ye shall abide in my love; even as I have kept my Father's commandments, and abide in his love. These things have I spoken unto you, that my joy might remain in you, and that your joy might be full. This is my commandment, That ye love one another, as I have loved you. Greater love hath no man than this, that a man lay down his life for his friends. Ye are my friends, if ye do whatsoever I command you. Henceforth I call you not servants; for the servant knoweth not what his lord doeth: but I have called you friends; for all things that I have heard of my Father I have made known unto you. Ye have not chosen me, but I have chosen you, and ordained you, that ye should go and bring forth fruit, and that your fruit should remain; that whatsoever ye shall ask of the Father in my name, he may give it you. These things I command you, that ye love one another. If the world hate you, ye know that it hated me before it hated you. If ye were of the world, the world would love his own; but because ye are not of the world, but I have chosen you out of the world, therefore the world hateth you. Remember the word that I said unto you, The servant is not greater than his lord. If they have persecuted me, they will also persecute you; if they have kept my saying, they will keep yours also. But all these things will they do unto you for my name's sake, because they know not him that sent me. If I had not come and spoken unto them, they had not had sin; but now they have no cloak for their sin. He that hateth me hateth my Father also. If I had not done among them the works which none other man did, they had not had sin: but now have they both seen and hated both me and my Father. But this cometh to pass that the word might be fulfilled that is written in their law, They hated me without a cause. But when the Comforter is come, whom I will send unto you from the Father, even the Spirit of truth, which proceedeth from the Father, he shall testify of me: And ye also shall bear witness, because ye have been with me from the beginning.

Chapter XV

BEARING FRUIT AND ABIDING

I am the true vine, and my Father is the husbandman. Every branch in me that beareth not fruit he taketh away: and every branch that beareth fruit, he purgeth it, that it may bring forth more fruit. Now ye are clean through the word which I have spoken unto you. Abide in me, and I in you. As the branch cannot bear fruit of itself, except it abide in the vine; no more can ye, except ye abide in me. I am the vine, ye are the branches. He that abideth in me, and I in him, the same bringeth forth much fruit; for without me ye can do nothing. If a man abide not in me, he is cast forth as a branch, and is withered; and men gather them, and cast them into the fire, and they are burned. If ye abide in me, and my words abide in you, ye shall ask what ye will, and it shall be done unto you. Herein is my Father glorified, that ye bear much fruit; so shall ye be my disciples.

The vine is a sort of tree, distinguished first of all by its capacity to bear fruit. No one uses the wood of the grape vine for any purpose, not even for fuel, and the ratio of the fruit to wood is quite unique. A single crop of grapes may outweigh many times the total weight of the vine that bears them. Probably that is the reason why Jesus chose this fugure. "Every branch in me that beareth not fruit, He taketh it away, and every branch that beareth fruit, He cleanseth it that it may bear more fruit."

"I am the vine, ye are the branches." What then is the fruit? Apparently two things were in Jesus' mind. In the first place, other people becoming Christians: "Except a grain of wheat fall into the ground and die, it abideth by itself alone, but if it die, it beareth much fruit." The fruit here is simply more wheat grains. And in the second place, perhaps still more fundamental, the fruit that God wants is borne in our individual hearts. Without this fruit of the Spirit, it would hardly be worth while to bring forth the fruit of multiplied Christians. "But the fruit of the Spirit is love, joy, peace, longsuffering, kindness, goodness, faith, meekness, self-control."

The second lesson is that of abiding. "Abide in me and I in you." That is the work of the Spirit, who is within us now that Jesus has gone. By means of the Spirit we can abide in Jesus even though we do not see Him. Seven times over in this short parable, this word emerges. The matter becomes more important when we realize that Jesus here is giving us a command. It is something that we can do, and must do. But the matter is not simple. How can we abide in Jesus, we who have only four meager records about Him?

One suggestion we get from the parable itself "If ye abide in me and my words abide in you." We can keep Jesus' words abiding in us. It is not easy but it can be done. We have met this lesson before. "If ye abide in my words then are ye my disciples indeed, and ye shall know the truth and the truth shall make you free." Jesus' words are Spirit and they are life. When we abide in them we abide in Him.

These things have I spoken unto you, being yet present with you. But the Comforter, which is the Holy Ghost, whom the Father will send in my name, he shall teach you all things, and bring all things to your remembrance, whatsoever I have said unto you.
But when the Comforter is come, whom I will send unto you from the Father, even the Spirit of truth, which proceedeth from the Father, he shall testify of me: And ye also shall bear witness, because ye have been with me from the beginning.

The Comforter, as He abides in us, is our teacher. "He will teach you all things," and here Jesus had in mind especially all the things that He had said to them. These "words" were the foundation of the Kingdom of God that Jesus was setting up. As Jesus presented them they were not understood, not even by the disciples. But they were remembered. We have noticed repeatedly how Jesus put these teachings into little unforgettable sentences. The day was coming now when all these "words" would be understood. The Comforter, the Spirit of truth, as Jesus called Him, working from within their minds and hearts, was going to illumine those "words."

"He will guide you into all the truth," said Jesus. "He will glorify me, for he will take of mine and declare it unto you." There is one corollary to that, which is often forgotten. The work of the Spirit of truth in our hearts is to go on through the centuries, and if those "words" of Jesus are really divine, infinite things straight from God, then we must expect His disciples, the Church as it is now, to see more and more in those "words" as the years and the centuries roll on. Eventually we are

to see "all the truth." That is aeons ahead, at Jesus' feet in the
heavenly city. But the process is going on now. We must not be
shocked and alarmed then, over a growing and changing understanding of Jesus and His works and words.   Such a growth
ought to be a constant experience of the Church, and will be
when its spiritual life is deep and sound. No greater honor can
come to a disciple than to be chosen by the Spirit of truth to
discover and give to the Church some deep new truth, previously
not clearly seen by the brotherhood.

And we must be careful not to quench the Spirit by our fear
of the unexpected and the unusual. There are going to be times
when the saints of the Church will look out with a sure vision into
the future. "He shall declare unto you the things that are to
come."

THE WORLD

If the world hate you, ye know that it hated me before it hated you.   If
ye were of the world, the world would love his own; but because ye are
not of the world, but I have chosen you out of the world, therefore the
world hateth you.   Remember the word that I said unto you, The servant
is not greater than his lord.   If they have persecuted me, they will also
persecute you; if they have kept my saying, they will keep yours also.
But all these things will they do unto you for my name's sake, because
they know not him that sent me.

Jesus had one other topic that He wanted to discuss with the
disciples. He was to leave them now, and they were to go out into
the world and work as His representatives for its salvation. Jesus
wanted to tell them of the treatment they were to receive at the
hands of the world. They were to work for and love every man
outside of the Kingdom. Their lives were to have no other purpose. But that did not mean that the world was going to love
them. Jesus did not discuss this point. He had told them probably
many times that the world hated Him. But apparently He was
not sure that the disciples were discriminating enough to realize
that they would share that hatred. This opposition was not devel-

If I had not come and spoken unto them, they had not had sin; but now they have no cloak for their sin. He that hateth me hateth my Father also. If I had not done among them the works which none other man did, they had not had sin: but now have they both seen and hated both me and my Father. But this cometh to pass, that the word might be fulfilled that is written in their law, They hated me without a cause.

---

oped on economic or political issues. The troubles carried a religious message, and would antagonize religious interests.

Jesus knew that He must prepare them for this shock. The disciples were not unusually stupid at this point. Where is the man or woman even now who does not assume in his heart that if he treats people well, they will treat him or her well? The disappointment, and even resentment, that the world's hatred stirs in our hearts can be very intense.

It seems strange that pure benevolence can arouse such antagonism even from the worst elements. Jesus' summary is very dreadful, "Now have they both seen and hated both me and my Father." The number who actually hated Jesus does not seem to have been large, but they were the leaders, and they were able to stir up the rank and file so that these hated Jesus too. During one of these episodes Jesus was crucified.

The disciples' need for instruction on this point runs deeper than simple information. One of the major lessons is that Jesus received this hatred without resentment or annoyance. He did not accuse the world. It was one of the inevitabilities. Indeed, as we have already seen in chapter 7, this is one of the stages in the journey of man's soul from the world to the Kingdom of God.

The disciples learned a number of things from these few sentences of Jesus. We must learn them too. When we meet the hatred of the world, it does not mean that our message is wrong, and it does not mean that our method is wrong. Moreover, whatever we do or fail to do, there will be times in our lives just as there were in Jesus' life, when we will be persecuted.

This hatred of Jesus and because of Him, this hatred of us, is a very deep and terrible thing. The most close and faithful imitation of Jesus will not save us from the world's hatred. We realize that here we are looking at the very foundations of human sin. But Jesus did not blame the world for this, and the disciples must not blame the world either. Our efficiency as evangelists will be completely ruined if we respond to this hatred with hatred from our side, or even if we respond with resentment. Jesus does not judge here, and His word to us is, "Judge not.   All these things will they do unto you for my name's sake because they know not him that sent me."

These things have I spoken unto you, that ye should not be offended. They shall put you out of the synagogues: yea, the time cometh, that whosoever killeth you will think that he doeth God service. And these things will they do unto you, because they have not known the Father, nor me. But these things have I told you, that when the time shall come, ye may remember that I told you of them. And these things I said not unto you at the beginning, because I was with you. But now I go my way to him that sent me; and none of you asketh me, Whither goest thou? But because I have said these things unto you, sorrow hath filled your heart. Nevertheless I tell you the truth; it is expedient for you that I go away: for if I go not away, the Comforter will not come unto you; but if I depart, I will send him unto you. And when he is come, he will reprove the world of sin, and of righteousness, and of judgment: Of sin, because they believe not on me; Of righteousness, because I go to my Father, and ye see me no more; Of judgment, because the prince of this world is judged. I have yet many things to say unto you, but ye cannot bear them now. Howbeit when he, the Spirit of truth, is come, he will guide you into all truth: for he shall not speak of himself; but whatsoever he shall hear, that shall he speak: and he will shew you things to come. He shall glorify me: for he shall receive of mine, and shall shew it unto you. All things that the Father hath are mine: therefore said I, that he shall take of mine, and shall shew it unto you. A little while, and ye shall not see me: and again, a little while, and ye shall see me, because I go to the Father. Then said some of his disciples among themselves, What is this that he saith unto us, A little while, and ye shall not see me: and again, a little while, and ye shall see me: and, Because I go to the Father? They said therefore, What is this that he saith, A little while? we cannot tell what he saith. Now Jesus knew that they were desir-

ous to ask him, and said unto them, Do ye inquire among yourselves of that I said, A little while, and ye shall not see me: and again, a little while, and ye shall see me? Verily, verily, I say unto you, That ye shall weep and lament, but the world shall rejoice; and ye shall be sorrowful, but your sorrow shall be turned into joy. A woman when she is in travail hath sorrow, because her hour is come: but as soon as she is delivered of the child, she remembereth no more the anguish, fo joy that a man is born into the world. And ye now therefore have sorrow: but I will see you again, and your heart shall rejoice and your joy no man taketh from you. And in that day ye shall ask me nothing. Verily, verily, I say unto you, Whatsoever ye shall ask the Father in my name, he will give it you. Hitherto have ye asked nothing in my name: ask, and ye shall receive, that your joy may be full. These things have I spoken unto you in proverbs: but the time cometh, when I shall no more speak unto you in proverbs, but I shall shew you plainly of the Father. At that day ye shall ask in my name: and I say not unto you, that I will pray the Father for you: For the Father himself loveth you, because ye have loved me, and have believed that I came out from God. I came forth from the Father, and am come into the world: again I leave the world, and go to the Father. His disciples said unto him, Lo, now speakest thou plainly, and speakest no proverb. Now are we sure that thou knowest all things, and needest not that any man should ask thee: by this we believe that thou camest forth from God. Jesus answered them, Do you now believe? Behold, the hour cometh, yea, is now come, that ye shall be scattered, every man to his own, and shall leave me alone: and yet I am not alone, because the Father is with me. These things I have spoken unto you that in me ye shall have tribulation: but be of good cheer; I have overcome the world.

Chapter XVI
THE COMFORTER AND THE DISCIPLES

These things have I spoken unto you, that ye should not be offended. They shall put you out of the synagogues: yea, the time cometh, that whosoever willeth you will think that he doeth God service. And these things will they do unto you, because they have not known the Father, nor me. But these things have I told you, that when the time shall come, ye may remember that I told you of them. And these things I said not unto you at the beginning, because I was with you.

The "world" in Jesus' mind was made up of those who hated Him. Their number was not large, but they occupied positions of power. They ruled. One wonders if the dreadful sin of hating Jesus is possible only to those who are possessed by the love of domination.

There is another corollary. Men hate Jesus because "they know not him that sent me." Then those who do not hate Jesus, who like the men in chapter 7 say, "He is a good man," such men to some little degree know "him that sent him." To know Jesus aright is life eternal. This knowledge even in its tiny beginnings is enough to keep us out of the list of those who hate Him.

The world hated Jesus and it hated the disciples, but that did not prevent their winning great victories, and seeing even in their own day great triumphs for the Good News. And as century follows century, the tone of society in at least part of the world has become less and less hostile.

The number of ordinary people in America who hate Jesus is very small indeed, and that is true of the leaders as well. The actual number of Jesus' disciples has grown, and with that there has grown up a very strong sense of the fundamental right of every human being to worship God as he thinks best. Hatred of Jesus does not live in such an atmosphere as that.

In Europe we have recently seen some very dreadful reversions to the hatred of the past, when the world did in all intensity hate Jesus and persecute and kill His disciples. That awful night-

I have yet many things to say unto you, but ye cannot bear them now. Howbeit when he, the Spirit of truth, is come, he will guide you into all truth: for he shall not speak of himself: but whatsoever he shall hear, that shall he speak: and he will show you things to come. He shall glorify me: for he shall receive of mine, and shall shew it unto you. All things that the Father hath are mine: therefore said I, that he shall take of mine, and shall shew it unto you.

mare has passed away in Germany, and we feel sure that it will pass away in Russia too.

The purpose of the Comforter is to teach the disciples about Jesus. He is not going to speak of Himself, and that is the reason why our impressions of the Spirit of truth are vague and uncertain. That is what the Holy Spirit desires. He came to extend and carry on the work that Jesus began. Under His guidance we meditate upon Jesus, His example, His teachings, and the whole significance of His life.

His purpose is to teach not about Himself, but about Jesus. His work in our hearts then will never result in a clear understanding of Himself. It will result in a commanding vision of Jesus, and a deep devotion to Him. Moreover, as far as we are told, there is no reason for expecting the emergence of the Comforter into the field of consciousness. He works unrecognized and unfelt, first to bring the human soul to a surrender to God, and after that to place before that redeemed mind such a vision of Jesus as will dominate every fraction of his conscious purpose. In that vision the believer finds his whole objective, and his whole motive, and the whole emotional coloring of his life. This is all the work of the Spirit. He is unrecognized and unfelt, because it is His desire to remain submerged and unseen. He reveals Jesus to us and in us and through us.

It is easy to say that apparently the main purpose of the Comforter is to teach the disciples about Jesus. But that is only a superficial view. Jesus quite surely would have disagreed with it. The world was what God wanted to save, and so it is also the work of the Comforter to convict the world of sin and of righteousness and of judgment. Jesus delayed discussing this until

He had spoken about the world itself and the disciples' relation to it. By testifying regarding Jesus He accomplishes these things, and it is by testimony of a specific character. The world is convicted of sin, because it has not believed in Jesus. The thought is not altogether easy to follow, but we feel that we are not completely helpless at this point. "Of righteousness because I go to the Father and ye behold me no more." Here part of the meaning lies along the line of establishing righteousness as God sees it, as it corresponds to His nature. That righteousness is the example that Jesus has given us. God the Heavenly Father's acceptance of Jesus validates that conception of righteousness. "Of judgment, because the prince of this world hath been judged." The Cross with Jesus dying on it, is what must be in mind here.

And part of the work of the Comforter, a very important part is to make it possible for us, His disciples, to abide in Jesus as branches abide in the vine.

This is the climax of the Comforter's work. First, He teaches us "all the truth." Gradually, to be sure, but eventually the Church will see it all. It is the truth about Jesus which we are to see more and more perfectly. But the ultimate goal is not a better vision of Jesus, the ultimate goal is abiding in Jesus. He is the vine, we are the branches. Jesus wants us to bear much fruit and this depends on our abiding in Him. We are not told specifically just what such "fruit" is. Other people who become Christians, perhaps. But the Apostle Paul, when he used this figure, meant the different Christian virtues, which he calls "the fruits of the Spirit, love, joy, peace," etc.

The point which concerns us most is that here we see something which we can do to make the work of the Comforter in our hearts possible. Just how can we "abide" in Jesus? Probably there are many different ways, far as our conscious understanding is concerned. To listen to the voice of Jesus in our hearts before we begin the day's work and then spend the day in carefully carrying out the directions we are given is surely one way to abide.

It is probably a matter of meditation in any case. We must let our mind and our affection rest on Jesus for at least a little while every day. Jesus Himself suggested that we keep ourselves, our minds particularly, in His words. "If ye abide in my words, then are ye truly my disciples." But the details He does not give us, and each one must work out his own program. Frank Laubach manages to keep himself in the consciousness of Jesus' presence all day long. Brother Lawrence did it long ago. No doubt we all do it in different ways. It is the climax of the Comforter's work in us.

But even when we do start out the day's work that way, most of us find it necessary many times during the day to renew our courage, or reassure our timidity, or reorient our course, by means of a conscious turning to Jesus for guidance and strength. This much of a contribution to the divine process of salvation we have to make. It keeps the channels open so that God's life can flow into ours. Then it is our life, and we can bear much fruit.

THE COMFORTER AND THE WORLD

Nevertheless I tell you the truth; It is expedient for you that I go away: for if I go not away, the Comforter will not come unto you; but if I depart, I will send him unto you. And when he is come, he will reprove the world of sin, and of righteousness, and of judgment: Of sin, because they believe not on me; Of righteousness, because I go to my Father, and ye see me no more; Of judgment, because the prince of this world is judged.

"And he when he is come will convict the world of sin, and of righteousness, and of judgment." This appears to be the reason why Jesus told the disciples that it was expedient that He go away. What God had in mind and what Jesus had in mind with His earthly visit was the world and its salvation. He had not reached all the world, and one of the things that He had to do in this last interview was to warn the disciples of the world's hostility. But it still remains that His major object was this world's salvation. That also is the major object of the Comforter's coming.

At first sight, the object of the Comforter's coming seems very incomplete. To convict the world of sin and righteousness and judgment does not reach either faith or salvation.

No doubt here we have a very profound glimpse into the process of salvation. This is the first step and it is the work of the Holy Spirit, not of any man, believer or unbeliever. The world, the man away from the Kingdom of God, must first be convicted by the Spirit of God. He is convicted of sin and of righteousness and of judgment. After that we must add our witness to the witness of the Spirit, just as Jesus says: "And bear ye also witness." And then, after our witness has been added to the witness of the Spirit of God, we are going to see the response of faith on man's part, and salvation as God's free gift. It is safe to say that any effort on our part to do the work of the Spirit, to convict outsiders of sin and righteousness and judgment, will result in failure. All that we can do is to add our simple witness to the Spirit's work. Then results will be great and powerful.

"Of sin because they believe not on me." We are talking here about the world's sin, and it is the world that is to be convicted. That means that men under the influence of the Spirit will recognize their own sins, frustrations fears, and resentments, that is they will see themselves as sinners.

The basis of this conviction is the fact that they have refused to believe on Jesus. Is that refusal an indication of sin, a symptom, as the doctors might say, or is it, in and of itself sin of the deepest and most deadly sort? And if this refusal to accept Jesus is of itself deadly and dreadful sin, then what of the man who has had no opportunity to either reject or accept Jesus? Has he no sin, or at least no serious sin? And there are myriads of men and women whose chance to see Jesus and accept Him has been extremely imperfect. Only God knows when we have had a sufficient opportunity to accept Jesus, and indeed He is the only one who needs to know. It is the business of no one else.

But all men, without any exceptions at all, are sinners. That probably must mean that they, too, have rejected Jesus. His person was not recognized when His teaching and attitudes were rejected. His name was not mentioned. But nevertheless when the good and the holy that He embodied were rejected, then *He* was rejected.

And the corollary of that of course is that when a rare soul accepts Jesus, presented without His name or His person being recognized, then he is a follower of Jesus. Cornelius apparently was in this category. No doubt when such men meet Jesus they will accept Him, as Cornelius did.

"Of righteousness because I go to the Father and ye behold me no more."

Jesus went to the Father and was accepted there, and that constituted a complete divine endorsement. Righteousness is what corresponds to the nature and will of God.

Here then we have a conception of righteousness established, that is the human life of Jesus. It was that human life that God endorsed, asserted that it was completely in accordance with His will, and therefore that it was a complete picture of righteousness.

This is the righteousness of God, the righteousness of Jesus. It is not the righteousness of men which at its best is a very imperfect thing. It is fully worthy of punitive justice and revenge, balanced and adjusted to be sure, but none the less revenge. But Jesus prayed, "Father forgive them for they know not what they do." That is the righteousness of God.

The world's conviction of sin can only be complete, when it is understood as a departure from the righteousness of God and from the life of Jesus.

"Of judgment because the prince of this world hath been judged."

Many questions emerge here. How was the prince of this world judged at the cross? for it was the cross that was in Jesus' mind here. The prince of this world is the prince of the men and women who hate Jesus.

We can see some ways in which the prince of this world was judged at the cross. In the first place he was judged to be so evil that the unspeakable sacrifice of the cross was required to to rescue the men under him. It was not only required, it was furnished, and the men were rescued.

There is a second way in which we can see that the prince of this world is judged at the cross. That prince has been an evil and bad ruler. The essence of this judgment is his displacement from his throne where he rules men and women. Jesus is going to rule them now. "I, if I be lifted up from the earth, will draw all men unto myself."

And with their prince, the world itself is judged. Every man who hates Jesus is included in the list. "Now is the judgment of this world, now is the prince of this world cast out."

Then said some of his disciples among themselves, What is this that he saith unto us, A little while, and ye shall not see me: and again, a little while, and ye shall see me: and, Because I go to the Father? They said therefore, What is this that he saith, A little while? we cannot tell what he saith. Now Jesus knew that they were desirous to ask him, and said unto them, Do ye inquire among yourselves of that I said, A little while, and ye shall not see me: and again, a little while, and ye shall see me? Verily, verily, I say unto you, That ye shall weep and lament, but the world shall rejoice; and ye shall be sorrowful, but your sorrow shall be turned into joy. A woman when she is in travail hath sorrow, because her hour is come: but as soon as she is delivered of the child, she remembereth no more the anguish, for joy that a man is born into the world.

After Jesus finished this teaching there was a time of simple, affectionate farewell with these twelve men He loved so much. There is much for us to learn in that last paragraph of the evening's talk.

We realize here as we have not done before, how very difficult the disciples found it to understand Jesus. They had been listening to some of His most profound utterances, but they were completely puzzled by the simple idea that He was leaving them.

And ye now therefore have sorrow: but I will see you again, and your heart shall rejoice, and your joy no man taketh from you. And in that day ye shall ask me nothing. Verily, verily, I say unto you, Whatsoever ye shall ask the Father in my name, he will give it you. Hitherto have ye asked nothing in my name: ask, and ye shall receive, that your joy may be full. These things have I spoken unto you in proverbs: but the time cometh, when I shall no more speak unto you in proverbs, but I shall shew you plainly of the Father. At that day ye shall ask in my name: and I say not unto you, that I will pray the Father for you: For the Father himself loveth you, because ye have loved me, and have believed that I came out from God.

John remembered this evening very vividly as he wrote the Gospel fifty years later. It may well have been his own question, "What is this that he saith, a little while?"

We can see now why Jesus had to look outside the disciples' circle for recipients of His great words. They would not have understood them well enough to even remember them. It must have been their preoccupation with a wrong idea of Jesus' coming Kingdom that shut their minds to what He told them, for they were far from being as stupid as this paragraph shows them.

And we realize how completely their later wonderful success in carrying Jesus' message depended upon the Comforter's help. He was to bring to their remembrance all the things they had forgotten, and more, He was to give comprehension of them. Every particle of intellectual understanding, and every grain of mystical union with God came from the same divine source.

But Jesus did not seem discouraged or disappointed by this. He was quite satisfied with His disciples, and even the prospect of their defection in the time of danger did not disturb Him. It was what He expected.

But had the disciples gained nothing at all from their three years with Jesus? They had gained a profound and firm faith in Him, and a love that never wavered. All the rest was to come from the indwelling Spirit.

But Jesus here is aiming at their immediate comprehension, and He wants to comfort their hearts. He started where real comfort must begin. The separation that was coming was a matter

I came forth from the Father, and am come into the world: again, I
leave the world, and go to the Father. His disciples said unto him, Lo,
now speakest thou plainly, and speakest no proverb. Now are we sure
that thou knowest all things, and needest not that any man should ask
thee: by this we believe that thou camest forth from God. Jesus answered them, Do ye now believe? Behold, the hour cometh, yea, is
now come, that ye shall be scattered, every man to his own, and shall
leave me alone: and yet I am not alone because the Father is with me.
These things I have spoken unto you, that in me ye might have peace.
In the world ye shall have tribulation: but be of good cheer; I have
overcome the world.

---

of tears. Separations always are. But He would see them again.
Their grief would be turned into joy, and that joy would be permanent.

And Jesus knew that He must put some real vividness into
their faith in their Heavenly Father. While He was with them,
it would seem that He had said very little on this subject. The
disciples had felt that their contact with the Father was through
Jesus and in this they were correct. Now their contact with the
Father was to be direct, and that for the most fundamental of
all reasons. The Heavenly Father loved them, just as Jesus did,
and would answer every request.

Jesus realized that even this was a little hard for them, so
He gave them an outline of His life, so simple that it could not
be missed. "I came out from the Father, and am come into
the world, again I leave the world, and go unto the Father." The
disciples caught the meaning here, and rejoiced to hear something which they could actually understand. This surely was no
dark saying, and they responded to it with a faith that was genuine and wholehearted, even if to us it seems disappointingly
meager.

Jesus left in their minds a word, not of criticism, still less of
condemnation, but rather a word of confidence and love. "Be
of good cheer, I have overcome the world." "In me," He said,
"ye shall have peace." The world was to be filled with discord
and trouble, but they would have, as their lot, peace in Him.

JOHN 17

These words spake Jesus, and lifted up his eyes to heaven, and said, Father, the hour is come; glorify thy Son, that thy Son also may glorify thee: As thou hast given him power over all flesh, that he should give eternal life to as many as thou hast given him. And this is life eternal, that they might know thee the only true God, and Jesus Christ, whom thou hast sent. I have glorified thee on the earth: I have finished the work which thou gavest me to do. And now, O Father, glorify thou me with thine own self with the glory which I had with thee before the world was. I have manifested thy name unto the men which thou gavest me out of the world: thine they were, and thou gavest them me; and they have kept thy word Now they have known that all things whatsoever thou hast given me are of thee. For I have given unto them the words which thou gavest me; and they have received them and have known surely that I came out from thee, and they have believed that thou didst send me. I pray for them: I pray not for the world, but for them which thou hast given me; for they are thine. And all mine are thine, and thine are mine; and I am glorified in them. And now I am no more in the world, but these are in the world, and I come to thee. Holy Father, keep through thine own name those whom thou hast given me, that they may be one, as we are. While I was with them in the world, I kept them in thy name: those that thou gavest me I have kept, and none of them is lost, but the son of perdition; that the Scripture might be fulfilled. And now come I to thee; and these things I speak in the world, that they might have my joy fulfilled in themselves. I have given them thy word; and the world hath hated them, because they are not of the world, even as I am not of the world. I pray not that thou shouldest take them out of the world, but that thou shouldest keep them from the evil. They are not of the world, even as I am not of the world. Sanctify them through thy truth: thy word is truth. As thou hast sent me into the world, even so have I also sent them into the world. And for their sakes I sanctify myself, that they also might be sanctified through the truth. Neither pray I for these alone, but for them also which shall believe on me through their word; That they all may be one; as thou, Father, art in me, and I in thee, that they also may be one in us: that the world may believe that thou hast sent me. And the glory which thou gavest me I have given them: that they may be one, even as we are one: I in them and thou in me, that they may be made perfect in one; and that the world may know that thou hast sent me, and hast loved them, as thou has loved me. Father, I will that they also, whom thou hast given me, be with me where I am: that they may behold my glory, which thou hast given me: for thou lovedst me before the foundation of the world. O righteous Father, the world hath not known thee: but I have known thee, and these have known that thou hast sent me. And I have declared unto them thy name, and will declare it; that the love wherewith thou hast loved me may be in them, and I in them.

Chapter XVII

THE PICTURE — JESUS PRAYING

These words spake Jesus, and lifted up his eyes to heaven, and said, Father, the hour is come; glorify thy Son, that thy Son also may glorify thee: As thou hast given him power over all flesh, that he should give eternal life to as many as thou hast given him. And this is life eternal, that they might know thee the only true God, and Jesus Christ, whom thou hast sent. I have glorified thee on the earth: I have finished the work which thou gavest me to do. And now, O Father, glorify thou me with thine own self with the glory which I had with thee before the world was. I have manifested thy name unto the men which thou gavest me out of the world: thine they were, and thou gavest them me; and they have kept thy word.

As a portrait of Jesus this prayer is the apex of the whole New Testament. It is our supreme picture of Him and particularly important because it shows Him in His dealings with His Heavenly Father. Things which are faint and vague elsewhere we see here with a beauty and clarity quite incomparable. He has "given us an example, that we should follow His steps." Here we see our model. We want to be just as much like Jesus as we can, and above all things, we want to be like Him in worship and consecration to God.

This is our model prayer. Jesus prayed as a man to His Heavenly Father. Love and loyalty pervade the chapter like a heavenly atmosphere.

There are some things which we do not find. There is no emotional storm, and no struggle for complete passivity so that the worshipper may melt into the divine. There is no tremendous soul-shaking worship which finally gains the presence of God and secures from Him great and far-reaching answers. Most remarkable of all from our point of view, there is no request for strength for the extremely difficult task ahead, and not even a request for guidance through these dreadful hours.

Jesus evidently had a completely easy and untroubled entrance into His Father's presence. He always stepped into the divine presence without hesitation or delay, as we see Him doing here.

Now they have known that all things whatsoever thou hast given me are of thee. For I have given unto them the words which thou gavest me; and they have received them, and have known surely that I came out from thee, and they have believed that thou didst send me. I pray for them: I pray not for the world, but for them which thou hast given me; for they are thine. And all mine are thine, and thine are mine; and I am glorified in them. And now I am no more in the world, but these are in the world, and I come to thee. Holy Father, keep through thine own name those whom thou hast given me, that they may be one, as we are. While I was with them in the world, I kept them in thy name: those that thou gavest me I have kept, and none of them is lost, but the son of perdition; that the Scripture might be fulfilled.

It was a prayer of faith, complete and unblemished faith in spite of the small success that He had seen. It was the report of complete faithfulness on His part. He had "finished the work" that He had been given to do. Opposition to His work had grown stronger and stronger. In a few hours He would be crucified, but His faith in His Father's program was undisturbed.

It was a prayer of faith, but even more a prayer of glory — the glory of redemptive self-sacrifice. Jesus had been given a task to perform. Now He makes a report. It was not a report of great success, but it was a report of a mission accomplished. It was a preliminary mission, but there was glory in it. "I glorified thee on earth, having accomplished the work which thou gavest me to do." That glory was a part of God's own divine radiance. A few men had been redeemed but Jesus' supreme glory is in the cross. That saved the world.

Jesus' first request is for the supreme glory which His preliminary faithfulness had made possible. This supreme task, the cross itself, is important beyond our utmost imagination. Its cost to Jesus was to be terrible. There are few more moving pictures of Jesus than this, on His knees earnestly asking for the cross, and in it His own and His Father' glory,

The agony in Gethsemane. His sweat turning into blood there, The sins of men in their slimy putridity, laid upon the purest and most sensitive soul the earth has ever seen.

And there was physical suffering there and abuse up to the last grain of physical endurance, and indeed beyond it, for Jesus had to have help in dragging His heavy cross up to the top of Calvary's hill. The dreadful crown of thorns was in that vision, and the awful nails.

The Pharisees hated Him with a steady, unresting hatred, which is the most awful thing that the whole New Testament shows. The Romans, from the governor down, looked on Him with contempt. They spat on Him. But most bitter of all was the response of the people. Their diseases He had healed, their babies He had blessed, their hunger He had shared. And they yelled, "Crucify him, crucify him."

How much of this did Jesus see, as He prayed, "And now Father glorify thou me with thine own self, with the glory that I had with thee, before the world was." No doubt He saw it all, but He did not feel it. He was to feel it soon enough, two or three hours was all that remained. And when the terrors of hell did close down on Him, it shook the last fiber of His being. "Oh my Father," He prayed, "if it be possible, let this cup pass from me." But it wasn't possible, and He drank that cup from His Father's hand.

There was also a report to be made. The philosopher with his tiny and groping mind will rise to ask some questions. What is the use of making a report to an omniscient God? This was a Son reporting to His Father. It is to the family circle that we must look for light here, not to philosophy. "For this cause I bow my knees unto the Father from whom every family in heaven and on earth is named."

It is a complete and detailed report of what Jesus had been able to accomplish in the hearts of a few men. No institution is mentioned, and no organization. Jesus tells how the work was done, and just what changes had taken place in the minds and hearts of the men He was working for.

Jesus did not listen for guidance this time. He did sometimes. He spent the night in prayer before He chose the disciples (Luke

And now come I to thee; and these things I speak in the world, that they might have my joy fulfilled in themselves. I have given them thy word; and the world hath hated them, because they are not of the world, even as I am not of the world. I pray not that thou shouldest take them out of the world, but that thou shouldest keep them from the evil. They are not of the world, even as I am not of the world. Sanctify them through thy truth: thy word is truth. As thou hast sent me into the world, even so have I also sent them into the world.

6:2). But this time His prayer was made up of requests which He wanted to present to God. "I pray for them," He said. He was going away, and the disciples, *twelve* distressed and bewildered men, were to be left behind. They would be alone. He wanted His heavenly Father to keep them. How little we know about God, and how much we owe to His care. Jesus had just been telling the disciples that He was to return to the Father. He had told them that anything they asked for in His name they would receive. So we might suppose that the thing needed now was that they themselves come and ask to be cared for by their Heavenly Father.

Jesus' mind was not following that line of thought at the moment. "Holy Father keep them in thy name," the name that God the Heavenly Father had given to Jesus. That name is a divine fortress. Jesus had kept them in it while He was with them, but He was not to be with them any longer. Now He wanted His Heavenly Father to keep them. That was on the positive side.

And on the negative side: "Keep them from the evil one." It is just as well that we understand so little about the evil one. It is the soul and not the body that he attacks. How are we to keep him out? It is not easy. How many boys are in the state prisons because they did not keep him out! Doubtless, the only way to do it is to be kept in God's name, that divine citadel of safety.

"Sanctify them in the truth. Thy word is truth." Accepting those words of Jesus puts up into God's name, and under His

And for their sakes I sanctify myself, that they also might be sanctified through the truth. Neither pray I for these alone, but for them also which shall believe on me through their word; That they all may be one; as thou, Father, art in me, and I in thee, that they also may be one in us: that the world may believe that thou hast sent me. And the glory which thou gavest me I have given them; that they may be one, even as we are one: I in them, and thou in me, that they may be made perfect in one; and that the world may know that thou hast sent me, and hast loved them, as thou hast loved me.

---

protection. Further study and meditation on these divine words sanctifies us for the Master's use. We are changed by those words.

We can feel the terrible, almost desperate grip on God in this prayer. Here is a prayer that we know will be answered. But it was not answered brilliantly or even obviously. It was simply added to the favorable factors in the years and the centuries to come. The temptations that torment and rack us can never quite overwhelm us because of that prayer.

Jesus was lifted out of some of His human limitations as He prayed. We are too, in a small way. It does not surprise us to see Him looking not at the disciples only now, as the prayer grew in intensity toward its end. He is not even looking at the Jewish nation. "Neither do I pray for these only, but for those who shall believe on me through their word." It included the whole world with its as yet undiscovered continents, and the centuries and millenniums that stretched down through the future. It is the universality of God Himself that we see here.

Here Jesus is not simply universal in point of earthly outlook, and not simply universal in point of time, He is praying a prayer that is utterly complete and universal in the depth of human personality which it reaches. "That they may all be one, as thou, Father, are in me and I in thee, that they may be one in us, that the world may believe that thou hast sent me." Complete union with each other, and complete union with Jesus and with His Heavenly Father, that is infinite eternity in terms of the human spirit.

Father, I will that they also, whom thou hast given me, be with me where I am; that they may behold my glory, which thou hast given me: for thou lovedst me before the foundation of the world. O righteous Father, the world hath not known thee: but I have known thee, and these have known that thou hast sent me. And I have declared unto them thy name, and will declare it; that the love wherewith thou hast loved me may be in them, and I in them.

The supreme lesson here is the picture it gives us of Jesus and His relations with His Heavenly Father. But there is a second picture hardly less beautiful. Jesus loved His disciples.

His first concern was to make a necessary report to His Heavenly Father, but the moment that had been attended to, Jesus poured out His heart in a very earnest prayer for them. He had not failed them. He had kept them in the Father's name while He was with them. But He was not going to be with them any longer. They were in the world and the world was their enemy. We would think of the fact that the whole enterprise of God's Kingdom was being left in their hands, and would expect an earnest prayer for them on that account.

But what we do find is different from that. Jesus' heart ached for those bewildered and grief-torn men. They would die martyrs' deaths, practically all of them. Subtle temptations would creep in to besmirch and mar the beauty of their souls. "Holy Father keep them." We have all of us prayed that kind of prayer. We can feel its intensity as we read the account. "Keep them from the evil one. Sanctify them in the truth."

The chapter ends on the loveliest note of all. Jesus loved His disciples. How much did He love them? "Father I desire that they also whom thou hast given me, be with me where I am, that they may behold my glory." Jesus asked His Heavenly Father that the love and effection which had previously been felt on earth might be made an eternal thing. Here we see something beyond the love of a teacher for His disciple. It is the love of one comrade for another. He makes out a good case for these disciples before their Heavenly Father, the case that intense personal love can always make for its beloved.

JESUS' TEACHING

"Father the hour is come." Jesus must have had a very definite idea of what He had been sent to do. He knew just when it was finished. The hour had come. Something of the world's history had been finished too. An old epoch had closed. Just around the corner, a few hours away, was the cross and a new epoch. There had been real glory in the old. Jesus felt that very keenly. But the incomparable glory of the ages was in the new era. "The glory which I had with thee, before the world was," was what He asked for now.

Jesus had been given authority over all flesh. He still has that authority. "All authority has been given unto me, in heaven and on earth." And this was for the purpose of giving eternal life to men. When the Comforter comes to take Jesus' place, then how wide salvation will be. And this is the glory of God, the glory of the ages, that men are to be given eternal life, God's own life, membership in His family.

And we see again what we have seen before, that the Heavenly Father was working with the Son. That is always the case.

We find here a new definition of eternal life. It is the natural growth and development from the new birth. It is Jesus living in us. "I am the bread of life" taught us that. Here the curtains are lifted a little further. "That they may know thee, the only true God, and Jesus Christ whom thou hast sent."

What an elusive thing is this little word "know." Eternal life by means of more information? That cannot be, but this is more than mere information, or, if we prefer that idea, it is a deep sort of information, the contact of one spirit with another, with surrender, and the fusion of spirits in it. Eternal life is union with God, and with His Son Jesus Christ. We think of knowing God with our intellect, but the deeper knowledge is that of the heart. We do not know even a human friend till we love him. No one ever new a man whom he hated. Nor can we love any one until in some degree we understand him. No one of us

will ever know the true God except through Jesus Christ whom
He hath sent.

Jesus reported His task as completed. He went on to tell
how He had accomplished the task. "I manifested thy name
unto the men whom thou gavest me out of the world." That is
an oriental way of speaking. We feel that we are in the presence
of a great truth which stands up before us like a mountain. The
authority and the nature of the omnipotent God are in His
"name." We have the same usage in the West. An employee
moved up to be a partner, thereafter speaks in the name of the
firm. Jesus had showed God's name to the disciples. His life was
a picture of the divine nature and beauty and authority and
power. The disciples moved up into the inner circle, and entered
that impregnable name. Jesus had kept them in it. Now they
were to go out into the hostile world in God's omnipotent name.
There is encouragement for us here, for the disciples at this time
were very imperfect. Nevertheless, they were in the Heavenly
Father's name, and so are we.

Jesus had one way of giving eternal life to these men. He
gave them the words that God had given unto Him. It is not
suggested in this prayer that the disciples reacted to Jesus' picture of God in any conscious way. Jesus lived with them for
about three years. Apparently His life and example soaked into
their lives unconsciously. His words stirred up definite reactions,
and by them these men were saved.

Their first reaction was that of obedience. "They have kept
thy words." The words were "received" too, which must mean
that they were loved and believed in. We may call this the voli-
tational part of faith. Jesus was also much interested in what
we may call the intellectual aspect of faith. These men had come
to hold certain convictions.

They knew "of a truth" that Jesus came from God. Men have
given different answers to the questions as to the nature of saving faith. What must a man do to be saved? Here is Jesus'
answer.

"They believed." This is less emphatic. It is not knowledge. It is faith. What did they believe? That God had sent Jesus. What this really does is to establish a new conception of God. Jesus is like God, He is divine. God is like Jesus. Jesus wanted both of these elements to be present in our faith. Jesus is God, and God is Jesus.

Jesus then passed on to present certain requests. They concerned the diciples whom He loved so much and whom He was leaving. It was a dreadful world that He was leaving them in. They were to be the means of redeeming it. "Holy Father keep them in Thy name." This does not surprise us. They were in the Father's name now. Everything depended on their remaining there. Jesus had done this while He was with them. Now He was going away.

But the reason comes with a shock of surprise. "That they may be one, as we are." Jesus' washing the disciples' feet, with His new commandment to love one another, comes before us clothed with a new and terrible importance. Everything depends on this one thing. And the disciples are to have the same sort of unclouded unity that Jesus and His Heavenly Father enjoyed.

Jesus states His request in a negative form. "Keep them from the evil one." Satan's attack always comes at just this point. The main emphasis however, is on the positive requests. "Sanctify them in the truth, thy word is truth." The words that Jesus brought from God were His one means of putting eternal life into men's souls. By their acceptance of these words, and their obedience to them they gained eternal life. By means of deeper acquaintance with these words they are to be fifted to carry the message and salvation of God to others. These words Jesus brought are a key to all the riches of grace in Christ Jesus.

And those requests, beautiful as Heaven itself, are extended to include you and me. We are to be one, just as Jesus and the Father are one. Thereby we join in the unity of the Heavenly Father and the Son. Even that is a means to an end. "That the world may believe that thou hast sent me" — saving faith for the whole world, far beyond the horizon of the disciples' imagination at this time. There is an additional touch here. To make this possible, Jesus has given us participation in His glory, which must mean that we are partners in His great task of world redemption.

When Jesus had spoken these words, he went forth with his disciples over the brook Cedron, where was a garden, into which he entered, and his disciples. And Judas also, which betrayed him, knew the place: for Jesus ofttimes resorted thither with his disciples. Judas then, having received a band of men and officers from the chief priests and Pharisees, cometh thither with lanterns and torches and weapons. Jesus therefore, knowing all things that should come upon him went forth, and said unto them, Whom seek ye? They answered him, Jesus of Nazareth. Jesus saith unto them, I am he. And Judas also, which betrayed him, stood with them. As soon then as he had said unto them, I am he, they went backward, and fell to the ground. Then asked he them again, Whom seek ye? And they said, Jesus of Nazareth. Jesus answered, I have told you that I am he: if therefore ye seek me, let these go their way: That the saying might be fulfilled, which he spake, Of them which thou gavest me have I lost none. Then Simon Peter having a sword drew it and smote the high priest's servant, and cut off his right ear. The servant's name was Malchus. Then said Jesus unto Pete, Put up thy sword into the sheath: the cup which my Father hath given me, shall I not drink it? Then the band and the captain and officers of the Jews took Jesus, and bound him. And led him away to Annas first; for he was father in law to Caiaphas, which was the high priest that same year. Now Caiaphas was he which gave counsel to the Jews, that it was expedient that one man should die for the people.

And Simon Peter followed Jesus, and so did another disciple: that disciple was known unto the high priest, and went in with Jesus into the palace of the high priest. But Peter stood at the door without. Then went out that other disciple, which was known unto the high priest, and spake unto her that kept the door, and brought in Peter. Then saith the damsel that kept the door unto Peter, Art not thou also one of the man's disciples? He saith, I am not. And the servants and officers stood there, who had made a life of coals, for it was cold; and they warmed themselves: and Peter stood with them, and warmed himself.

the high priest then asked Jesus of his disciples, and of his doctrine. Jesus answered him, I spake openly to the world; I ever taught in the synagogue, and in the temple, whither the Jews always resort; and in secret have I said nothing. Why askest thou me? ask them which heard me, what I have said unto them: behold, they know what I said. And when he had thus spoken, one of the officers which stood by struck Jesus with the palm of his hand, saying, Answerest thou the high priest so? Jesus answered him, If I have spoken evil, bear witness of the evil: but if well ,why smitest thou me? Now Annas had sent him bound unto Caiaphas the high priest. And Simon Peter stood and warmed himself. They said therefore unto him, Art not thou also one of his disciples? He denied it, and said, I am not. One of the servants of the high priest, being his kinsman whose ear Peter cut off, saith, Did not I see thee in the garden with him? Peter then denied again; and immediately the cock crew.

Then led they Jesus from Caiaphas unto the hall of judgment: and it was early; and they themselves went not into the judgment hall, lest they should be defiled; but that they might eat the passover. Pilate then went out unto them, and said, What accusation bring ye against this man? They answered and said unto him, If he were not a malefactor, we would not have delivered him up unto thee. Then said Pilate unto them, Take ye him, and judge him according to your law. The Jews therefore said unto him, It is not lawful for us to put any man to death: That the saying of Jesus might be fulfilled which he spake, signifying what death he should die. Then Pilate entered into the judgment hall again, and called Jesus, and said unto him, Art thou the King of the Jews? Jesus answered him, Sayest thou this thing of thyself, or did others tell it thee of me? Pilate answered, Am I a Jew? Thine own nation and the chief priests have delivered thee unto me: what hast thou done? Jesus answered, My kingdom is not of this world: if my kingdom were of this world, then would my servants fight, that I should not be delivered to the Jews: but now is my kingdom not from hence. Pilate therefore said unto him, Art thou a king then? Jesus answered, Thou sayest that I am a king. To this end was I born, and for this cause came I into the world, that I should bear witness unto the truth. Every one that is of the truth heareth my voice. Pilate saith unto him, What is truth? And when he had said this, he went out again unto the Jews, and saith unto them, I find in him no fault at all. But ye have a custom, that I should release unto you one at the passover: will ye therefore that I release unto you the King of the Jews? Then cried they all again, saying, Not this man, but Barabbas. Now Barabbas was a robber.

Chapter XVIII

THE TRIAL OF JESUS

THE PICTURE

When Jesus had spoken these words, he went forth with his disciples over the brook Cedron, where was a garden, into the which he entered, and his disciples. And Judas also, which betrayed him, knew the place: for Jesus ofttimes resorted thither with his disciples. Judas then, having received a band of men and officers from the chief priests and Pharisees, cometh thither with lanterns and torches and weapons. Jesus therefore, knowing all things that should come upon him, went forth, and said unto them, Whom seek ye? They answered him, Jesus of Nazareth. Jesus saith unto them, I am he. And Judas also, which betrayed him, stood with them. As soon then as he had said unto them, I am he, they went backward, and fell to the ground. Then asked he them again, Whom seek ye? And they said, Jesus of Nazareth. Jesus answered, I have told you that I am he: if therefore ye seek me, let these go their way: That the saying might be fulfilled, which he spake, Of them which thou gavest me have I lost none.

We enter the last scenes of Jesus' life, our final picture. Jesus is not teaching except for a moment as He tries to reach Pilate. This is a very unusual picture. We see Jesus. Everything else is subordinated to that. Judas is present, and so is Peter, the high priest and other background figures. They are put in be- cause of some relationship to Jesus.

But the writer is drawing a very special kind of picture. It is not evident at first just what his purpose is, but he is very

Then Simon Peter having a sword drew it, and smote the high priest's scrvant, and cut off his right ear.   The servant's name was Malchus. Then said Jesus unto Peter, Put up thy sword into the sheath: the cup which my Father hath given me, shall I not drink it?   Then the band and the captain and officers of the Jews took Jesus, and bound him.   And let him away to Annas first; for he was father in law to Caiaphas, which was the high priest that same year.   Now Caiaphas was he, which gave counsel to the Jews, that it was expedient that one man should die for the people.

And Simon Peter followed Jesus, and so did another disciple: that disciple was known unto the high priest, and went in with Jesus into the palace of the high priest.   But Peter stood at the door without. Then went out that other disciple, which was known unto the high priest, and spake unto her that kept the door, and brought in Peter. Then saith the damsel that kept the door unto Peter, Art not thou also one of this man's disciples?   He saith, I am not.   And the servants and officers stood there, who had made a fire of coals, for it was cold; and they warmed themselves: and Peter stood with them, and warmed himself.

---

plainly striving for a definite effect. His most vivid material he omits — the dreadful traitorous kiss of Judas, Jesus' look that melted the heart of Peter, the initial bribery of Judas, and his pathetic end. Even more important items are left out, the bloody sweat in Gethsemane and the entire vivid and dreadful trial before Caiaphas.

But we gain little by listing the items which have been left out. What has been put in? As we read the account in its vivid brevity, we have a shivery feeling that all these details are a kind of epiphenomena without real significance. The narration is detached and impersonal, with no blame and no praise, even when telling of dreadful sin and treachery, or picturing the poise and dignity of Jesus.

Underneath we see tremendous currents of Satanic power. "This is your hour and the power of darkness" (Luke 22:53). Jesus meets pure sin here. Every human being whom this dreadful current touched, went down. Judas betrays Him, Peter denies Him, the Pharisees murder Him. Pilate, the passover

The high priest then asked Jesus of his disciples, and of his doctrine. Jesus answered him, I spake openly to the world; I ever taught in the synagogue, and in the temple, whither the Jews always resort; and in secret have I said nothing. Why asketh thou me? ask them which heard me, what I have said unto them: behold, they know what I said. And when he had thus spoken, one of the officers which stood by struck Jesus with the palm of his hand, saying, Answerest thou the high priest so? Jesus answered him, If I have spoken evil, bear witness of the evil: but if well, why smitest thou me? Now Annas had sent him bound unto Caiaphas the high priest. And Simon Peter stood and warmed himself. They said therefore unto him, Art not thou also one of his disciples? He denied it, and said, I am not. One of the servants of the high priest, being his kinsman whose ear Peter cut off, saith, Did not I see thee in the garden with him? Peter then denied again; and immediately the cock crew.

---

crowds, His own disciples all render at different times such assistance to Jesus' murderers as might be needed.

"This is your hour and the power of darkness." It was Luke and not John who reported this remark of Jesus. But it helps us understand the sequence of events. God apparently withdrew the support that He usually gives His children, and the powers of darkness had undisputed sway over Caiaphas. He was the principal tool of the powers of darkness. The Satanic drive that overcame all opposition came from him. But Judas went down almost as completely, and Peter and Pilate, and most dreadful of all, the Passover crowds, the men and women whose diseases Jesus had healed and whose hunger he had fed. Surely it was the hour of the powers of darkness.

It was Luke too, who recorded for us Jesus' lovely word, "Father forgive them, for they know not what they do." That took in Caiaphas, and Judas, and Peter, and Pilate. It took in the great disloyal crowd. They had gone down before that dreadful current of evil. Because God intended that they should, He left them unsupported for the purpose. So Jesus forgave them all.

But these details we have been considering are really only the background of the picture that John is drawing. He wants us

Then led they Jesus from Caiaphas unto the hall of judgment: and it was early; and they themselves went not into the judgment hall, lest they should be defiled; but that they might eat the passover.   Pilate then went out unto them, and said, What accusation bring ye against this man?   They answered and said unto him, If he were not a malefactor, we would not have delivered him up unto thee.   Then said Pilate unto them, Take ye him, and judge him according to your law.   The Jews therefore said unto him, It is not lawful for us to put any man to death: That the saying of Jesus might be fulfilled, which he spake, signifying what death he should die.   Then Pilate entered into the judgment hall again, and called Jesus, and said unto him, Art thou the King of the Jews?   Jesus answered him, Sayest thou this thing of thyself, or did others tell it thee of me?   Pilate answered, Am I a Jew?   Thine own nation and the chief priests have delivered thee unto me: what hast thou done?   Jesus answered, My kingdom is not of this world: if my kingdom were of this world, then would my servants fight, that I should not be delivered to the Jews: but now is my kingdom not from hence.

---

to see Jesus as He walks and talks and loves, in that awful ocean of sin.   There are three scenes in which Jeus is the central figure in each.

First, the scene in the garden, as Jesus meets the soldiers with Judas at their head.   His dignity is still with Him, and there is nothing in the occurrence which surprises or disturbs Him. When He dismissed Judas from the table in the upper room, He knew what was going to happen.

How easy it would have been for Him to decline to be arrested. The soldiers, hardened veterans of oppression and cruelty, were abashed and fell backward when faced by Jesus' simple dignity. It was only a week since He had cleared the whole temple court by the simple frown on his face.

Jesus excused the disciples.   None of them could be trusted to drink His cup that night.   Their time would come and every one of them would drink it, but one was ready now.

The second scene was enacted before Annas and Caiaphas. Here was sin in its most malignant form, cold-blooded murder by the high priest.   Not only were Annas and Caiaphas full of sin, but they asserted that God was full of the same sin that filled them.   That is the worst sin of all.   Jesus was brutally abused

Pilate therefore said unto him, Art thou a king then? Jesus answered, Thou sayest that I am a king. To this end was I born, and for this cause came I into the world, that I should bear witness unto the truth. Every one that is of the truth heareth my voice. Pilate saith unto him, What is truth? And when he had said this, he went out again unto the Jews, and saith unto them, I find in him no fault at all. But ye have a custom, that I should release unto you one at the passover: will ye therefore that I release unto you the King of the Jews? Then cried they all again, saying, Not this man, but Barabbas. Now Barabbas was a robber.

---

and insulted and spat upon, but His dignity did not leave Him. nor did He cringe before any of them. His rebuke to the brutality of the soldier was mildness itself, but it still remained a rebuke. Apparently Jesus felt that leaving it unnoticed would constitute a kind of endorsement of it and the official iniquity it represented.

In the final scene, we see Jesus before Pilate. Here Jesus bows to legitimate authority. Jesus had made no effort to reach out for Annas and Caiaphas, but He did reach out for Pilate. There must have been a deep-lying particle of sincerity in the Roman governor. Pilate was the most cruel of them all, but it stirred up no resentment in Jesus' soul. He knew it would work out that way.

THE TEACHING

The picture of Jesus coming to the cross to die for us is doubtless the most important picture of Jesus we have. There is no formal teaching. But there are important lessons which John wants us to learn.

We have noted the deep currents of evil. "It is your hour and the power of darkness." Satan himself was behind these things. Jesus did not resist. He made no effort to defend Himself. Indeed, we can see that He actively assisted. He was careful to go to the usual place so Judas would have no trouble in finding Him. When the soldiers came Jesus identified Himself to them. They were terrified at meeting the man who had cleared the temple courts a week before. Thy wanted to run away. There was no frown on Jesus' face this time, rather a smile as He waited for them to get over their fright so the arrest could be made.

But the greatest lesson is from Jesus' lips after Malchus' ear had been healed. "The cup which the Father hath given me, shall I not drink it?" Luke caught the irresistible currents of Satanic power underneath, but it was John who understood the real situation. The cup which Jesus was asked to drink did not come from Satan, even though it was Caiaphas, one of Satan's own children who gave it to Him.

There were many kinds of sin in Jesus' world. He might have infuriated the slave owners and been stoned by them, on account of His teachings which might have robbed them of hundreds and thousands of slaves. The bandits and the criminals of that day might have joined together to kill a man who preached effectively against them. Indeed, even the prostitutes might have conspired to kill a man who was taking away their livelihood. But God chose none of these to be His cup-bearer. Caiaphas was chosen. He bore the cup and gave it to Jesus.

Underneath the power of Satan and the sin of his servants we catch a glimpse of the silent and irresistible movement of the will of God. The drama unfolds, moving from one scene to the next with the inevitability of a planet in its orbit. The prophets of old had foretold these things, they were all in God's plan.

And there are some other lessons too, not quite as important perhaps, but still worth our notice. What had happened to Judas? He yielded to the temptation of avarice. That would seem a little crack, but Satan's power can seep in through it, and as we see Judas betraying Jesus with a kiss, we realize that his ruin was very complete.

But really it is Caiaphas who represents the greatest problem. Why did he hate Jesus? He had been immersed since childhood in the Old Testament Scriptures. Had continual study of God's revelation done nothing for him? For his ruin was far more complete than that of Judas. Judas did not hate Jesus. Was avarice the crack through which Satan entered Caiaphas' soul too? We know that he was enormously wealthy because of his misuse of temple privileges. For a man in Caiaphas' position drunkenness and adultery or even laziness hardly offer any temptation at all, but avarice and pride have longer arms. No matter how high we climb they can still reach us.

And what about Peter and Pilate? It was not avarice and pride with them, and still less drunkenness and adultery. Theirs was the sin of simple cowardice. For cowardice is a sin, and sometimes it is the worst sin of all. How hard it is to be courageous. All they had to fear was the disapproval of their fellows. How trifling that looks in retrospect, but how dreadful and irresistible at the time.

But it is a mistake to look too long at the sins of Caiaphas and Judas, and more so still to gaze at Peter and Pilate. The most dreadfully sinful thing in this picture is the evil legalistic religion that bound them all. It was not only Caiaphas but all the others who remained outside the pretorium lest they tread upon spittle or in some inadvertent way disqualify themselves from the solemn blessings of the passover.

They were brutally murdering Jesus, but they were as religious as ever. God, their God, was an active partner in it all, with His blessing and approval. To assert such a thing about God is the supreme sin.

Then Pilate therefore took Jesus, and scourged him. And the soldiers platted a crown of thorns, and put it on his head, and they put on him a purple robe, and said, Hail, King of the Jews and they smote him with their hands Pilate therefore went forth again, and saith unto them, Behold, I bring him forth to you, that ye may know that I find no fault in him. Then came Jesus forth, wearing the crown of thorns, and the purple robe. And Pilate saith unto them, Behold the man! When the chief priests therefore and officers saw him, they cried out, saying, Crucify him, crucify him. Pilate saith unto them, Take ye him and crucify him: for I find no fault in him. The Jews answered him, We have a law, and by our law he ought to die, because he made himself the Son of God.

When Pilate therefore heard that saying, he was the more afraid. And went again into the judgment hall, and saith unto Jesus, Whence art thou? But Jesus gave him no answer. Then saith Pilate unto him, Speakest thou not that I have power to crucify thee, and have power to release thee? Jesus answered, Thou couldest have no power at all against me, except it were given thee from above: therefore he that delivered me unto thee hath the greater sin. And from thenceforth Pilate sought to release him: but the Jews cried out, saying, If thou let this man go, thou art not Cesar's friend: whosoever maketh himself a king speaketh against Cesar.

When Pilate therefore heard that saying, he brought Jesus forth, and sat down in the judgment seat in a place that is called the Pavement, but in the Hebrew, Gabbatha. And it was the preparation of the passover, and about the sixth hour: and he saith unto the Jews, Behold your King! But they cried out, Away with him, away with him, crucify him. Pilate saith unto them, Shall I crucify your King? The chief priests answered, We have no king but Cesar. Then delivered he him therefore unto them to be crucified. And they took

Jesus, and led him away. And he bearing his cross went forth into a place called the place of a skull, which is called in the Hebrew Golgotha: Where they crucified him, and two others with him, on either side one, and Jesus in the midst.

And Pilate wrote a title, and put it on the cross. And the writing was, JESUS OF NAZARETH THE KING OF THE JEWS. This title then read many of the Jews; for the place where Jesus was nigh to the city: and it was written in Hebrew, and Greek, and Latin. Then said the chief priests of the chief priests of the Jews to Pilate, Write not, The King of the Jews; but that he said, I am King of the Jews. Pilate answered, What I have written I have written.

Then the soldiers, when they had crucified Jesus, took his garments, and made four parts, to every soldier a part; and also his coat: now the coat was without seam, woven from the top throughout. They said therefore among themselves, Let us not rend it, but cast lots for it, whose it shall be: that the Scripture might be fulfilled, which saith, They parted my raiment among them, and for my vesture they did cast lots. These things therefore the soldiers did.

Now there stood by the cross of Jesus his mother, and his mother's sister, Mary the wife of Cleophas, and Mary Magdalene. When Jesus therefore saw his mother, and the disciple standing by whom he loved, he saith unto his mother, Woman, behold thy son! Then saith he to the disciple, Behold thy mother And from that hour that disciple took her unto his own home.

After this, Jesus knowing that all things were not accomplished that the Scripture might be fulfilled, saith, I thirst. Now there was set a vessel full of vinegar: and they filled a sponge with vinegar, and put it upon hyssop, and put it to his mouth. When Jesus therefore had received the vinegar, he said,

It is finished: and he bowed his head, and gave up the ghost. The Jews therefore, because it was the preparation, that the bodies should not remain upon the cross on the sabbath day, (for that sabbath day was a high day,) besought Pilate that their legs might be broken and that they might be taken away. Then came the soldiers, and brake the legs of the first, and of the other which was crucified with him. But when they came to Jesus, and saw that he was dead already, they brake not his legs: But one of the soldiers with a spear pierced his side, and forthwith came there out blood and water. And he that saw it bare record, and his record is true; and he knoweth that he saith true that ye might believe. For these things were done, that the Scripture should be fulfilled, A bone of him shall not be broken. And again another Scripture saith, They shall look on him whom they pierced.

And after this Joseph of Arimathea, being a disciple of Jesus, but secretly for fear of the Jews, besought Pilate that he might take away the body of Jesus: and Pilate gave him leave. He came therefore, and took the body of Jesus. And there came also Nicodemus, (which at the first came to Jesus by night,) and brought a mixture of myrrh and aloes, about a hundred pound weight. Then took they the body of Jesus, and wound it in linen clothes with the spices, as the manner of the Jews is to bury. Now in the place where he was crucified there was a garden; and in the garden a new sepulchre, wherein was never man yet laid. There laid they Jesus therefore because of the Jews' preparation day; for the sepulchre was nigh at hand.

Chapter XIX

THE CRUCIFIXION

John's Account

This account of Jesus' crucifixion begins really with the last part of the previous chapter. It is disappointing in that no further light is thrown on the somber mystery that surrounds the cross. The exhibition of pure human sin was focussed in the court of Caiaphas. There we saw a further dreadful chapter added to the world's long record of cruelty and pride and iniquity. And we learned from Jesus' own mouth that this cup was given Him by the Father.

Sin exulted in a great victory over righteousness that day, but it was sin's suicide, for out of that very victory of sin, God gained His eternal victory of righteousness. Men were eternally saved by that cross, the crystallized sin of the whole race.

That in a way is an introduction, a pedestal on which the cross stands. And here, even more than before, it is to an impersonal commentator that we listen. The account divides itself into three fractions. First, the trial before Pilate. It is a mistake to call it a trial. Jesus had been condemned to death by the supreme tribunal of the Jewish nation. Like colonial powers of our own day, Rome tried to interfere as little as possible in the local domestic and religious affairs of her subject states. Jesus was a local problem, and it is evident that Pilate realized this.

But nothing would satisfy Caiaphas and his underlings except Jesus' death. Jewish courts were not allowed to punish in that way. Moreover, there was something particularly disgraceful and contaminating in a pagan crucifixion. Jesus had claimed to be the Messiah. To see Him hanging from a Roman cross would rout that idea out of His most earnest disciples!

The trial before Caiaphas was a pure mockery. This one before Pilate equally so. It would seem that they expected Pilate to acquiesce without protest in their request for Jesus' death. Important religious questions were involved and getting rid of a troublesome Jew should not trouble a man like Pilate.

But Pilate was also a man of religious principles, though he would not have called them such. Love for his enemies was no part of Pilate's creed. But fair play and honesty did mean a great deal to this Roman. He flatly acquitted the prisoner. Jesus' claim to being a King constituted no danger to the Roman state.

There followed a wrestling match between bitter Jewish fanaticism and Roman justice. Roman justice failed, just as contemporary Jewish religion had failed. The fierce devilish push of Caiaphas and his men overcame this second obstacle as it had the first. Pilate wanted to release the prisoner, but when it became evident that a riot was developing, and that he himself would be accused of disloyalty to Rome if he refused to yield, then Jesus was given up. Certainly every prisoner should be handled with justice and fair play. But when his own personal position was threatened, and when the interests of the state?

Then Pilate therefore took Jesus, and scourged him. And the soldiers platted a crown of thorns, and put it on his head, and they put on him a purple robe, And said, Hail, King of the Jews! and they smote him with their hands. Pilate therefore went forth again, and saith unto them, Behold, I bring him forth to you, that ye may know that I find no fault in him. Then came Jesus forth, wearing the crown of thorns, and the purple robe. And Pilate saith unto them, Behold the man!

---

seemed to be genuinely implicated, then expediency ruled, and Jesus was sacrificed.

Jesus hung on the cross from nine in the morning to three in the afternoon. The second fraction of the account covers this period. John omits some items, the account of the repentent thief, and Jesus' beautiful word, "Father forgive them for they know not what they do."

The third section recounts some of the events that followed immediately after Jesus died. They are of interest chiefly as they show that it was certain he had actually died. When John wrote this Gospel that was an important consideration, for the whole tremendous episode of the resurrection depended on it.

THE PICTURE

Here we see Jesus crucified. There is little or no teaching. It is another picture. Evidently when Jesus told His disciples that He was to be delivered up into the hands of men, there was a very somber and dreadful meaning in His words. Before this, Jesus had always been able to control the situations in which He found Himself. "The Father is with me," Jesus said repeatedly, and no one could even arrest Him, for as the writer explains, "His hour had not yet come."

But now evidently "His hour" had come — the Devil's hour, too, and God's. His Father is no longer protecting Him. He has been delivered up into the hands of men. In this dreadful situation evil is dominant and it does to Jesus anything it wishes. He is insulted, abused, betrayed, and He submits with hardly a word. He Himself had predicted this. These were the evil men

When the chief priests therefore and officers saw him, they cried out, saying, Crucify him, crucify him. Pilate saith unto them, Take ye him, and crucify him: for I find no fault in him. The Jews answered him, We have a law, and by our law he ought to die, because he made himself the Son of God.

When Pilate therefore heard that saying, he was the more afraid; And went again into the judgment hall, and saith unto Jesus, Whence art thou? But Jesus gave him no answer. Then saith Pilate unto him, Speakest thou not unto me? knowest thou not that I have power to crucify thee, and have power to release thee? Jesus answered, Thou couldest have no power at all against me, except it were given thee from above: therefore he that delivered me unto thee hath the greater sin.

---

into whose hands He was to be delivered. Their determined purpose was to murder Him.

Jesus was attending the Passover feast. We would have supposed that it might prove extremely difficult to force His judicial murder, with so many of His friends in Jerusalem. Religious leaders supervised the arrangements and conducted the ceremonies. Bands of Roman soldiers kept the crowds in order. Pilate in his castle directed the city's affairs. But the situation was really in the hands of the priests with Caiaphas at the head.

Caiaphas knew just what he wanted. First of all, he must transform this crowd of religious pilgrims into a fierce and blood-thirsty mob shouting for Jesus' death. He appears to have had little difficulty in accomplishing this. It was indeed the hour of the powers of darkness. No voice was heard asking for Jesus' release. They shouted savagely for His crucifixion. These were the men that He had come to save. It was His last contact with them.

With the help of this savage mob, Caiaphas hoped to force Pilate to execute Jesus in the regular legal way. There are many easier ways to murder a man than this. But Caiaphas had both seen and hated both Jesus and His Father. There was something of the sadistic in Caiaphas. He wanted to destroy Jesus' life, to violate and insult the respectability of this man. Caiaphas represented the forces of evil He intended that there should be something extreme and excessive in Jesus' suffering. They wanted to

And from thenceforth Pilate sought to release him: but the Jews cried out, saying, If thou let this man go, thou art not Cesar's friend: whosoever maketh himself a king speaketh against Cesar.

When Pilate therefore heard that saying, he brought Jesus forth, and sat down in the judgment seat in a place that is called the Pavement, but in the Hebrew, Gabbatha. And it was the preparation of the passover, and about the sixth hour: and he saith unto the Jews, Behold your King! But they cried out, Away with him, away with him, crucify him. Pilate saith unto them, Shall I crucify your King? The chief priests answered, We have no king but Cesar. Then delivered he him therefore unto them to be crucified. And they took Jesus, and led him away.

---

brutilize the whole episode. They tore the body of Jesus with thorns and disgraced it with a Roman cross. They spat upon it.

There are many questions we would like to ask as we study this picture. That it was necessary for Jesus to die we know very well, but was it necessary for Him to suffer in this dreadful way, and if so, why? Hebrews has given us at least part of the answer. It was necessary for Jesus to suffer without the gate, the place of contempt and loathing, so that He could sanctify His people with His own blood.

Facing this pitiless mob whose determined purpose was His death, Jesus stood deserted and alone. His physical strength gave way, but His composure was unbroken, and His spirit was untroubled and quiet. His enemies spat on Him and insulted Him, but it roused no resentment. After all, these were the men He had come to save, and this surely showed that they needed saving.

Jesus could have helped Pilate in his struggle with the terrible mob, for Pilate tried hard to acquit Him. Jesus was careful not to do so. Whatever the forces of evil wanted to do with Him they were to do. Jesus did not oppose them, so with very little delay Pilate handed Jesus over to be crucified.

Even so we are surprised to see that this whole episode lasted only a few hours. Jesus apparently wanted His trial to be finished as rapidly as possible. John does not tell us the reason, but in Luke we get a glimpse of at least part of it. Jesus' human

And he bearing his cross went forth into a place called the place of a skull, which is called in the Hebrew Golgotha: Where they crucified him, and two others with him, on either side one, and Jesus in the midst.

And Pilate wrote a title, and put it on the cross. And the writing was, JESUS OF NAZARETH THE KING OF THE JEWS. This title then read many of the Jews; for the place where Jesus was crucified was nigh to the city: and it was written in Hebrew, and Greek, and Latin. Then said the chief priests of the Jews to Pilate, Write not, The King of the Jews; but that he said, I am King of the Jews. Pilate answered, What I have written I have written.

Then the soldiers, when they had crucified Jesus, took his garments, and made four parts, to every soldier a part; and also his coat: now the coat was without seam, woven from the top throughout. They said therefore among themselves, Let us not rend it, but cast lots for it, whose it shall be: that the Scripture might be fulfilled, which saith, They parted my raiment among them, and for my vesture they did cast lots. These things therefore the soldiers did.

Now there stood by the cross of Jesus his mother, and his mother's sister, Mary the wife of Cleophas, and Mary Magdalene. When Jesus therefore saw his mother, and the disciple standing by, whom he loved, he saith unto his mother, Woman, behold thy son! Then saith he to the disciple, Behold thy mother! And from that hour that disciple took her unto his own home.

---

body was part of his personality just as ours is and that day it had to carry very heavy burdens.

The day's task began as Jesus knelt in Gethsemane and there, after a pause when His soul quailed before this dreadful "cup," He drank it. He sweat drops of blood then. As He knelt there, the slimy and putrid sins of Caiaphas and of you and me were wrapped around His sensitive and shrinking soul. Jesus bore these sins, that intolerable, repulsive load. He carried that fearsome burden to the cross. Evidently, His body, strong as it was, untainted by dissipation, or sin and disease, unweakened as yet by age, was able to carry that dreadful burden, only so long. It was not quite able to meet the day's demands, and another carried His heavy cross the last part of that awful half mile.

So with Jesus' own assistance Caiaphas had Him crucified, and when finally the last lap of that pitiful journey was com-

After this, Jesus knowing that all things were now accomplished, that the Scripture might be fulfilled, saith, I thirst. Now there was set a vessel full of vinegar: and they filled a sponge with vinegar, and put it upon hyssop, and put it to his mouth. When Jesus therefore had received the vinegar, he said, It is finished: and he bowed his head, and gave up the ghost. The Jews therefore, because it was the preparation, that the bodies should not remain upon the cross on the sabbath day, (for that sabbath day was a high day), besought Pilate that their legs might be broken, and that they might be taken away. Then came the soldiers, and brake the legs of the first, and of the other which was crucified with him. But when they came to Jesus, and saw that he was dead already, they brake not his legs:

---

pleted, we can imagine with what relief Jesus stretched out His hands for the nails. For the few hours that were left, He would not have to carry the burden with His own muscles. The nails would do it.

It is a somber and awful picture, this vision of the beauty and the love of God deliberately letting itself be carried down into the bottomless pit of evil. The surrounding clouds and the dark mountains are black and forbidding. Sin never seemed so dark and hideous before. But as our trembling soul looks at that picture, there gradually takes shape, right in the clouds and the darkness of the scenes that we are looking at, a great snow-capped mountain with the beauty of God shining from its summit, and the fragrance of the roses of Heaven on it.

We caught the first glimpse of this in the dialogue between Pilate and Jesus. "Are you a king then" and Jesus said "Yes, I am a King of the Kingdom of truth. Every one who is of the truth is my subject."

Pilate was much impressed by this reply even though he tried to ridicule the Jews by means of it. He realized that this remarkable prisoner was in some deep sense a king. He was not king of the Jews, at least not of these Jews, but He was a king right that moment.

But Pilate was a child of his times and of its limitations. So he scourged Jesus, perhaps to stir the crowd to pity. He should have known better. Men like Caiaphas are not stirred to pity.

But one of the soldiers with a spear pierced his side, and forthwith came there out blood and water. And he that saw it bare record, and his record is true; and he knoweth that he saith true, that ye might believe. For these things were done, that the Scripture should be fulfilled, A bone of him shall not be broken. And again another Scripture saith, They shall look on him whom they pierced.

And after this Joseph of Arimathea, being a disciple of Jesus, but secretly for fear of the Jews, besought Pilate that he might take away the body of Jesus: and Pilate gave him leave. He came therefore, and took the body of Jesus. And there came also Nicodemus, (which at the first came to Jesus by night), and brought a mixture of myrrh and aloes, about a hundred pound weight.

The soldiers followed suit. They wove thorn twigs together, and made a crown and forced it on His head. There appeared a little trickle of blood where each thorn pierced the skin. Some faded old robe of royal purple was brought out and put on the prisoner and now they had a real king, crown, robe, and all.

Then Pilate presented Him to the people a second time. This time He was a real King and a very great one, the King of suffering. We shrink from suffering, and the philosopher has a hard time to accommodate this element in his universe. But God gives it a large place. Every woman in that great company who had borne babies, every man who had suffered from the ravages of pain and disease, the slaves and the prisoners, were all looking at their King. His back was cut to pieces by the whips. His head was bleeding and aching from the thorns. His heart was utterly sick and nauseated by the sins He was carrying. And as a dreadful climax He looked out over a massed exhibition of sin as the mob shouted for His death.

The scene changes and the picture moves on. Jesus is King now in a new and final sense. This is the final picture. The King has two retainers, one on each side. They are in eternity, those three men. Their world has been wound up and finished. "To-day," said Jesus to one of them, "thou shalt be with me in paradise." This is the King of eternity. He speaks the final word, "Father, into thy hands I commend my spirit." It is the King of life speaking. The flesh that housed that life for thirty-three

Then took they the body of Jesus, and wound it in linen clothes with the spices, as the manner of the Jews is to bury. Now in the place where he was crucified there was a garden; and in the garden a new sepulchre, wherein was never man yet laid. There laid they Jesus therefore because of the Jews' preparation day; for the sepulchre was nigh at hand.

---

years was about exhausted, so to that failing body, and its flagging heart He bowed in courteous appreciation, and gave up His spirit.

Jesus was not alone as He died. One friend hung next to Him, but it was not one of the disciples. It seems remarkable that after these years of association not one of the disciples remained loyal. Any emperor in ancient Japan, Napoleon a hundred and fifty years ago, Lenin of Russia or Bin Saoud of Arabia in our own time, any one of these men executed by a hostile government would have had a dozen faithful followers glad to show their loyalty by dying with their chief. Jesus had none. He gained no such blind personal loyalty, and what is more, it is obvious that He did not want it. All of which brings up a very profound question as to just what loyalty Jesus wants.

The scenes around the cross introduce us again to Jesus' mother. She was there suffering as only mothers can suffer. Evidently Jesus' departure was to leave her in need of support and filial loyalty, so Jesus provided for her. Many questions are suggested as to their relations during the year of Jesus' public ministry. Unquestionably many beautiful things in Jesus' life are left unmentioned in our records.

And so the somber, uncolored narrative moves to its close. Pilate"s timid resistance was overcome. The mob shouted for Jesus' death. They took Him to the place of the skull and there "they crucified Him;" and then they buried Him in a nearby tomb.

THE TEACHING

Here the lesson is the picture, and many of the things which God wants us to learn, we have seen already. But there are

deeper lessons which do not lie on the surface. We have already
noticed that Jesus does not fight against the current of evil which
is carrying Him to the cross. He offers no resistance, nor even
protest. He clears away obstacles so that delays are avoided.
There are times when He seems to turn away intentionally from
an avenue of escape.

He did not want to escape. The world's salvation depended
on Jesus' complete surrender to evil, grievous, unopposed evil,
with its final triumph in the execution of a completely innocent
man. So Peter's sharp resistance was stopped, and Jesus healed
the ear. The divine offering would not have been quite "without
blemish" if it had been ushered in by means of a general fight.

Part of Caiaphas' program was forcing the Roman governor
to be Jesus' executioner. Jesus could have defeated this scheme
very easily, but He did not do so. That morning evil was allowed
to do anything it wished. There is little profit in speculating on
why Caiaphas wanted to kill Jesus this way. The real question
is why God wanted His eternal sacrifice offered in that manner.

Jesus took a calm satisfaction in seeing the great divine tragedy
work out to its predetermined end. He saw the Satanic currents
of incredible power and He knew that for the moment they were
irresistible.

But He saw something else, something that with the Spirit's
help we must see if we are to understand this lesson. We have
a deep view into eternal reality here. Pure sin was victorious
over pure righteousness, but Jesus saw His Father's face in it
and we are not surprised at His poise and dignity.

Jesus saw the Satanic currents, but He also saw something
deeper and more powerful.

That cup did not come from Satan no matter what the appear-
ances were. Underneath that dreadful human sin, far down below even the Satanic power that directed this evil, Jesus saw the
unhurried will of God moving on to complete eternal triumph,
and most unbelievable of all, the triumph of God was by means
of this very victory of Satan.

Satan's victory was complete. Jesus died. Every evil desire was completed to the last detail, the brutality, the contempt, the spitting, the scorn. It was the unopposed will of the devil. Our imagination sees the devils of hell dancing around the foot of the cross in unrestrained exultation. It was their moment of complete victory.

Among all the impossible things we are allowed to see and marvel over, this is surely the farthest removed from the divine nature. The very excess of Satan's victory, the cold, bitter hatred of Caiaphas, the treachery of Judas, the contemptuous pride of Pilate, it was means of these that the omnipotent grace of God won its eternal victory. This was foreseen by the prophets, was indeed the essence of their vision. "He was wounded for our transgressions. He was bruised for our iniquities. The chastisement of our peace was upon Him, and by His stripes we are healed."

"By His stripes we are healed." Even in heaven we will not understand that but we can see it. These stripes of Jesus are spread out before us here with dreadful vividness, the addition of a dreadful list of new sins to the melancholy record of the past. The theologian tries to see here a vindication of the righteousness of God, but no righteousness is in this picture, neither of God nor of man, only pure evil.

But God the Father knew that it was necessary. He insisted that His beloved Son should drink this cup. In that cup were the slimy, putrid sins of men, and the frown of a Fatherly God.

The one thing that we must not let slip, no matter how impossible it seems, is that the contempt, and the spitting, and the scorn, and the cruelty were all necessary parts of our redemption. Like the beasts of old, Jesus' body was offered without the camp, where filth and contempt are. Jesus suffered this way so that He could sanctify us by His own blood.

The very completeness of Satan's triumph, the contempt, the loathing, the brutality, the treachery, it was by means of these that God's grace won its eternal victory. Why were these things

necessary.   How could God use them to such an end?   We
cannot see it and probably we never will.   Such things belong in
the deep counsels of God.

In the other Gospels much space is devoted to the part which
the Roman governor played in the trial and execution.   John
leaves most of this out.   Pilate was simply one of the tools that
Satan used that day.

This was all in fulfillment of Old Testament prophecy.   Death
by stoning was the Old Testament way.   The whole entrance of
Rome into the story looks incongruous.   But Rome represented
the world, and God is saving the world.   Pilate had his place in
it.   Jesus was put to death by the religious sins of religious people.   The justice and fair play of pagan Rome were unable to
save Him.

JOHN 20

The first day of the week cometh Mary Magdalene early, when it was yet dark, unto the sepulchre, and seeth the stone taken away from the sepulchre. Then she runneth, and cometh to Simon Peter, and to the other disciple, whom Jesus loved, and saith unto them, They have taken away the Lord out of the sepulchre, and we know not where they have laid him. Peter therefore went forth, and that other disciple, and came to the sepulchre. So they ran both together: and the other disciple did outrun Peter, and came first to the sepulchre. And he stooping down, and looking in, saw the linen clothes lying; yet went he not in. Then cometh Simon Peter following him, and went into the sepulchre, and seeth the linen clothes lie, And the napkin, that was about his head, not lying with the linen clothes, but wrapped together in a place by itself. Then went in also that other disciple, which came first to the sepulchre, and he saw, and believed, For as yet they knew not the Scripture, that he must rise again from the dead. Then the disciples went away again unto their own home.

But Mary stood without at the sepulchre weeping: and as she wept, she stooped down, and looked into the sepulchre. And seeth two angels in white sitting, the one at the head, and the other at the feet, where the body of Jesus had lain. And they say unto her, Woman, why weepest thou? She saith unto them, Because they have taken away my Lord, and I know not where they have laid him. And when she had thus said, she turned herself back, and saw Jesus standing, and knew not that it was Jesus. Jesus saith unto her, Woman, why weepest thou? whom seekest thou? She, supposing him to be the gardener, saith unto him, Sir, if thou have borne him hence tell me where thou hast laid him, and I will take him away. Jesus saith unto her,

Mary. She turned herself, and saith unto him, Raboni; which is to say, Master. Jesus saith unto her, Touch me not: for I am not yet ascended to my Father: but go to my brethren, and say unto them, I ascend unto my Father, and your Father; and to my God, and your God. Mary Magdalene came and told the disciples that she had seen the Lord, and that he had spoken these things unto her.

Then the same day at evening, being the first day of the week, when the doors were shut where the disciples were assembled for fear of the Jews, came Jesus and stood in the midst, and saith unto them, Peace be unto you. And when he had so said, he shewed unto them his hands and his side. Then were the disciples glad, when they saw the Lord. Then said Jesus to them again, Peace be unto you: as my Father hath sent me, even so send I you. And when he had said this, he breathed on them, and saith unto them, Receive ye the Holy Ghost: Whosoever sins ye remit, they are remitted unto them; and whosesoever sins ye retain, they are retained.

But Thomas, one of the twelve, called Didymus, was not with them when Jesus came. The other disciples therefore said unto him, We have seen the Lord. But he said unto them, Except I shall see in his hands the print of the nails, and put my finger into the print of the nails, and thrust my hand into his side, I will not believe.

And after eight days again his disciples were within and Thomas with them: then came Jesus, the doors being shut, and stood in the midst, and said, Peace be unto you. Then saith he to Thomas, Reach hither thy finger, and behold my hands; and reach hither thy hand, and thrust it into my side; and be not faithless, but believing. And Thomas answered and said unto him, My Lord any my God. Jesus saith unto him

Thomas, because thou hast seen me, thou hast believed: blessed are they that have not seen, and yet have believed.

And many other signs truly did Jesus in the presence of his disciples, which are not written in this book: But these are written, that ye might believe that Jesus is the Christ, the Son of God; and that believing ye might have life through his name.

Chapter XX

THE RESURRECTION

The first day of the week cometh Mary Magdalene early, when it was yet dark, unto the sepulchre, and seeth the stone taken away from the sepulchre. Then she runneth, and cometh to Simon Peter, and to the other disciple, whom Jesus loved, and saith unto them, They have taken away the Lord out of the sepulchre, and we know not where they have laid him. Peter therefore went forth, and that other disciple, and came to the sepulchre. So they ran both together: and the other disciple did outrun Peter, and came first to the sepulchre. And he stooping down, and looking in, saw the linen clothes lying; yet went he not in. Then cometh Simon Peter following him, and went into the sepulchre, and seeth the linen clothes lie,

We find here the same brevity, the same economy of incidents that surprised us in John's account of the crucifixion. The vivid stories of the other Gospels are not here. The sealing of the tomb, the angel rolling away the stone, the walk to Emmaus are all omitted. We feel a little annoyed at the parsimony of the writer.

In the matter of emotional expression, the case is even worse. John spills no tears over the crucifixion, and no joy bubbles out here. It is difficult to be sure just what the writer is trying to do. This is a picture of Jesus, given no doubt to show that He is the Christ, the Son of God, but it is a surprising picture. There is no new vision of God's redemptive grace, and no new light on Jesus' divine character.

This is history at its colorless best, or worst. John's was a difficult task. He had lived through a memorable day, and seen remarkable things. From these things he concluded that Jesus the crucified leader, had risen from the dead. John reports what he saw without any emotional embroidery. The hope is that his readers will draw the same conclusion which he had drawn.

And the napkin, that was about his head, not lying with the linen clothes, but wrapped together in a place by itself. Then went in also that other disciple, which came first to the sepulchre, and he saw, and believed. For as yet they knew not the Scripture, that he must rise again from the dead. Then the disciples went away again unto their own home.

But Mary stood without at the sepulchre weeping: and as she wept, she stooped down, and looked into the sepulchre. And seeth two angels in white sitting, the one at the head, and the other at the feet, where the body of Jesus had lain.

Moreover, this was a matter of immeasurable importance. Men's eternal salvation down through the centuries depended on believing his story.

This Gospel appeared fifty years afterward. It was written for a Greek church. John saw that he must demonstrate three things. First that Jesus rose, that the corpse which was put into the grave three days before, had been revivified by God's power, and come forth a living man. Two incidents support this. In the moonlit dark of the very early morning, Mary saw that the stone had been rolled away from the tomb's door. These stones are very large and cut from the rock. It takes a number of men to move such a stone.

Two incidents support this. In the moonlit dark of the very early morning, Mary saw that the stone had been rolled away from the tomb's door. These stones are very large and cut from the rock. It takes a number of men to move such a stone.

John was not with Mary when she saw this, so he does not comment on her story. Later this same Mary (Magdalene) was quoted as having seen an angel descend and by means of an earthquake roll the gigantic stone away. Apparently John does not feel sure enough of this to use it. He himself saw the displaced stone, and he reported just what he saw.

John saw one other thing which showed that the corpse of Friday night rose a living man on Sunday morning. He and Peter entered through the door of the tomb, wide open now that the stone had been rolled away. They saw Jesus' grave clothes ly-

And they say unto her, Woman, why weepest thou? She saith unto them, Because they have taken away my Lord, and I know not where they have laid him. And when she had thus said, she turned herself back, and saw Jesus standing, and knew not that it was Jesus. Jesus saith unto her, Woman, why weepest thou? whom seekest thou? She, supposing him to be the gardener, saith unto him, Sir, if thou have borne him hence, tell me where thou hast laid him, and I will take him away. Jesus saith unto her, Mary. She turned herself, and saith unto him, Rabboni; which is to say, Master. Jesus saith unto her, Touch me not; for I am not yet ascended to my Father: but go to my brethren, and say unto them, I ascend unto my Father, and your Father; and to my God, and your God.

---

ing untouched on the floor. Those grave clothes proved to John that Jesus had risen.

That is not quite as unreasonable as it sounds. We know how bodies were prepared for burial in those days. Long bandage-like strips of cloth were wrapped snugly around the body and lumbs. Ointment and spices were liberally smeared on in the process. Now if a snow man were wrapped up that way, and then taken where it was warm, after a little time the snow would melt and disappear. An empty and undisturbed shell would be left. John caught the significance of this at a glance.

These two incidents took care of John's most difficult task. But there were others equally important. He must show that the risen Jesus was in all truth the same Jesus who had been crucified and buried. The incredulous sceptic in the Greek church would ask many questions. The possibility of mistaken identity, of ghosts and apparations all had to be considered. John summons his witnesses. Mary Magdalene, Peter and John. The whole group of disciples with Thomas absent, and then the whole group with Thomas present.

Not an impressive list, but John thought it adequate, and who will disagree with him? These men and women knew Jesus intimately. They were glad to meet Him again after the devastating experiences of the crucifixion and burial. Their testimony was spontaneous and sincere, and the identity of the risen Jesus seems adequately established.

Mary Magdalene came and told the disciples that she had seen the Lord, and that he had spoken these things unto her.

Then the same day at evening, being the first day of the week, when the doors were shut where the disciples were assembled for fear of the Jews, came Jesus and stood in the midst, and saith unto them, Peace be unto you. And when he had so said, he shewed unto them his hands and his side. Then were the disciples glad, when they saw the Lord. Then said Jesus to them again, Peace be unto you: as my Father hath sent me, even so send I you. And when he had said this, he breathed on them, and saith unto them, Receive ye the Holy Ghost: Whosesoever sins ye remit, they are remitted unto them; and whosesoever sins ye retain ,they are retained.

John was concerned to show another thing. This was indeed Jesus, the individual with whom they had lived. They had seen Him being crucified and buried. But he had changed. Mary did not know Him at first.

However, He still belonged to this world. His body was a definite material thing. It showed the scars of the nails and the spear. Thomas felt of those scars and found that they belonged to a normal human body. That convinced him, sceptic though he was. Moreover, falling back on the Appendix (chap. 21) which John (probably) added afterward, we see that Jesus, risen from the dead, could eat fish just like the rest of us.

But Jesus belonged to the next world even more. His body passed at will through solid doors. It was this startling ability of Jesus' body to pass through material things which convinced John in the first place.

John was an observant young man. He noticed that when Jesus appeared to the disciples on that Sabbath evening, He did not just happen along and walk in and join them. He came right through a closed door. A week later when Thomas was with them, the same thing occurred.

The greatest surprise of all is His casual discussion of the Holy Spirit. This, of course, is merely John's selection of material. We know from the other accounts that Jesus did discuss this with the disciples very carefully.

These are the surface details, meager but adequate, emotionally completely colorless, but perhaps all the more convincing on that account. With meditation and a prayer for the Spirit's guidance, we will try to penerate below the surface of the narrative which is for all the world, and enter into the deeper things which were for the beloved disciples.

It was to Mary that the first word came. "Touch me not, for I am not yet ascended unto the Father." What was behind that? Jesus belonged to eternity. He had been through a purifying fire, and before anything else He must ascend to the purity of His Father. But Jesus belonged to men, for this caution to Mary was a temporary thing. In a few hours, Thomas was invited to reach out and search Jesus' body for the crucifixion scars.

We pause to consider His next word, "But go unto my brethren." He had never called them that before. They had been His "disciples,' and even His "friends." From now on they were brethren, and brethren in what family! "I ascend unto my Father and your Father, and my God and your God."

We remember that discipleship began by entering a family circle, with Jesus as our elder brother. That is an eternal thing. Jesus belongs to us. He is our elder brother through the years and centuries of the future, and out into the uncharted millenia of eternity. Now we are to see the peak of this great mountain. Jesus speaks to the entire group. It is a new revelation. His divine commission for them. Jesus gives this great commission in eight words. It would be impossible to add to its vivid completeness with eighty more." As My Father hath sent me, even so send I you." Under the omnipotent Father we are Jesus' brethren, comrades, and more, in the eternal task of redeeming the world.

There is fellowship in that. "He that sent me is with me, the Father hath not left me alone." There is power in it. "All power is given unto me in Heaven and on earth." Jesus is to work with us as our constant partner. Men's salvation is Jesus' work. We do not have any share in that. But carrying it

But Thomas, one of the twelve, called Didymus, was not with them when Jesus came. The other disciples therefore said unto him, We have seen the Lord. But he said unto them, Except I shall see in his hands the print of the nails, and thrust my hand into his side, I will not believe.

And after eight days again his disciples were within, and Thomas with them: then came Jesus, the doors being shut, and stood in the midst, and said, Peace be unto you. Then saith he to Thomas, Reach hither thy finger, and behold my hands; and reach hither thy hand, and thrust it into my side; and be not faithless, but believing. And Thomas answered and said unto him, My Lord and my God. Jesus saith unto him, Thomas, because thou hast seen me, thou hast believed: blessed are they that have not seen, and yet have believed.

And many other signs truly did Jesus in the presence of his disciples, which are not written in this book: But these are written, that ye might believe that Jesus is the Christ, the Son of God; and that believing ye might have life through his name.

---

to the world is a partnership task. Jesus works above and we below.

Jesus adds a word not concerning the work of the disciples, but concerning their souls. "Peace be upon you." He repeats that three times. We would surely have emphasized faith and courage and diligence. Jesus does not even mention love. His final gift was peace, peace with God and peace with each other, and peace with the world. They were to be men of peace.

He left them a word about faith. "Blessed are they that have not seen and yet have believed." He was looking down the years and the centuries. We have all believed that way.

The story ends and the book ends. "These are written that ye might believe that Jesus is the Christ, the Son of God, and that believing ye might have life in His name. . ."

After these things Jesus shewed himself again to the disciples at the sea Tiberias; and on this wise shewed he himself. There were together Simon Peter, and Thomas called Didymus, and Nathanael of Cana in Galilee, and the sons of Zebedee, and two other of his disciples. Simon Peter saith unto them, I go a fishing. They say unto him, We also go with thee. They went forth, and entered into a ship immediately; and that night they caught nothing. But when the morning was now come, Jesus stood on the shore; but the disciples knew not that it was Jesus. Then Jesus saith unto them, Children, have ye any meat? They answered him, No. And he said unto them, Cast the net on the right side of the ship, and ye shall find. They cast therefore, and now they were not able to draw it for the multitude of fishes. Therefore that disciple whom Jesus loved saith unto Peter, It is the Lord. Now when Simon Peter heard that it was the Lord he girt his fisher's coat unto him, (for he was naked,) and did cast himself into the sea. And the other disciples came in a little ship, (for they were not far from land, *but as it were two hundred cubits,) dragging the net with fishes. As soon then as they were come to land,* they saw a fire of coals there, and fish laid thereon, and bread. Jesus saith unto them, Bring of the fish which ye have now caught. Simon Peter went up, and drew the net to land full of great fishes, a hundred and fifty and three: and for all there were so many, yet was not the net broken. Jesus saith unto them, Come and dine. And none of the disciples durst ask him, Who art thou? knowing that it was the Lord. Jesus then cometh, and taketh bread, and giveth them, and fish likewise. This is now the third time that Jesus shewed himself to his disciples, after that he was risen from the dead. So when they had dined, Jesus saith to Simon Peter, Simon, son of Jonas, lovest thou me more than these? He saith unto him, Yea, Lord; thou knowest that I love thee. He saith unto him, Feed my lambs. He saith to him again the second time, Simon son of Jonas, lovest thou me? He saith unto him, Yea, Lord: thou knowest that I love thee. He saith unto him, Feed my sheep. He saith unto him the third time, Simon, son of Jonas, lovest thou me? Peter was grieved because he said unto him the third time, Lovest thou me? And he said unto him, Lord, thou knowest all things; thou knowest that I love thee. Jesus saith unto him, Feed my sheep. Verily, verily, I say unto thee, When thou wast young, thou girdedst thyself, and walkedst whither thou wouldest: but when thou shalt be old, thou shalt stretch forth thy hands, and another shall gird thee, and carry thee whither thou wouldest not. This spake he, signifying by what death he should glorify God. And when he had spoken this, he saith unto him, Follow me. Then Peter, turning about seeth the disciple whom Jesus loved following; which also leaned on his breast at supper, and said, Lord, which is he that betrayeth thee? Peter seeing him saith to Jesus, Lord, and what shall this man do? Jesus saith unto him, If I will that he tarry till I come, what is that to thee? follow thou me. Then went this saying abroad among the brethren, that that disciple should not die; yet Jesus said not unto him, He shall not die; but, If I will that he tarry till I come, what is that to thee? This is the disciple which testifieth of these things, and wrote these things: and we know that his testimony is true. And there are also many other things which Jesus did, the which, if they should be written every one, I suppose that even the world itself could not contain the books that should be written. Amen.

Chapter XXI

APPENDIX

This appendix gives us an additional story. Jesus whom they had known and followed for three years was in all truth He who had risen from the dead. Its value is obvious, though the evidence already brought forward seems adequate.

But there are other elements of interest here. Jesus saved Peter and his companions from a fresh defection. There is a bit of the supernatural here. Jesus knew of their danger and saved them.

Jesus did not rebuke them. Evidently He expected almost nothing from them until the Comforter could abide in them and lead them, lead them in external things, and far more important, lead them in their faith and loyalty.

Here Jesus recognizes Peter's leadership. It had a physical element. Hauling ashore a great overfilled net single-handed was a considerable feat. Peter receives his commission. His mind was filled at this moment with the evil dream of a military kingdom, as the account of Luke in Acts shows us. The last thing that Peter should appreciate as Jesus talked to him was that humility and unceasing service to his fellow disciples was the one qualification for leadership in the church. It was not necessary that he understood this at the moment. All he needed was to remember it, and that he did.

One wonders if this appendix was added to the Gospel at some later time just to show that Peter's leadership was based on a direct word from Jesus Himself. Perhaps John put it in to check some over-zealous group of admirers who wanted to put John into Peter's place.